Aa Bb Cc Dd
Ee Ff Gg Hh
Ii Jj Kk Ll
Mm Nn
Oo Pp Qq Rr
Ss Tt Uu Vv
Ww Xx Yy Zz

Aa　　　　　Bb　　　　　Cc

Ff　　　　　Gg　　　　　Hh

Ii　　　　　Jj　　　　　Kk

Ll　　　　　Mm　　　　　Nn

Qq　　　　　Rr　　　　　Ss

Vv　　　　　Ww　　　　　Xx

NERD

Aa ～ Zz

Your
Reference
to ~~Literally~~
FIGURATIVELY
Everything You've
Always Wanted
to Know

T. J. Resler

NATIONAL GEOGRAPHIC
WASHINGTON, D.C.

RAD ROBOTS, PAGE 120

INTRODUCTION

Think you're a nerd? You know, the kind of kid with smarts, passion, expert knowledge, and the kind of Einstein cool other kids can only dream about? If so, read on.

This book is packed full of nerdy awesomeness. It has the details on everything nerd from A to Z—aardwolves to zombies. Hundreds of nerd-worthy topics—everything you need to seriously up your nerd cred.

Most are encyclopedia-style entries that give you the inside scoop on a subject.

Some topics—stuff like artificial intelligence, pirates, or UFOs—get extra attention. Sounds cool, right? You're not the only one who thinks so. You'll meet many Nerds of Note who pursued their passions and made their mark on the world.

Whatever your type of nerdiness, you'll find something of interest. Are you a **SCIENCE SCHOLAR?** You'll read about all kinds of fascinating and bizarre animals, catch up on the latest dinosaur discoveries, and find out what goes on inside your brain. **CULTURE CONNOISSEURS** can dive into the world of superheroes and mythical creatures, explore art movements and music genres, or learn about role-play. If you're the type of **GEOGRAPHY GENIUS** who marvels over mysterious designs carved into the Earth, caves that sparkle with glowing worms, or phantom islands, you'll be able indulge your interests, too.

But, wait, there's more! **DESIGN DEVOTEES** will learn the secrets of buildings with missing floors, how decor can float in the air, and how designers can make mind-blowing tree houses. **HISTORY HEROES** can nerd out over the details of storming castles, the exploits of Vikings, or the storied past of circus acts. If you're a **TECH TITAN,** who prefers the latest cutting-edge inventions, read up on amazing robots and super spacecraft. And more. Much, much more.

If you want to follow a particular passion, look for the icons attached to each entry. They'll flag which nerdy category or categories the subject fits in. But no need to choose just one area of nerdiness. We know the passions of nerds can't be contained. Nerds don't let others tell them what to like or how to be. They define their own cool.

SCIENCE SCHOLAR

CULTURE CONNOISSEUR

GEOGRAPHY GENIUS

DESIGN DEVOTEE

HISTORY HERO

TECH TITAN

DEVCALEDONIVS

Thule insula

OCEANVS

Orcades

MAP MISTAKES, PAGE 94

S

Explore tremendous tree houses on page 140.

What's really going on at Area 51? Find out on page 145.

DINO DISCOVERIES, PAGE 32

WHAT KIND OF NERD ARE YOU?

START HERE!

WHAT WOULD YOU DO IN A TREE HOUSE?

Make it even more awesome.

HOW CAN A TREE HOUSE GET ANY MORE AWESOME?

DESIGN DEVOTEES have a flair for architecture, game design, and applied art.

I'd just chill.

HOW?

Building some models.

Reading.

WHAT'S YOUR FAVORITE THING TO READ?

Comics.

Novels.

Playing some games.

Just hanging out, watching all the animals.

Listening to some tunes.

Spy on people on the ground.

HOW WOULD YOU KEEP TRACK OF THEM?

A field journal.

I'd map how they come and go.

GEOGRAPHY GENIUSES know their way around planetary features, population facts, and mapmaking.

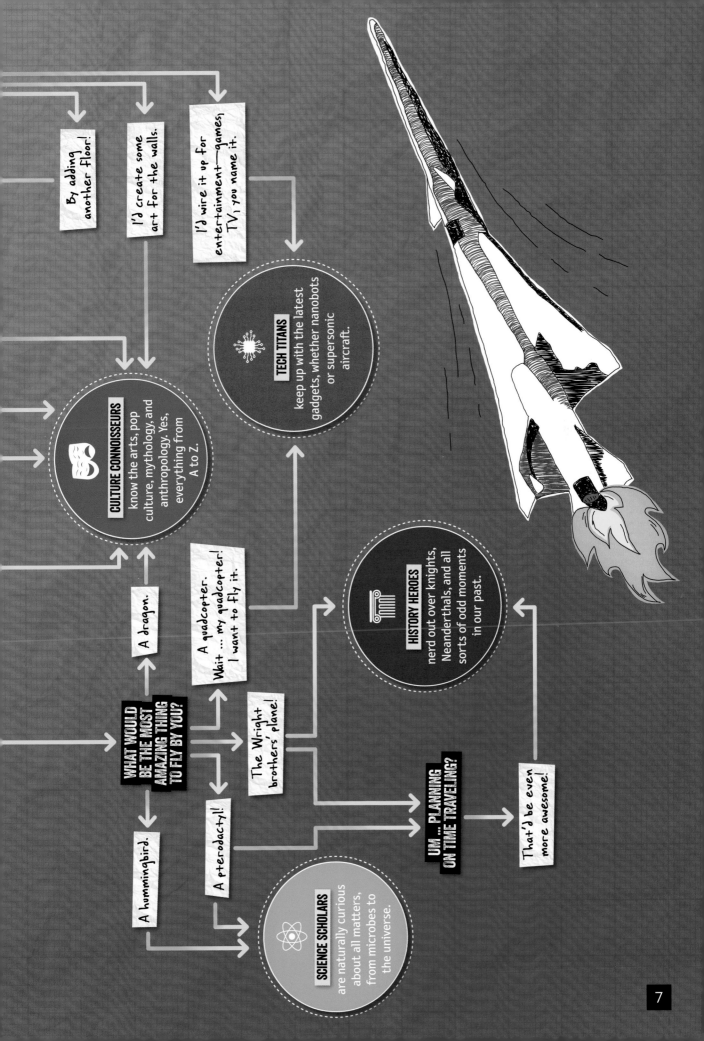

By adding another floor!

I'd create some art for the walls.

I'd wire it up for entertainment—games, TV, you name it.

TECH TITANS
keep up with the latest gadgets, whether nanobots or supersonic aircraft.

CULTURE CONNOISSEURS
know the arts, pop culture, mythology, and anthropology. Yes, everything from A to Z.

A dragon.

A quadcopter. Wait ... my quadcopter! I want to fly it.

HISTORY HEROES
nerd out over knights, Neanderthals, and all sorts of odd moments in our past.

WHAT WOULD BE THE MOST AMAZING THING TO FLY BY YOU?

The Wright brothers' plane!

A hummingbird.

A pterodactyl!

UM ... PLANNING ON TIME TRAVELING?

That'd be even more awesome!

SCIENCE SCHOLARS
are naturally curious about all matters, from microbes to the universe.

"People challenge my nerd cred all the time. I just show them the photo of me winning my middle-school science fair, wearing my Casio calculator watch and eye-glasses so big they look like they can see the future."

AISHA TYLER, actor, comedian, talk-show host

AARDWOLF

DON'T BE FOOLED BY THE NAME. This cute little critter is not a mix of aardvark and wolf. It's actually a member of the hyena family that lives in the shrubby areas of eastern and southern Africa. Very shy animals, aardwolves burrow by day but come out at night. Like their almost namesake, aardvarks, aardwolves feast on termites. They use their long tongues to lap up about 200,000 of the little insects in a single night! Their name actually means "earth wolf" in Afrikaans.

AIR CAPTURE

YES, WE'RE TALKING ABOUT CAPTURING AIR—as in that stuff floating around us. Why would anyone want to do that? To clean it! Air is a mix of invisible gases (mainly oxygen and nitrogen), but it gets polluted with all sorts of harmful gases, smoke, and dust. Some gases, such as carbon dioxide (or CO_2) trap heat around Earth, making climate change worse. Lucky for us, some companies in Canada, Switzerland, and the United States are building direct air-capture facilities that blow air through filters to trap CO_2, cleaning the air. The world would need a lot of these plants to tackle climate change, but it's a move in the right direction.

ALCATRAZ

JUST CALL IT THE ROCK. This island, 1.25 miles (2 km) offshore from San Francisco, California, U.S.A., is best known as the site of an infamous U.S. federal penitentiary from 1934 to 1963. Its inmates included America's most notorious criminals: gangster Al Capone, George "Machine Gun Kelly" Barnes, and Robert Franklin Stroud, the "Bird-man of Alcatraz." Surrounded by strong, bone-chilling currents, the fortified prison had a reputation for being impossible to escape. But in 1962, three inmates broke out and sneaked off the island in a makeshift raft. After years of searching for them, federal officials concluded they must have drowned—but no one knows for sure.

LONG-LEGGED SAC SPIDER

ANANSI, THE SPIDER

THIS MISCHIEVOUS SPIDER, one of the most popular animal tricksters in West African folklore, can disguise himself as a person or other animals, such as a rabbit or a fox. In some stories, Anansi appeals to the sky god Nyame on behalf of humans—for example, he persuades the god to give both rain and night. But most of the time, Anansi tricks people, other animals, or even the gods to make life more fun for himself—or more difficult for others. Tales of Anansi's antics have spread all over the world, including to the Caribbean and Americas. In some parts of North America, the trickster is known as Aunt Nancy or Miss Nancy, and in parts of the Caribbean, he's known as Kompa Nanzi.

AQUARIUS REEF BASE

IF YOU WANT TO STUDY OCEANIC LIFE, there's no better place to do it than under the sea. Dive on down to the Aquarius Reef Base, a research laboratory some 60 feet (18 m) underneath the water's surface in the Florida Keys National Marine Sanctuary in the United States. Researchers have used the base for three decades to study the health of the nearby Conch Reef, the ocean's health, and climate change. But they're not the only ones who use it. NASA also sends astronauts there to practice techniques for exploring space.

AQUARIUS AQUANAUTS PEER THROUGH THE LAB'S PORTHOLE

9

ARCHERY

THE INVENTION OF THE BOW AND ARROW was a game changer—and for more reasons than experts first realized. Prehistoric humans replaced their old spear-throwers with more accurate bows at least 11,000 years ago in Europe and probably much earlier in Africa. These more effective hunting tools helped them expand their diets, adding small animals to the mix. The shift to bows also occurred as individuals became specialists at doing certain tasks in society. Before bows, all members of a community may have hunted. But using bows took more strength and experience—in other words, the most expert hunters. When people divided tasks by who could do what best, all of society changed. Think of that the next time you're asked to do a chore.

ARCHIMEDES PALIMPSEST

IN 1998, a book collector paid $2 million for this old prayer book. Why? Part of the 13th-century book was written on top of a 10th-century manuscript that included important works by the brilliant ancient Greek scientist Archimedes. Parchment is made from specially treated, stretched, and dried animal skin. And it cost a lot back when it was used: something like $20 a sheet, if you bought it today. So writers washed or scraped off old text and reused parchment over and over for years, even centuries. (A reused parchment book is a palimpsest.) Lucky for us, traces of the old text could be seen with special, advanced imaging equipment.

CHRYSLER BUILDING

ART DECO

THIS CREATIVE MOVEMENT, popular in the United States and western Europe from about 1925 into the 1930s, transformed urban architecture and had a major impact on art, fashion, and even furniture. The movement is known for simple and streamlined designs, sleek geometric ornamentations, edgy sunrise and floral patterns, and shapes inspired by Native American artwork. Often used on public buildings, including the Chrysler Building in New York City, and apartment buildings, it was both cool-looking and practical: Its fancy features could be mass-produced for much less cost than earlier ornamentation, which was often hand-carved by artists.

AUGMENTED REALITY BRINGS 2D IMAGES TO LIFE.

AUGMENTED REALITY

TAKE REAL LIFE and add a layer of computer-generated information, and you've got augmented reality (AR). If you've ever seen Pokémon GO, you already know about AR: You're exploring a real scene and find a computer-generated Squirtle or Eevee. Augmented reality ("augment" means to add) isn't just fun and games, but it is plenty awesome. It can give you a deeper experience of the world by adding details about the scene you're viewing. You could view an archaeological site full of ruins, and AR could layer on a computer-generated image of the houses and people who lived there when it was a thriving community. AR also could help turn 2D drawings into 3D images that you can move around and explore. AR is becoming more available. Some AR requires special equipment, but some requires only the smartphone you hold in your hand.

AVALANCHE MAPPING

DURING AN AVALANCHE, a huge slab of snow breaks loose and slides down a mountain at speeds up to 80 miles an hour (130 km/h). It's the last thing you want to experience when you're out skiing in the backcountry. Avalanches are most common when a winter storm dumps a lot of fresh snow on top of existing snowpack, which cracks the weaker layers underneath. Luckily, avalanche forecasters predict which areas are most at risk for avalanches—and sometimes have snow blasted loose when nobody's around. They traditionally rely on their knowledge of terrain, snowpack conditions, weather forecasts—and their experience—to determine avalanche risks. But new, high-tech equipment, including radar and even satellite imagery, can look into the layers of snow, help identify likely avalanches, and map their locations.

AXOLOTL

AXOLOTLS, rare Mexican salamanders, never grow up. Unlike other amphibians, such as frogs, which transform from tadpoles to much different-looking adults, axolotls (pronounced ACK-suh-LAH-tuhls) keep their tadpole-like fins and external gills all their lives. But that's not the only awesome thing about these water dwellers. They also can regrow body parts that get damaged—their legs, tails, jaws, even skin and spinal cords! Those amazing feats have attracted the attention of scientific researchers, who wonder if we can learn any lessons from the axolotl to help people heal better. No wonder the ancient Aztec revered them.

ARTIFICIAL
Intelligence ✳

Machines that think like people do. Impossible? Nope. That's what artificial intelligence (AI) does. AI lets machines understand speech, identify objects, make decisions, translate between languages, and so on. It's mind-blowing.

To understand why, consider this: Ever run on a slick floor in socks and try to round a corner at top speed? Your feet slide out from under you, and BAM!

Down you go. The next time you sprint on a slick floor, you slow down to round a corner—or maybe wear sneakers. That's because you're intelligent. You tried something (socks + speed + slick), remembered how it worked out (ouch), then changed what you did (sneaker traction), so you wouldn't face-plant again. In other words, you learned.

For years, the most powerful computers—the ones that sent astronauts into space or crunched through tons of scientific data—couldn't learn diddly-squat. They were super fast and accurate, but they could only do what we programmed them to do. The same went for robots. Nothing like *Star Wars'* C-3PO or BB-8.

AI is changing all that. It makes machines think for themselves and learn from their experiences so they keep getting "smarter." Intelligent machines process information much like our brains do: recognizing things, classifying them, and drawing on all that information to make decisions. They even learn from their mistakes, so they can make better decisions and tackle harder problems.

If you've ever asked Google, Siri, or Alexa a question, you've interacted with AI. The same goes for those movies, songs, and videos recommended for you by streaming sites. The sites pay attention to what you play, classify it, and suggest entertainment similar to your tastes. In self-driving cars, AI figures out how to avoid obstacles. One day, AI machines may even learn how to make new AI technology.

REFERENCE • REFERENCE • REFERENCE • REFERENCE • REFERENCE • REFERENCE •

WANT TO SEE WHERE AI DOES SOME OF ITS BEST WORK? CHECK OUT THE ROBOTS ON PAGES 120-121.

FAQ

DO AI ROBOTS HAVE FEELINGS?

AI robots don't feel real human emotions—at least, not yet! But some are learning to understand our emotions and even act like they have their own, so they seem more like real buddies. Some are also programmed to have "personalities," like Siri, who's known for sometimes giving snarky replies. Some developers want AI robots to have real emotions and desires, but that raises big questions: Would they still be treated like tools that people use to do things, or would they deserve the respect and care we give living beings? People are already debating what kind of rights AI robots should have—like could they sue people who don't treat them well?

WILL AI GET SO SMART THAT IT OVERTHROWS HUMANITY?

Many experts predict that AI will keep getting smarter until it outperforms us—but we'll still be around, maybe doing more creative things. Some people look forward to that day. AI robots will help find solutions to hard problems, like curing diseases or easing climate change—and they won't be like people, who try to satisfy their own desires. But other experts aren't so sure. They're worried that superhuman AI robots could become so focused on meeting their goals that they wouldn't let anything get in their way—even us trying to give them new directions.

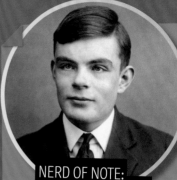

NERD OF NOTE:
ALAN TURING

AI IS HOT TODAY, but its roots go back decades. One of its pioneers was Alan Turing, the brilliant English mathematician who broke the Nazi's Enigma code during World War II and went on to design some of the first computers. In the 1950s, he began to wonder whether machines of the future could "think" and act as intelligently as people. And if they could, how would we even know?

Turing invented a simple test: People sit on one side of a screen and chat with others behind the screen. But here's the trick: Most of the conversation partners are people, but one is a computer chatbot. If the people can't tell if they are talking to a machine or another human, the AI passes the test. Turing set a pretty low bar: The people would only have to be fooled about a third of the time during a short conversation. But even then, it's been a tough test for AI to pass. One machine came close in 2012 by pretending to be a 13-year-old Ukrainian boy speaking imperfect English. Other AI machines have produced sounds—like leaves crunching underfoot or cars crashing—that people thought were real.

IMAGINING AI
SCIENCE FICTION HAS GIVEN US SOME OF THE COOLEST—AND CREEPIEST!—AI ROBOTS.

- **BB-8,** an astromech droid from recent *Star Wars* movies, has tons of personality and showed a range of emotions through his body language, squeals, and bleeps. Plus, his body rolls but his head always manages to stay on top.

- **HAL 9000 FROM THE MOVIE *2001: A SPACE ODYSSEY*** was a charming superintelligent computer that was programmed to hide critical information from his crewmates and to complete his mission—no matter what. The conflict drove him mad, and he turned on his crew.

- **LIEUTENANT COMMANDER DATA,** the wise and sensitive android from the *Star Trek* series, defined what many people think of as the ideal artificially intelligent robot. Ironically, Data was constantly striving to become more human.

"Here's my nerd code of conduct: Be open and be honest. Don't pretend you know what you don't know (often a little too easy to do). Show the world as it is, rather than the way you wish it would be. Respect facts; don't deny them just because you don't like them. Move forward only after you trust your design."

BILL NYE, science guy

BAMBOO HOUSES

IF YOU THINK OF BAMBOO HOUSES, you might picture simple huts of bamboo lashed together. But in the hands of architect Elora Hardy, bamboo houses soar six floors high, forming magical curves and peaks. Lightweight and renewable, bamboo is a fast-growing grass—not a tree—that's super strong. It holds up to tension as well as steel does, and it's as good as concrete at handling heavy loads. Used to build homes and bridges in tropical regions for tens of thousands of years, bamboo eventually rots or is eaten by insects. But Elora uses a natural coating to protect it. Her bamboo homes can last a lifetime.

BANYAN TREES

BANYAN TREES GROW FROM THE TOP DOWN.
Their seeds blow into the branches of other trees and then sprout vine-like tendrils that grow to the forest floor, where they take root. As the treetop grows wider, it sends more and more tendrils to the ground, and the tree keeps spreading wider. One 550-year-old banyan tree in India—believed to be the largest in the world—has a canopy that covers as much ground as a football field (without the end zones).

BIKE PATH THAT TWINKLES

A BIKE PATH IN THE NETHERLANDS, inspired by artist Vincent van Gogh's "The Starry Night," twinkles with thousands of lights embedded in the path. They're arranged in swirling patterns like the sky in that famous painting. Developed by artist and designer Daan Roosegaarde, the bike path gets energy from the sun's rays during the day and shines for eight hours at night.

BIODIVERSITY

BIODIVERSITY IS THE VARIETY OF LIFE in a particular ecosystem—and the Amazon has a lot of it. The amazing Amazon, which spans nearly 40 percent of South America, contains more than half of our planet's remaining rainforest and is home to more species of animals and plants than any other land ecosystem on Earth. Researchers discover hundreds of new species in the Amazon every year—sometimes averaging one species every two days. And all that diversity benefits the entire planet. The variety of plant life works together in the ecosystem, like pieces that join to create a big jigsaw puzzle—a really lush, green puzzle. The plants don't just thrive on the rain and nutrients they absorb from the soil. As part of their photosynthesis process, which produces the energy they need to grow, they also soak up harmful carbon dioxide emissions from cars, airplanes, and power plants, and produce clean oxygen for us to breathe. That's earned the Amazon a nickname: the lungs of the Earth.

BIONIC PROSTHETICS

PROSTHETICS ARE ARTIFICIAL LIMBS, like arms or legs, that people can wear if they don't have a natural limb. For many years, prosthetics were mechanical devices that lacked a sense of touch. By operating something like a pulley system on their shoulders, people could open or close prosthetic hands, but they couldn't tell how strongly they were grabbing something. They broke a lot of eggs and delivered some crushing handshakes. But researchers have recently developed bionic prosthetics embedded with lots of sensors. A bionic hand can be wired directly into the nerves on someone's arm. It can send signals to the person's brain and be controlled like any hand. Now people with high-tech prosthetic hands can even feel textures and enjoy holding hands.

15

BIRD CHIRPS

BIRDS COMMUNICATE BY CHIRPING.
(Like you didn't know that, right?) But it's not just any chirping. Some birds, such as Japanese tit birds, chirp entire sentences. And just like our own sentences, they make sense only if the words—or chirps—are in the right order. If a predator threatens a flock, Japanese tit birds will tweet a specific series of chirps that mean, "Danger, come now!" Then other flock members will fly in and mob the predator. But if the "come now" chirps aren't tacked on to the end of the sentence, the birds won't ruffle a feather. Or if the chirps are in the wrong order, the birds won't even pay attention. Researchers found that out by recording chirps and playing real and garbled sentences back to the birds to see their reaction.

BLACK DEATH

YOU WOULDN'T WANT TO BE NEAR EUROPE between 1347 and 1351. The Black Death, a pandemic probably caused by the plague, swept from Asia through Europe, killing a larger percentage of that continent's population than had died from any war or disease up to that point. Plague was an infectious disease caused by a specific kind of harmful bacteria. Scientists thought rats spread the disease, but it may have been the work of infected fleas and human body lice. The Black Death had such an impact that it changed culture. Even art and poetry—which had earlier celebrated the saints' lives or knights' heroic deeds—turned to focus on death and the afterlife.

LICE

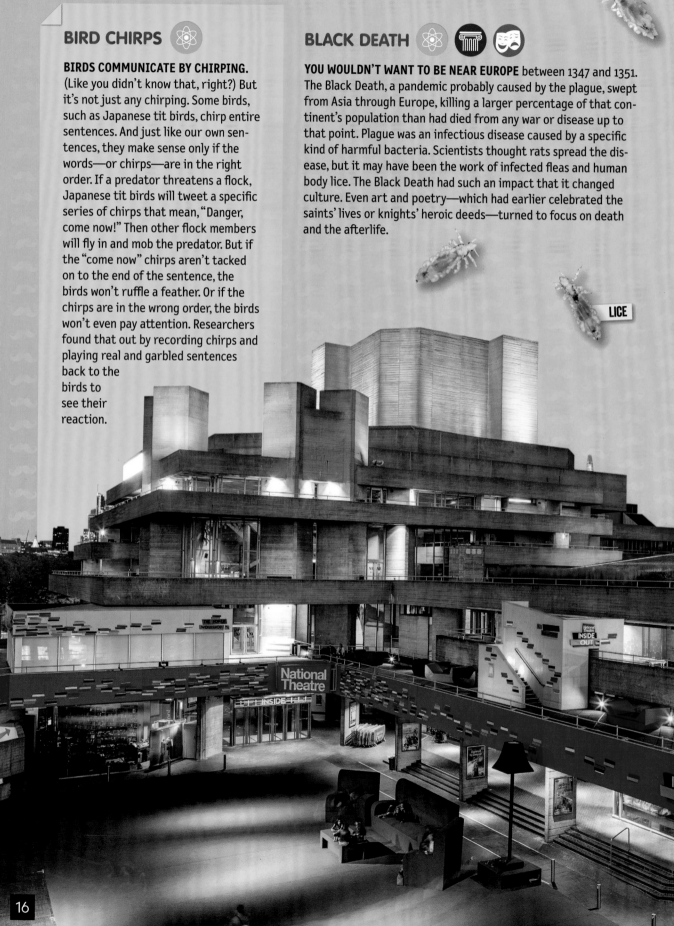

BRAIN-COMPUTER INTERFACE

IMAGINE BEING ABLE TO CONTROL all sorts of things by thought alone: robots, video games, artificial limbs. It's not just science fiction. It's possible through a brain-computer interface—or mind-machine interface. We've long had medical sensors that can pick up the strength of various brain waves. Researchers now are fine-tuning that technology and linking it to computers that can translate the signals to operate apps, machines, or robots. To make it work, a person often wears a cap embedded with sensors that pick up the signals and controls things simply by thinking. The technology has already worked for playing video games, operating a computer, flying a drone, and operating bionic prosthetics. In 2014, a dramatic display of the technology's potential occurred at the soccer World Cup in Brazil. A 29-year-old man paralyzed from the waist down wore a robotic "exoskeleton," which he controlled with his thoughts, and made the ceremonial first kick.

BRANE CRAFT SPACECRAFT

THEY'RE NOT AS CUTE AS WALL-E, but Brane Craft may be just as awesome. The little spacecraft, still in the development stage, would clean up space trash—particles of spent rocket fuel or bits of spacecraft that have broken up. The Brane Craft are nearly flat, flexible spacecrafts with embedded solar cells, sensors, propulsion, and so on. They'd nab trash in space and wrap it up in their thin, flexible membrane. Then they'd use their thrusters to slow down, fall out of orbit, and plummet toward Earth—where both the craft and its load of trash would burn up in Earth's atmosphere. A smart solution. Maybe it should be called Brain Craft instead.

NATIONAL THEATRE, LONDON

BRUTALISM

THIS HARSH SOUNDING NAME is actually a style of modern architecture that was especially popular from the mid-1940s to the 1980s. It gets its name from the French term *béton brut,* which means "rough or raw concrete"—which kind of gives it all away. The style used a lot of molded and shaped concrete, sometimes with bricks, in massive, fortress-like buildings. Many university and government buildings—some of which still stand today, such as Boston City Hall—used brutalist architecture. Brutalism's rugged look was a reaction to what people saw as the light, frivolous styles of the 1930s and early 1940s. (We're looking at you, art deco.)

BUNGEE JUMPING

JUMPING FROM WAY UP HIGH with only a thick elastic cord tied to you ... yikes. Bungee jumping became an extreme type of recreational fun in 1979, but its roots are way deeper. Every spring for centuries, young men living on Pentecost Island, in the South Pacific nation of Vanuatu, have performed ritual land dives. They build 75-foot (23-m)-tall towers, tie vines around their ankles, and fling themselves down. The idea is to bless the soil—ensuring a bountiful yam harvest—by brushing the earth with the top of their heads. (You know not to ever, ever try that, right?)

17

BURIALS

Burials have always reflected people's beliefs and traditions—many rooted in religion, which often has elaborate rituals surrounding death. Many cultures view burial as a step toward an afterlife, and some include objects in the graves to help the deceased person make the journey. In many Western countries, "burial" means a boxy coffin buried six feet (1.8 m) under the ground in a solemn cemetery.

But some people want something more modern for their final resting places. They want their deceased bodies to nourish nature or hang with some fishies for eternity—or maybe even be turned into serious bling. These people have made their wishes clear: When they die, they want unusual burials. They're often willing to break with tradition to focus on other priorities.

"Green burials" skip the traditional casket—a container designed not to degrade—and focus on returning bodies' organic matter quickly to the earth. Yep, bodies become fertilizer. There are different ways of doing it. In a process invented by a Swedish biologist and avid gardener, bodies would be quickly frozen using liquid nitrogen—a chemical element that turns tissue into a brittle, frozen brick—then vibrated into dust by a special machine and freeze-dried to remove liquid. After metals are removed, the remains would be buried in a small grave, where they'd turn into fresh soil within six to 18 months.

Another eco-friendly approach, created by Italian designers, would use egg-shaped burial pods for the departed. A tree or tree seed would be planted over the pod, which would use the nutrients from the decaying body as fertilizer. Instead of cemeteries with rows of tombstones, the designers envision forests of trees to honor the dead.

Some people set their sights deeper—as in the bottom of the ocean. Cremated remains are cast into concrete memorials and placed in an artificial reef, where they create a habitat for fish and coral. If you want to visit their graves, you can suit up in scuba gear.

But if glitz and glamor are more your style, several companies are ready to provide a memorial with bling appeal. They put cremated remains under high pressure and heat—like the conditions deep inside Earth that create diamonds from carbon—and compress them into diamonds. And, yes, you can make the diamonds into jewelry. They view it as a way for people to keep their loved ones with them forever.

CAPSULA MUNDI, AN EGG-SHAPED BURIAL POD

FUN FACT

Neanderthals—who often get a bad rap as being brutish cave dwellers—actually had complex ways of burying their dead, including putting stone tools and animals in the shallow graves, at least 50,000 years ago.

REFERENCE · REFERENCE · REFERENCE · REFERENCE · REFERENCE · REFERENCE ·

LOOKING FOR MORE AFTER-DEATH ARRANGEMENTS?
READ ABOUT MUMMIES ON PAGE 97.

FAQ

CAN PEOPLE GET BURIED ANY WAY THEY WANT?

It depends where they live—or, um, die. Different countries have their own rules and laws—most are related to public health concerns, like burying remains deeply enough that wild animals won't dig them up. Some U.S. states require bodies to be buried in cemeteries, and the cemeteries may allow only certain types of burials and containers. But others may give permission for unusual burials on private land.

ST. LOUIS CEMETERY, NEW ORLEANS, LOUISIANA

CAN PEOPLE BE FROZEN AND THEN BROUGHT BACK TO LIFE?

Some people sure hope so! They've paid many times the cost of a typical funeral to be specially frozen in hopes of being thawed and brought back to life someday—usually after science has figured out a way to cure a disease, such as cancer, that they had. Cryogenic techniques, where something is completely frozen and then slowly warmed back up, have worked with very small, live things. Will it be able to bring back a person who's died? It's never been tried—and many scientists don't think it's possible ... at least for now.

IMAGINING THE END

IN STORIES AND MYTHOLOGY, DEATH ISN'T JUST A STATE OF BEING; IT'S A CHARACTER THAT COMES LOOKING FOR PEOPLE TO ESCORT TO THE AFTERLIFE.

- **IN EUROPEAN TRADITION,** the grim reaper—a mysterious skeletal figure shrouded in a long, black, hooded robe—comes carrying a scythe, a long-handled tool with a curved blade. Farmers use scythes to harvest crops ready to be plucked from the earth. The grim reaper uses it to harvest souls.

- **IN GREEK MYTHOLOGY,** the god Hades rules the shadowy underworld, where souls go after death. The only god who didn't live on Mount Olympus, Hades was much feared by ordinary Greeks in ancient times—so much so that his name would not be spoken.

- **TIME'S UP.** That's how death works in the 2016 movie *Alice Through the Looking Glass*, based on the Lewis Carroll novel. The character Time, the personification of death, maintains rows of watches, one for each person in the land. You don't want the final tick to come.

NERD OF NOTE: JAE RHIM LEE

JAE RHIM LEE ISN'T CREEPY. She just happens to spend a lot of time thinking about death. Oh, and mushrooms, too: She's consumed with the cool things these edible fungi can do.

On the death side, Jae Rhim thinks we need to think about the impact modern burial traditions make on our planet.

As we go through life, our bodies absorb toxins from pollution, pesticides, preservatives, and other chemicals. After we die and our bodies decay, those toxins seep into the environment.

That's where the mushrooms come in. Mushrooms and other fungi can break down toxins, making them pretty harmless for the environment.

So Jae Rhim put death and mushrooms together and came up with a way mushrooms can eat our dead bodies, leaving behind clean, pollutant-free compost for the ground.

She designed full-body burial suits embedded with mushroom filaments. When bodies are buried in the suits, the mushrooms can grow and do their work.

She sees it as a way "to understand and accept death and to minimize the impact of our death on the environment." Not so creepy after all.

WHAT KIND OF
SCIENCE
SCHOLAR
ARE YOU?

START HERE.

ARE YOU A PEOPLE PERSON?

People are way too confusing.

HOW ABOUT ANIMALS?

Eh ... I'm not a big fan.

LIKE HANGING OUT IN NATURE?

Yes, yes, yes!

Only if they are long gone.

WHAT INTERESTS YOU THE MOST?

Elephant societies.

Rainforest animals.

Protecting them!

Well, I'm a person, so ... yeah, of course.

ARCHAEOLOGISTS AND PALEONTOLOGISTS dig into the ancient history of people, animals, and plants. Sounds like you might want to join those **HISTORY HEROES.**

WHAT'S THE MOST INTERESTING THING ABOUT THEM?

How our bodies work.

HOW THEY FUNCTION, DEVELOP, OR RELATE TO OUR ENVIRONMENT?

All of the above.

How our hearts and muscles and stuff work.

More like what gives us certain traits.

Braaaaiiiinnnnnnns!

WHAT ABOUT THEM? (AND DON'T GO ALL ZOMBIE ON US AGAIN.)

How they work.

Why we do what we do, what motivates us, why we dream—that kind of stuff.

20

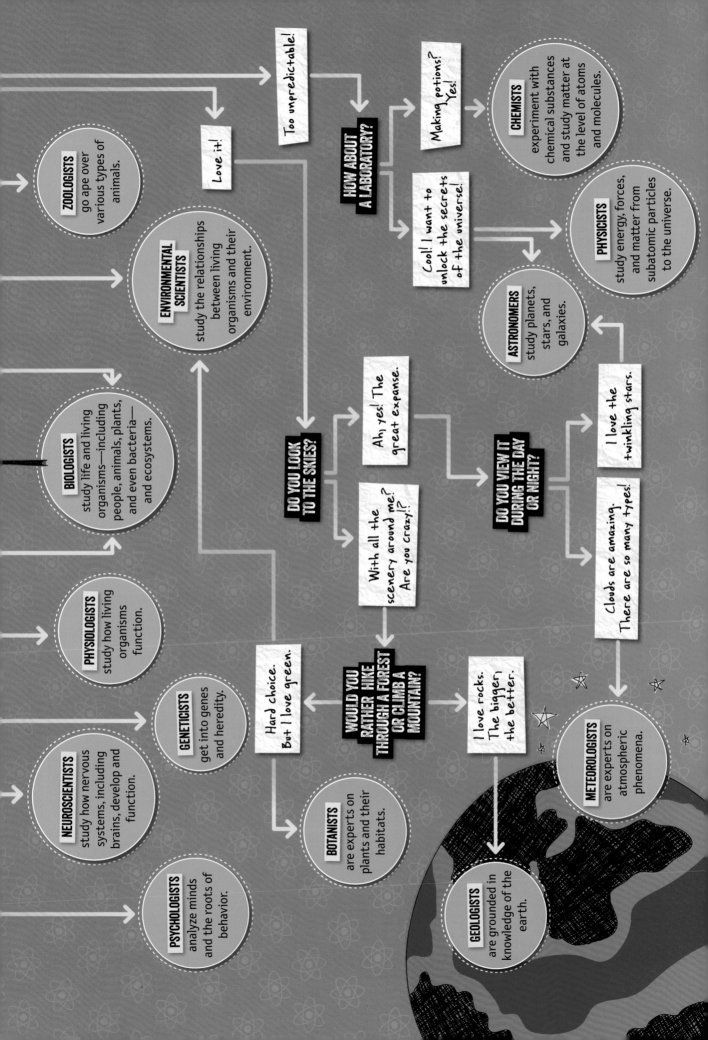

CARBON DATING
C
CROP CIRCLES

"Everyone's a nerd inside. I don't care how cool you are."

CHANNING TATUM, actor

CARBON DATING

OLD BONES, ANCIENT WOODEN SPEARS, MUMMIES—they're treasures archaeologists dig up from thousands of years ago. But how do they know how old they are? Scientists often use carbon dating (or radiocarbon dating), a way to figure out the age of things that lived as long as 50,000 years ago. All living things—people, animals, plants—have an element called carbon in them. Plants absorb carbon dioxide naturally as part of photosynthesis, and people and animals take in carbon when they eat plants. A very small portion of the carbon is radioactive, and it starts to decay when a living thing dies. The rest of the carbon isn't radioactive, and it doesn't change. Scientists know how long it takes radioactive carbon to decay, so they can look at how much a fossil's radioactive carbon has decayed—and compare it to the stable carbon— to figure out roughly how old the fossil is.

CASTLES

THESE FORTIFIED STRUCTURES didn't start out awesome. The first castles, built in the early 1000s, were simple wooden forts on mounds of earth, called motte (mound) and bailey (yard next to it). They were pretty easy to attack, so castle-makers started strengthening them by building a ring of stone on top of the mound. By the late 1200s, castles had tall stone towers, called keeps, in the middle, surrounded by defense walls on the outside. Over the centuries, they grew larger and more strongly fortified, with thicker walls and rings of extra outer walls around them. They gained lots of defensive features, such as moats, arrow slits where archers could fire on attackers, and "murder holes" through which guards could dump hot oil or rocks on invaders. But no matter how strong castles became, attackers figured out how to bring them down. The glory days of castles ended around the 1500s, when cannons became too powerful for

CARDIFF CASTLE,
WALES, U.K.

CENOTES

CENOTES (pronounced sih-NO-tees) are flooded caves or natural sinkholes most often found on the Yucatán Peninsula in Mexico. But these are no ordinary holes in the ground! For centuries, the ancient Maya have viewed cenotes as sacred. They believed the rain god Chaac lived in them, and they may have made offerings to the gods in them, too. Underwater passages within cenotes have led to temples and depictions of mythically important animals, such as jaguars. For the Maya, cenotes—and caves—represented the entrance to the underworld, the sacred world of the supernatural.

CERN

PART OF CERN'S PARTICLE COLLIDER

CERN, the European Organization for Nuclear Research laboratory, which straddles the Swiss-French border, exists to uncover the secrets of the universe: How did it begin? What's it made of? The laboratory is home to the Large Hadron Collider, the largest and most powerful single machine in the world. It can smash subatomic particles together at nearly the speed of light, re-creating conditions similar to those during the earliest moments of the universe. To house the Large Hadron Collider, CERN sits on more than 1,360 acres (550 ha)—a patch of land bigger than all four of Disney World's Florida theme parks combined.

CHAMBERED NAUTILUS

IT'S OFTEN CALLED A LIVING FOSSIL, and it's not hard to see why. This mollusk—a relative of the octopus, squid, snail, and clam—is older than the first dinosaurs by about 265 million years. And it has barely changed in more than 400 million years. It has 90 tentacles that grab its prey, which it locates by smell. Its shell is also one of the marvels of nature. The shell's chambers are arranged in a mathematically perfect spiral known as a Fibonacci sequence or "golden ratio." Art and architecture based on the golden ratio is extra pleasing to our eyes.

CIRCUSES

Step right up

and see the show! Amazing acts of acrobatics, dazzling feats of daring, kooky antics of clowns—circuses have them all.

Circus acts have deep roots going back centuries, when traveling entertainers delighted royalty and street performers showed off their skills to earn their suppers. But today's modern circus really got its start in Europe in the late 1700s, when trick riders showed off their "feats of horsemanship" in the circular arenas—or circuses—of their riding schools. To keep the audiences coming, they soon added acrobats, jugglers, and clowns to their riding shows. Soon every major European city had at least one permanent circus.

In 1793, one of the trick riders, a young Scotsman named John Bill Ricketts, took his troupe of riders, acrobats, and clowns to the United States, where they performed in cities along the East Coast. The young country didn't have entertainment venues, so the troupe had to build their own wooden arenas as they traveled from town to town. Other European circuses soon followed to America.

When showman Joshua Purdy Brown came to Wilmington, Delaware, in 1825, he found that city leaders had banned "public amusements" from the city as part of a religious revival. Brown came up with a creative solution. He erected a canvas tent, a "pavilion circus," just outside the city limits—and forever changed the American circus. Traveling circuses began pitching tents throughout America, following settlers as they pushed westward, and expanding from one-ring shows to three or more.

Always looking for new ways to attract crowds, American circuses began including exotic animals, such as lions, tigers, and elephants. P. T. Barnum also added sideshows of people with unusual physical traits. After he merged with his rivals, J. A. Bailey and later the Ringling brothers, they included new, exciting performers, such as tightrope dancers, trapeze artists who swung from one rope to another, and human cannonballs. By the 1920s, what was to become the "Greatest Show on Earth" had 1,600 performers and filled a 100-car train.

But the big, multi-ringed extravaganzas, like the Ringling Bros. and Barnum & Bailey Circus, were not to last. In the 1970s and 1980s, artsy one-ring circuses, such as Cirque du Soleil, breathed new life into the circus arts with elaborate stories, amazing costumes, and awesome acrobatics. They ensured that the show would go on—in a new style.

CAN'T GET ENOUGH OF CRAZY ACTS? CHECK OUT DAREDEVILS ON PAGE 30 AND FIRE WALKING ON PAGE 45.

FAQ DO CONTORTIONISTS—THOSE PERFORM-ERS WHO TWIST THEMSELVES UP LIKE LIV-ING PRETZELS—HAVE UNUSUAL JOINTS?

Some famous contortionists have been able to slip bones in and out of their natural locations. But that kind of dislocation is really rare. Most contortionists train really hard to become super flexible in key areas, especially their backbones. The spine's joints, held together by connective tissue, are slightly movable. If the performers' muscles are stretchy enough, they can pull the spine into extreme positions.

In the mid-1900s, the famous contortionist Paul Brachard would do a handstand, then slowly move into a back bend so extreme that he'd end up sitting on his own head. He'd then clamp his teeth on a special brace and lift his hands off the ground, so his entire, twisted body would be supported only by his teeth!

DON'T FIRE-EATERS USE TRICK FLAMES THAT AREN'T REALLY HOT?

Nope. The flames are the real deal. They can burn. But fire-eaters learn how to carefully place the flaming torches in their mouths and snuff them out without getting hurt. Remembering that heat rises, they keep the flames above their faces—and they make sure not to inhale! As they place the torches in their mouths, they either blow the flames out or snuff them out by closing their lips around the torch and cutting off the oxygen necessary for the fire. No matter how they do it, it's still dangerous. Don't try it!

DO PEOPLE REALLY RUN OFF AND JOIN A CIRCUS?

Back in the late 1800s, definitely. In fact, circus innovator James A. Bailey—of Ringling Bros. and Barnum & Bailey Circus fame—ran away with a circus when he was 13 years old. These days, though, joining a circus takes more than an itch to travel and willingness to try risky stunts. Circus performers spend years training and perfecting their acts—often in special circus schools—and must audition and beat out many other hopefuls to join the best circuses.

FUN FACT
Traveling circuses were a big deal in the late 1800s—especially in rural areas of the United States. When the circus came to town, nearby mills, shops, and even schools would close for "Circus Day."

NERD OF NOTE: ROSA RICHTER

IT WAS APRIL 2, 1877, and Rosa Richter was getting ready for her aerial act at the newly constructed Royal Aquarium in London. Better known by her stage name, Zazel, the British teenager was already an experienced acrobat, entertaining crowds by dancing along a high wire. But that day was different. She had a new grand finale to her act.

Zazel waved to the crowd and slid into the long metal barrel of a cannon. Moments later, a loud boom split the air, and Zazel was hurled 70 feet (21 m) into the air, over spectators' heads, and into a woven safety net. The brave teenager had become the first human cannonball—and an instant celebrity. She went on to thrill huge crowds in England and America.

More amazing than the act was Zazel's bravery. Just because it wasn't a real cannon didn't make it any less dangerous. Circus aerialists usually rely on their strength, skills, and experience to pinpoint where they go. But when she was shot from the cannon, Zazel had no control over her flight—and the cannon mechanism was a bit unpredictable. One horrible day, a misguided launch sent her flying far from the safety net. She crashed to the ground, suffering an injury that ended her career. Luckily, she lived to tell about it.

CHIMPANZEES

CHIMPANZEES SHARE 98.8 PERCENT OF OUR DNA— and, it turns out, our competitive spirit. In case you had any doubts, check this out. In Japan, five chimps learned how to play rock-paper-scissors at the same level as a typical four-year-old human. OK, it took them a little longer to learn, but once they did, they played it with no problem. That means they understood that rock beats scissors, and so forth, and they made decisions fast. Awesome— but maybe not surprising considering that they're such close relatives of ours.

CONCUSSIONS

MOST PEOPLE KNOW THAT A HARD BUMP to your head can give you a concussion. But what's really going on? Your brain is protected by the bone of your skull and cushioned by fluids inside. If your head gets hit hard enough, your brain smacks up against the inside of your skull. It can get hurt that way, even enough to change how it works for a little bit. You have to let your brain recover, or it'll be easier to get hurt again. If you get a hard knock on your noggin, tell a grown-up right away, and have a doctor check out any possible concussion—especially if the hit makes you feel dizzy or sick to your stomach, or if it gives you a headache or makes it hard to concentrate. Your brain is your body's boss. Treat it well!

COSMETICS

MAKEUP HAS A LONG—AND SOMETIMES DEADLY—HISTORY. As far back as 4000 B.C., Egyptians used makeup to decorate their eyes in distinctive shapes. A thousand years later, Chinese elites painted their fingernails to show their social class—with golds, silvers, and reds reserved for royalty. Women in ancient Greece painted their faces white. Using makeup to lighten faces eventually spread across Europe. Trouble is, some makeup back then was toxic. Women applied arsenic, mercury, lead, and even leeches to make their skin lighter—sometimes creating problems like paralyzed muscles, facial tremors, and even death!

PERFUME AND COSMETICS JARS FROM ANCIENT EGYPT

DRAGON BALL Z
COSPLAYERS

COSPLAY

TAKE "COSTUME" AND ADD "PLAY," and you've got cosplay. It's a hobby in which you dress up like your favorite character from comic books, movies, cartoons, or even video games. Cosplay is an entire subculture. You can meet with other cosplayers and even go to competitions or conventions for fans of different genres. It's Halloween all year, OK, without the candy. But definitely with all the fun.

COYOTE

THE COYOTE, that wild cousin of dogs, can adapt to life almost anywhere—prairies, deserts, forests, mountains, and even cities. Maybe that's why the coyote has a reputation for being clever. In some Native American folklore, Coyote lived even before the age of humans. He is sometimes a creator, sometimes a trickster, sometimes a fool—and sometimes all three at once. In some tales, Coyote brought fire and daylight to people; in others, his actions show the dangers of greed or recklessness.

CROP CIRCLES

CROP CIRCLES—those mysterious patterns that suddenly appear in farmers' fields, especially in the United Kingdom—are real. The question is: Who made them? Crop circle fans have lots of ideas: weird wind patterns, energy fields, time travelers, aliens, or hedgehogs. Researchers try to find the truth by examining the patterns—to see if they hold meaning—and the crops themselves, which can reveal evidence that people crushed them. They've figured out that most were made by pranksters. But others ... they still can't explain.

27

Amy Winston didn't know until she was 17 years old that she really was **AMETHYST,** A PRINCESS OF GEMWORLD. She uses her **sword skills** and **magical powers** to defend the fictional otherworldly realm where the Faerie live.

A mutant with ANIMAL-LIKE SENSES, an amazing power to heal, and retractable claws, **WOLVERINE**—raised as James Howlett—mastered multiple martial arts to become a **crime fighter.**

INSPIRED BY AN ENCOUNTER WITH BATMAN, socialite Kate Kane, daughter of career military officers, donned her own **mask** and **cape** and became **BATWOMAN.**

After suffering a grave injury, Victor Stone was saved with advanced mechanical parts. **Half machine and half human, CYBORG,** who debuted in 1980, uses his SUPERHUMAN STRENGTH and ability to interface with computers to help superheroes fight crime.

T'Challa, the **BLACK PANTHER,** is an Avenger and king of the fictional African nation of Wakanda. Mystically connected to the WAKANDAN PANTHER GOD, he has superhuman **strength, speed,** and **senses.**

Created in 1994, Angelo Espinosa, a member of Generation X, is called **SKIN**—because he has a lot of it. When he's at rest, his skin sags. But in a fight, he can control his extra, SUPERTOUGH SKIN to help in many ways, letting him **hold onto enemies** or **swing though the air.**

First appearing in 1967, Carol Danvers, AIR FORCE PILOT TURNED SUPERHERO **CAPTAIN MARVEL,** gained her **superhuman strength** and ability to fly after an explosion fused her genes with alien Kree genes.

One of the FEARLESS DEFENDERS, Cheyenne mutant Danielle Moonstar, aka **MIRAGE,** can create visible images of people's greatest fears.

Created in 1992, MUTANT Doreen Green flees the taunts of high school peers and heads into the woods, where she discovers she can **marshal forces of squirrels.** As **SQUIRREL GIRL,** she protects New York City's Central Park but is recruited into the Great Lakes X-Men/Champions.

26 COOL COMIC BOOK HEROES

Volunteering to take a SUPER-SOLDIER SERUM, Steve Rogers became **CAPTAIN AMERICA,** a highly skilled superhero trained in multiple martial arts. First appearing in 1941, he uses his skills, **extraordinary strength,** and endurance to keep the peace.

First appearing in 1964, attorney Matt Murdock becomes **DAREDEVIL** at night to **fight crime.** Blinded as a child, he found his other heightened senses gave him SUPERPOWERS.

Sooraya Qadir, **a mutant from Afghanistan,** joined the X-Men as **DUST,** who can transform into a SANDSTORM strong enough to blind enemies or strip away their flesh.

When a lightning bolt hit his lab, forensic scientist Barry Allen gained the ability to **run at near light speed**—even up the side of buildings and across oceans. As **THE FLASH,** a character created in 1940, he CONTINUES TO FIGHT CRIME, but up close and personal now.

The X-Men's "WEATHER WITCH," superhero **STORM,** a natural leader whose real name is Ororo Munroe, can **control the weather and fly on the wind.** The superhero debuted in 1975.

Already SUPER SMART, David Alleyne became **PRODIGY,** a Young Avenger, who can **mimic the skills, knowledge,** and **abilities** of everyone he's met, including other X-Men.

Debuting in 1979, Canadian Jean-Paul Beaubier—known as **NORTHSTAR**—can harness the KINETIC ENERGY of his body's molecules to **move and fly at superhuman speed.**

Not a bird, not a plane ... it's **SUPERMAN,** the MAN OF STEEL, who rocketed to Earth from the planet Krypton. Raised as Clark Kent, he uses his superpowers—like x-ray and heat vision—to **protect people.** The superhero was created in 1938!

Created in 1939, **BATMAN,** the SUPERHERO PERSONA of **millionaire Bruce Wayne,** doesn't have any superpowers. But he has smarts, determination, and a whole lot of high-tech tools and vehicles to help him fight crime.

Brainy billionaire Anthony Edward "Tony" Stark used his **genius and money** to transform himself into **IRON MAN.** He creates super high-tech armor and gadgets, which he uses to help MAKE THE WORLD A SAFER PLACE.

LUKE CAGE, aka **Power Man,** gained extraordinary strength and steel-hard skin during an experimental procedure. First appearing in 1972, he uses those powers to FIGHT FOR JUSTICE in New York City.

Vietnamese-born Xi'an "Shan" Coy Manh, the superhero **KARMA,** has PSYCHIC POWERS that let her control several people at once by **possessing their minds.**

First appearing in 2013, nerdy Pakistani-American teen Kamala Khan was exposed to **alien mist,** awakening her Inhuman ability to SHAPE-SHIFT. She takes the name **MS. MARVEL**—a connection to her idol, Captain Marvel—and defends Jersey City.

Hal Jordan, the **GREEN LANTERN,** wears a POWERFUL RING that lets him create anything he wants out of pure energy. He uses his powers as part of a universe-wide PEACEKEEPING force, the Green Lantern Corps.

A RADIOACTIVE SPIDER bit high-school student Peter Parker and gave him the **senses, strength, and agility of a spider.** As **SPIDER-MAN,** a superhero since 1962, he uses his powers to protect people—when he's not fanboying all over the Avengers.

With her LASSO OF TRUTH and shielded bracelets, **WONDER WOMAN,** Princess Diana of the immortal Amazons, uses her superhuman strength and speed to stop wars and to **better humanity.** This powerful princess joined the ranks of superheroes in 1941.

Magician **ZATANNA ZATARA** can invoke anything she imagines by reciting spells backward. She uses her magical abilities alongside superheroes of the Justice League to BATTLE THE DARK ARTS.

•DADA•

D

•DRONES•

"The nerds are the ones that make the films and do loads of other really cool stuff in their life."

DANIEL RADCLIFFE, actor

DADA

NO, we're not talking about a baby's first word. Dada was an art and literary movement that developed in reaction to World War I. It didn't focus on creating beautiful works. Its main goal was to mock materialism (the value we put on owning things) and to shock people into thinking about what's important in society. Some Dada artists, like Marcel Duchamp, bought everyday objects—like restroom urinals!—and made them works of "art."

DAREDEVILS

DAREDEVILS ARE PEOPLE who risk their lives for thrills and fame. Our hearts pound and adrenaline surges even just watching their stunts: scaling the sides of skyscrapers, like Alain Robert, the "French Spider-Man"; tightrope walking, like Nik Wallenda, who crossed Niagara Falls on a 1,800-foot (550-m) tightrope in 2012; going over the falls in a barrel, like Annie Edson Taylor, a 63-year-old teacher who, in 1901, became the first person to do that stunt; and motorcycle jumping over buses or canyons, like Robert "Evel" Knievel, who was as famous for his crashes as for his spectacular jumps. Daredevil stunts are super risky, and a lot of daredevils get busted up— or worse.

(Don't try this at home.)

EVEL KNIEVEL

DARK STAR CAVE

INSIDE A REMOTE MOUNTAIN in the Central Asian country of Uzbekistan, a massive cave system winds through layers of blue ice and rock. It's Dark Star. Most of the cave system is unmapped, but expeditions have already found 11 miles (18 km) of passageways, some lying 3,000 feet (914 m) below the surface—and it may turn out to be the deepest high-altitude cave system in the world. To enter Dark Star, you either rappel or climb to a hole in the side of a cliff. Inside, you scramble over rocks, crawl through narrow tunnels, and zip-line over an icy cold lake. It's not just awesome to explore: The minerals lining the cave's walls could give scientists thousands of years of information about how Earth's climate has changed over time.

DAYDREAMING

EVER GET IN TROUBLE for daydreaming when you were supposed to be paying attention to something else (like your teacher)? Maybe this info will help you defend yourself: Research shows that daydreaming might be a sign you're really smart and creative. People whose brains have a lot of capacity to think can zone out during lectures or easy tasks but then tune back in without missing important points or steps. (But we're not telling you to try this out at school!)

DELPHI

LYING ON THE SLOPES of Mount Parnassus in southern Greece, the sacred site of Delphi was considered by the ancient Greeks to be the center of the world. Especially from the sixth to fourth centuries B.C., both rulers and ordinary citizens from Greece and beyond traveled to Delphi to consult the oracle when they had to make important decisions. The oracle, known as the Pythia—the name given to any priestess of Apollo—channeled the wisdom of the gods.

ACCORDING TO CULTURE CALCULATIONS ...

Zeus, the Greek god of sky and thunder, sent two eagles from each end of the universe to find the center of the world. They circled the globe and met at Delphi. Legend aside, the site's importance is reflected in geography. The most sacred sites of Greece are spaced exactly the same distance from Delphi.

For years, paleontologists thought that **T. REX'S** tiny clawed arms were pretty useless. But recent research shows they were STRONG ENOUGH TO MAKE DEEP SLASHES in any prey that the massive dinosaur had locked in its jaws.

T. REX turns out to be EVEN MORE AWESOME than we knew. A recent study revealed **it crunched down on bones** with forces equaling the weight of three small cars ... way more than the other dinos.

A recently rediscovered fossil turned out to be the earliest member of the titanosauriform family of **huge plant-eating dinosaurs.** It's named **VOUIVRIA DAMPARISENSIS.**

EPIDENDROSAURUS was extreme. It was extremely small—**only the size of a sparrow!** But it had SUPERLONG, CLAWED HANDS.

A **dog-size cousin** of *Triceratops*, discovered in China in 2002, had strange furrows and bumps of bone on its face. Dubbed **HUALIANCERATOPS WUCAIWANENSIS,** the 160-million-year-old fossil was one of the OLDEST PLANT-EATING, BEAKED DINOSAURS EVER FOUND.

Huge, long-necked sauropods that lived in southern Africa were more like the sauropods of South America than the other dinosaurs living in Africa at the time. SCIENTISTS MADE THE DISCOVERY after unearthing **SHINGOPANA** in 2002.

It may have been **turkey-size**, but the meat-eating, feathered **SINO-SAUROPTERYX** likely had CAMOUFLAGE MORE LIKE A RACCOON AND SHARK: face mask, dark back, light belly.

Paleontologists had thought the dinosaurs of southern Africa were either large plant-eaters or smaller meat-eaters. That's before they found the footprints of **KAYENTA-PUS AMBROKHOLOHALI,** a giant, **two-legged meat-eater** about three-fourths the size of *T. rex*—or about four times the size of a lion.

Think the long spiny sail running down the back of *Spinosaurus* is impressive? Well, **AMARGASAURUS** had two of them. The **jagged double rows on the spine** of this dino, found in Argentina in the early 1990s, may have been JUST FOR SHOW.

During the **Cretaceous period,** 145 million to 66 million years ago, the central region of North America was flooded, dividing the continent for about 30 million years. The western side, called **LARAMIDIA,** has become fertile ground for several RECENT DINOSAUR DISCOVERIES.

Like birds today, some **BIRDLIKE DINOSAURS** ROOSTED TOGETHER TO SLEEP, MAYBE AS A FAMILY. Scientists made the surprising discovery by examining a fossil of three young dinosaurs snoozing together.

Dinosaurs recycled! Well, kind of. The large veggie-loving **SAURO-PODS** ate so many plants and traveled so far that their DUNG PROVIDED TONS OF FERTILIZER, creating habitats lush with ... more plants.

They look **seriously scary,** but the NUMEROUS POINTY HORNS on dinosaurs like **KOSMOCERATOPS,** a cousin of *Triceratops*, were probably just for show. They wouldn't have protected the dinosaurs from attacks—but they probably helped them find mates.

Hatching a dinosaur egg was a **serious commitment.** It takes 42 days to hatch an ostrich, but scientists think that dinosaurs didn't break through their shells until THREE TO SIX MONTHS OF INCUBATION.

Some **plant-eating dinosaurs** may not have been strict vegetarians after all. Scientists have found SHELLS OF CRUSTACEANS—the ancestors of crabs, shrimp, and krill—in fossilized dinosaur dung.

Dinosaurs with **fancy horns and head ridges** evolved to become bigger. Researchers found that large two-legged **THEROPODS** with head displays took GREAT LEAPS IN BODY SIZE over millions of years.

EPIDENDROSAURUS

26 DINO-MITE
DINOSAUR DISCOVERIES

TITANOSAURUS

Baby **LIMUSAURUS INEXTRICABILIS** dinos, a type of **two-legged dinosaur,** were born eating meat. But as they grew older, they lost their teeth and had to switch to plants. Researchers RECENTLY RECORDED THE AMAZING CHANGE by studying fossils of the dinosaur at different parts of their lives.

A tiny horned dinosaur, **AQUILOPS AMERICANUS,** discovered in the late 1990s in North America, was about THE SIZE OF A BUNNY RABBIT.

In 2011, a miner in western Canada accidentally unearthed an amazing dino discovery: the best fossil of the nodosaur family ever found. The **minivan size plant-eater,** named **BOREALOPELTA MARKMITCHELLI**, was ARMORED, WITH LONG SPIKES ON ITS SHOULDERS.

As heavy as a space shuttle, **PATAGOTITAN MAYORUM** lumbered through the forests of Patagonia about 100 million years ago. Discovered in Argentina in 2014, the giant sauropod, a long-necked plant-eater, was the LARGEST CREATURE EVER TO WALK EARTH—that we know of yet!

A **pheasant-size** dinosaur, **SERIKORNIS SUNGEI,** discovered in China in 2014, had FOUR FEATHERED WINGS—but it couldn't fly.

Dinosaurs don't look like **touchy-feely types,** but high-tech scans of a large meat-eater, **NEOVENATOR SALERII,** revealed that their snouts were sensitive enough to help them pick the tiniest scrap off a bone or even to stroke a mate's face. YES, KIND OF LIKE A DINO KISS.

Dinosaurs ALL LAID EGGS—or so we thought. But it was recently discovered that one of the dino relatives, a 245-million-year-old long-necked sea creature called **DINOCEPHALOSAURUS,** gave birth to live young.

Its name says it all: **NASUTOCERATOPS TITUSI** means "BIG NOSE HORNED FACE." The dino, whose fossil was discovered recently in Utah, U.S.A., sported a small horn on a large nose with **spearlike horns over its eyes.** Despite its huge schnoz, its sense of smell probably wasn't any better than other dinosaurs'.

Fossils have revealed that small, feathered dinosaurs shared behaviors with birds—which means they MAY HAVE DANCED, hopping around in fancy shows **to attract their mates.**

A **dragon-looking dinosaur** discovered in South Dakota was named **DRACOREX HOGWARTSIA,** in honor of Harry Potter's school.

SPINOSAURUS

DODO

THE DODO BIRD GETS A BAD RAP. For centuries, sayings like "dumb as a dodo" and "go the way of the dodo" made it seem like the large, flightless bird was responsible for its own demise. But the dodo was actually an evolutionary success—perfectly adapted to life on Mauritius, an island off the coast of Madagascar with no predators and tons of fruit lying around for the birds to eat. Over millions of years, dodos adapted to store more fat, so they'd make it through times when food was scarce. But with their increasing size, they lost the ability to fly. So when people arrived on the island in the 16th and 17th centuries, dodos were easy prey. These explorers, and the animals they brought with them, were the real cause of the dodo's extinction.

DOGS DOING GOOD

ANIMALS HELPING OTHER ANIMALS: That's a serious "awe" moment! Some dogs use their super schnozes to save endangered wildlife. These dogs help track endangered animals so conservationists can tell how they're doing. Some of the dogs even sniff out illegal traps set by poachers or locate poachers' guns and ammunition. Others find invasive animals, insects, and plants that threaten habitats. They're helping keep protected areas safe for wildlife.

DOGS TELLING TIME

DOGS' NOSES ARE WAY TOO AWESOME to mention just once. So, here's another amazing way dogs may use their sense of smell: to tell time. They can smell how scents change over the day, and researchers think that gives them a sense of the passage of time. Their person's scent may fade during the day—or move about the room as hot air rises. Researchers think that dogs can track these changes. That may be how they predict when you come home from school— they link your return to how much your smell has faded since the morning.

DRAGONS

THESE HUGE, serpent-like beasts show up in the mythology of ancient cultures around the world. But their characters differ a lot depending on where they're from. In European tales, fierce dragons inspired terror. Heroes slew dragons—or at least tried to. To them, dragons represented evil and greed, as they often hoarded treasure. In the Middle East, where snakes are often deadly, dragons also were seen as symbols of evil power. But in Asia, they were quite different: kind and protective. Revered as forces of nature that controlled weather, they also brought wisdom, luck, and power. Emperors chose dragons as symbols of their power and good fortune.

DREAM CHASER

MISSED THE LAST SPACE SHUTTLE launch in 2011? No problem. Stand by for Dream Chaser. Like a mini space shuttle, the small, reusable "spaceplane" is slated to fly cargo up to the International Space Station (ISS) in the 2020s. It'll ride into space on a rocket, dock with the ISS, and then glide back to Earth and land on a runway. The spaceplane is about 30 feet (9 m) long with a wingspan of 23 feet (7 m) and will carry up to 12,125 pounds (5,500 kg) of cargo. Developed by the Sierra Nevada Corporation, Dream Chaser is based on designs developed by NASA in the 1980s after Western spies took pictures of a similar Soviet spacecraft.

DRONES

DRONES ARE REMOTE-CONTROLLED aircraft that range in size from a cupcake to a small passenger jet. And they aren't just for fun or military uses—or delivering packages. Drones can zoom to places that are hard for people to reach and relay images back to them. That makes them valuable to photographers, scientists, aid organizations, and conservation groups. Amazing aerial photography—both stills and scenes for blockbuster movies—are captured by drones. They can locate armed poachers that threaten wildlife and help conservationists keep track of the numbers of endangered species. Scientists have used them to map coral reefs. Medical centers in remote areas of Africa have drones deliver blood supplies for injured patients. Drones can even plant seeds to grow new forests as they zip over ground.

"I love space movies, from Star Trek to Star Wars to my all-time favorite—The Dish, an Australian comedy that celebrates that first moment when Neil Armstrong stepped down onto the surface of our moon."

ELLEN STOFAN, planetary scientist

EASTER ISLAND STATUES

THE GIANT STONE HEADS ON EASTER ISLAND (also called Rapa Nui) have mystified people for ages. Averaging twice the height of a typical grown-up and weighing as much as two to three full-grown African elephants, these statues—called moai—were carved, transported, and stood up in their places between the 10th and 16th centuries. What a lot of people don't know is that the statues aren't just heads. They have bodies, too, buried deep in the ground. Transporting the statues was difficult, and only about a third made it to the ceremonial sites. Archaeologists think the moai represent the spirits of ancestors, chiefs, or other important men and—bridging earth and sky—may have served as sacred links with the gods.

ECHOLOCATION

BATS ARE MOST FAMOUS FOR IT, but other animals—and even people—use echolocation to find their way around. To echolocate, animals send out a sound, which bounces off everything nearby and comes back as a quiet echo. By listening to the echo, they can tell how close something is, how big it is, and even how its shaped. Bats and other animals, such as some whales and dolphins, are naturals at using echolocation, but people can learn how to do it, too. Some people—usually those who are visually impaired or blind—have learned to listen to the echoes from tapping their canes or making clicking sounds with their mouths.

ACCORDING TO OUR CALCULATIONS ...

Ears are exquisitely excellent. The tiniest bones in our ears—the hammer, anvil, and stirrup—work together to pull off a major feat. They take the vibrations of our eardrums and make the movements 22 times larger! That helps our inner ears get the signals ready to send to our brains.

ECLIPSE MYTHS

IMAGINE YOU LIVE IN AN ANCIENT SOCIETY and one day the sun (or moon) gets blotted out of the sky. Today, you just think, "Cool! An eclipse." But back then—without the benefit of current science—people were terrified. Some thought a terrible beast gobbled up the sun. Dragons, toads, and bears were all blamed, depending on the culture. Others believed it was an omen from above that meant they should stop— or maybe start—a war. In one West African legend, people believed eclipses meant the sun and moon had a fight and people had to encourage them to make up. After the eclipse was over, the people rebuilt their own friendships. If it was good for heavenly bodies, it was good for people, too.

ELECTRIC ANIMALS

ALL ANIMALS CREATE ELECTRIC FIELDS as their muscles and nerves do their jobs, but some animals have truly shocking electrical abilities. The most famous is the electric eel (really a type of fish), which senses its environment using low-voltage pulses—and creates a big zap to protect itself. But other animals get charged up, too. The Oriental hornet is solar-powered! Its exoskeleton transforms the sun's energy into electricity, which it may use for energy. Sharks and rays follow electrical signals to find food. Their heads have hundreds to thousands of tiny pores filled with jellylike stuff that picks up the signals. The odd-looking platypus has that shocking ability, too.

ELECTRONICS THAT DISINTEGRATE

ELECTRONICS THAT FALL APART on purpose? Sounds like a serious design flaw! But, no. Researchers have created disintegrating electronics, and lots of people are excited about that. The disintegrating devices could erase sensitive information after a certain period of time—*Mission: Impossible* style— or they could be used inside medical devices that go inside people's bodies to help detect health problems. The secret to their disappearing act is a safe, organic acid built into the device's base. This base holds the device's electric circuits and dissolves in moisture—like, say, someone's stomach. When the base dissolves, the acid is released and begins to break down the electric circuitry.

AN ELECTRONIC CIRCUIT DISSOLVES IN WATER.

37

ELECTRIC
Cars

Get ready to say goodbye to your family's gasoline-guzzling people mover. In the near future, electric cars may rule the roadways. That may seem like a long time from now, but most people actually can't imagine the world switching from gasoline to electric cars that fast! After all, when you look at all the cars on the road, hardly any are electric vehicles, or EVs. And even if they were, there aren't many places to charge them. Plus, it's just hard to get people to change.

But we've done it before.

Time travel back to 1910. Ford's Model T, the first mass-produced car, started rolling off the assembly line two years ago, but it's ridiculously expensive—like four times more than we'd pay for a typical car today. Gasoline is hard to find, stop signs don't exist, and most roads aren't even paved. And driving these newfangled horseless carriages isn't anything like driving a buggy or riding a horse. People crash and "turtle" them—flipping

them over. But in only 10 to 15 years, cars almost totally replace horses.

Compared to the challenges of that transition, going from one kind of car to another is easy-peasy. Carmakers are getting ready for the switch.

EVs are super high-tech. They can go as fast as any car, and when they're taking off from a stop, they're even faster than gas-powered cars. The instant you push the accelerator, EVs zoom off. That's because they create instant torque, a rotational force that turns the car's wheels as soon as electrical current flows. But a gas-powered car, which must ignite fuel inside the engine's cylinders to move, can't do that right away. EVs also are really quiet—perfect, if you like traveling in stealth mode. Best of all, they use less energy than gas-powered vehicles, and they don't produce exhaust gas. Switching to EVs will cut carbon emissions a lot—and that's good news for our health and Earth.

REFERENCE • REFERENCE • REFERENCE • REFERENCE • REFERENCE • REFERENCE

LOOKING FOR MORE ON GREEN TRANSPORTATION? READ UP ON THE HYPERLOOP, PAGE 62, AND SOLAR BIKE PATH, PAGE 129.

FAQ

CAN ELECTRIC CARS DRIVE THEMSELVES?

Yes and no. Self-driving—or autonomous—cars will be EVs. But not all EVs have the advanced technology needed for autonomous driving. Self-driving cars need a lot of sensors to see what's around them and advanced computer programs (with artificial intelligence) to figure out where they are and where they need to go. Once they calculate all that—and they do it multiple times every single second—they send signals to control the car's speed, steering, and braking. Even if self-driving cars aren't zipping down the roadways yet, many cars already have a lot of the smarts needed for autonomous driving. They have sensors that can detect cars and other obstacles nearby, alert you if you start to drift out of your lane, and even put on the brakes to make sure you stay a safe distance from the car in front of you.

SELF-DRIVING CAR SENSOR

DO ELECTRIC CARS RUN OUT OF BATTERY POWER?

Yes, they can. Just like small, remote-controlled vehicles or electric toys, EVs run on batteries that need to be recharged. EV batteries are huge—like the size of a bed mattress—and they store a lot of energy. But it takes a lot of power to move a big vehicle at high speeds. So after you drive about 90 to 300 miles (145 to 483 km)—how far depends on the car—you need to recharge the battery. You do that by plugging in the car!

EVs also make some of their own energy. When a motor doesn't need to power the wheels forward, like when you're going down a hill or trying to slow down, it turns into a generator, creating and storing electricity in the car's battery.

FUN FACT

EVs may be uncommon on Earth, but they've dominated the driving scene on Mars and our moon. All NASA rovers have been powered by electricity. And because it's a pretty far drive to the nearest charging station, they've used solar panels and onboard energy sources to fuel up.

NERD OF NOTE:
WILLIAM MORRISON

ELECTRIC CARS seem like the latest and greatest innovation in car technology, but they're not. They were the first! Before gasoline-powered cars puttered along the roads, EVs were quietly rolling along.

In the late 1800s, inventor William Morrison worked in a secret laboratory in Des Moines, Iowa, U.S.A., where he built the first successful electric vehicle in the United States. In 1890, the vehicle, which looked like a fancy, doorless passenger carriage—minus the horse—cruised along in a parade, amazing the parade-watchers. It could reach 14 miles an hour (23 km/h) and go about 50 miles (80 km) between charges.

Morrison's horseless carriage fueled demand for electric cars. Within four years, electric taxis were carrying people around New York City. And by 1900, EVs made up a third of all the vehicles in the United States. People loved that they were quiet and didn't emit smelly pollutants—unlike gas-powered cars.

So what happened to them? In short: the Model T. The gas-powered Fords were cheaper and could go farther. By 1935, EVs had pretty much disappeared from streets until now.

ELEPHANT SOCIETY

ELEPHANTS ARE NOT JUST GENTLE and magnificent giants; they also form societies—close-knit communities that come together for a purpose—that are similar in complexity to the groupings of humans and other primates. The elephants' leaders are older females that make important decisions for the group while balancing the needs of all its members. The leaders remember where food and water are located and decide when and how far the group should travel to get to them. The other members of the elephant society also look to their leaders to decide how to stay safe—including if it's OK to let new elephants join their group.

ELEVATOR, EVERY WHICH WAY

IT'S LIKE SOMETHING straight from Willy Wonka's factory: an elevator that goes every which way, not just up and down. And it's real. A German company has created an elevator that zooms up and down, side to side, and even diagonally. It doesn't move on cables, like most elevators. Instead, it relies on magnetic levitation technology (like the Hyperloop, page 62), which uses superstrong magnets to move it along guide rails. The company, thyssenkrupp, calls its groundbreaking elevator the MULTI. (But we'll keep calling it the Wonkavator.)

EXERCISE

YOU ALREADY KNOW THAT EXERCISING makes your body stronger, more agile, and all-around healthier. But being active also makes you smarter! Exercise that gets your heart and lungs pumping increases the creation of new brain cells, especially in the part of your brain involved in learning and remembering stuff. And it's not a short-term benefit. Researchers have discovered that being active when you're young may pay off all your life.

EXPERIENTIAL SCULPTURE

WHEN YOU THINK OF SCULPTURE, you usually imagine something that you look at, maybe in a museum. But sculptures don't have to be static and still. That's where the "experiential" part comes in. Artist Janet Echelman, for one, wants you to get lost in her sculptures. She creates experiential sculptures the size of buildings or city blocks. Her artworks transform environments, so you experience your surroundings in a new way. To pull off her colossal art, she uses all sorts of unusual materials, such as fishing nets and even mist, which change with the wind and light.

EXPERIMENTAL ROCK

EXPERIMENTAL ROCK isn't about playing music in a science lab. It's all about taking chances, trying new things, and seeing what happens. Starting in the 1960s, experimental rock artists became the "mad scientists" of the music world, mixing things up and making new sounds. Forget the usual verse-chorus-verse song structure. Experimental rock might not have it. In fact, a song might not even have lyrics! Experimental rock may add layers of recorded tracks on top of each other

to create a full sound or use electronic synthesizers. Some artists created entire experimental albums, such as the Beatles' *Sgt. Pepper's Lonely Hearts Club Band,* which pushed rock into a new art form.

EXTRASENSORY PERCEPTION

CAN YOU SEE WITHOUT USING YOUR SENSE OF SIGHT? If so, you might have extrasensory perception, or ESP! Also called a sixth sense or second sight, ESP is when you receive information, or perceive, without using your usual senses. It's like sensing something just with your mind. There are different kinds of ESP, including seeing the future, being aware of stuff that others don't know, or communicating thoughts directly with another (no speaking or writing involved!). It's hard to prove that ESP even exists—and many scientists say it doesn't—but investigators sometimes consult people with ESP to help locate missing people or things.

WHAT KIND OF
CULTURE
CONNOISSEUR
ARE YOU?

START HERE.

WOULD YOU LIKE TO JUMP INTO THE MADE-UP WORLD OF A STORY?

This world is weird enough.

If it's about stuff I like to do.

I totally live for stories!

**UM ...
HAVE TROUBLE SORTING FACT FROM FICTION?**

SOCIOCULTURAL ANTHROPOLOGISTS
study the art, customs, and traditions of societies past and present.

WHAT'S YOUR FAVORITE TYPE OF STORYTELLING?

SOCIOLOGISTS
study how we act in groups and how society affects us.

Whatever's cool.

SUCH AS?

I'm really into art.

CAN YOU DRAW?

Tunes! I love music.

Sports. Go, team!

DO YOU PLAY?

Does a bird fly? I'm a natural!

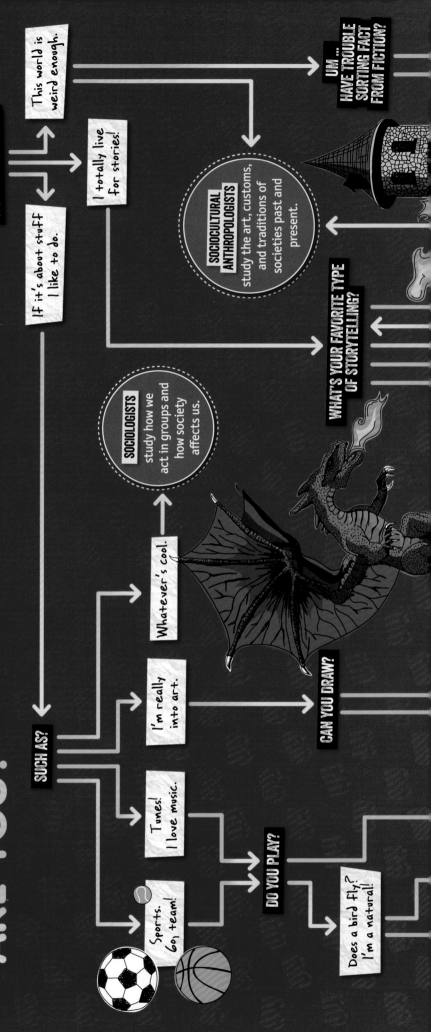

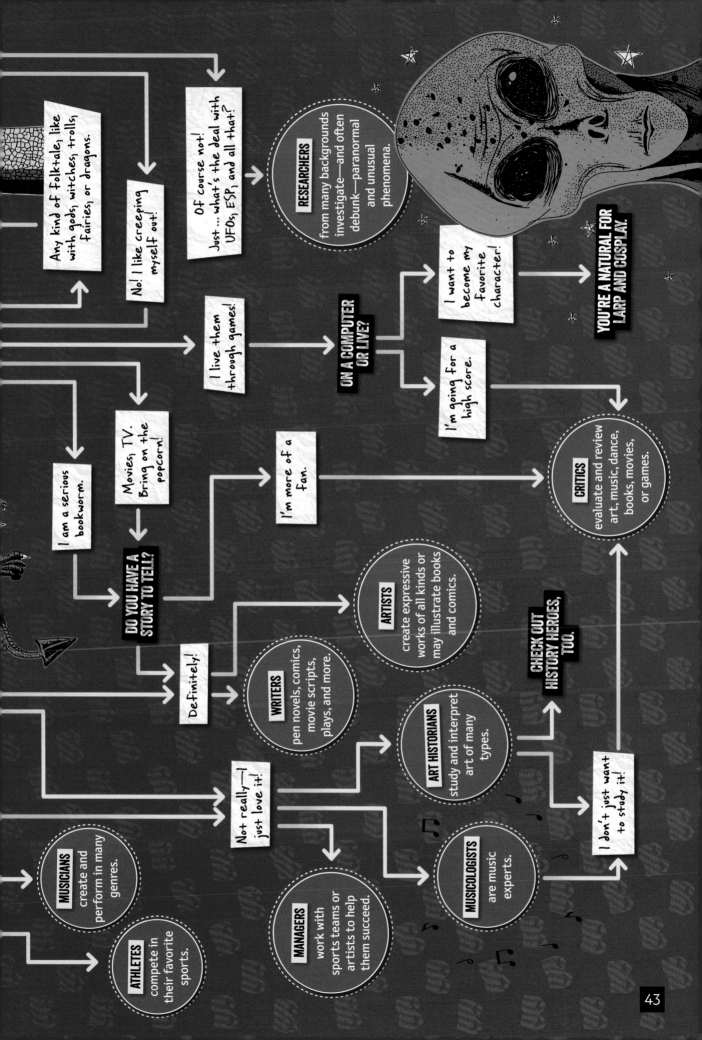

Any kind of folktale, like with gods, witches, trolls, fairies, or dragons.

No! I like creeping myself out!

Of course not! Just ... what's the deal with UFOs, ESP, and all that?

RESEARCHERS from many backgrounds investigate—and often debunk—paranormal and unusual phenomena.

I want to become my favorite character!

YOU'RE A NATURAL FOR LARP AND COSPLAY.

I live them through games!

ON A COMPUTER OR LIVE?

I'm going for a high score.

Movies, TV. Bring on the popcorn!

I'm more of a fan.

I am a serious bookworm.

CRITICS evaluate and review art, music, dance, books, movies, or games.

DO YOU HAVE A STORY TO TELL?

ARTISTS create expressive works of all kinds or may illustrate books and comics.

CHECK OUT HISTORY HEROES, TOO.

Definitely!

WRITERS pen novels, comics, movie scripts, plays, and more.

ART HISTORIANS study and interpret art of many types.

Not really—I just love it!

I don't just want to study it!

MUSICIANS create and perform in many genres.

MANAGERS work with sports teams or artists to help them succeed.

MUSICOLOGISTS are music experts.

ATHLETES compete in their favorite sports.

F-35 HELMET
FOOD FIGHTS

"The idea of recognizing your strengths and using them in as versatile a way as you can is cool to me."

FRANK OCEAN, singer, songwriter, rapper

F-35 HELMET

WHEN YOU THINK ABOUT the cool things on the new F-35 fighter jet, you may not focus on the pilots' helmets. But you should. They're technological marvels. Microphones pick up pilots' voice commands, night-vision systems help them see in low light, and an advanced display shows flight information. But that's just the start. The helmets link to computers on the jets and use six infrared cameras mounted on the aircraft, so the pilots can see in every direction. Seriously, every direction. If the pilots look down, they don't see the jets' floor. They see the ground below! It's awesome technology, but don't think of getting one for your bike. One helmet alone costs $400,000.

FANTASY GEOPOLITICS

MAYBE YOU'VE HEARD OF FANTASY SPORTS, a type of game where you choose players and put them together on a virtual team. Your fantasy team competes with others based on how well the players do in real life. Well, if sports are too tame for you, how about world domination? That's right. You can also play fantasy geopolitics, where you become the leader of a group of countries. You compete based on how well your countries do in a variety of economic and demographic areas. If one of your countries' citizens gets a Nobel Prize, you get more points. Does one of your presidents speak at the United Nations? Rack up another point. But if one of your countries elects a corrupt leader, watch out: You can lose points. Choose wisely.

RUNWAY FASHIONS
INSPIRED BY *STAR WARS*

FASHIONS FROM SCI-FI

IF SOMETHING SEEMS familiar about the models strutting down the fashion runways, there's a good reason. They may be wearing clothes inspired by your favorite sci-fi movie. Not long after Rey and BB-8 scavenged on the dusty surface of Jakku in *Star Wars: The Force Awakens,* breezy, sand-colored outfits debuted in fashion lines. Bold primary colors showed up on uniform-styled clothing, thanks to Federation uniforms seen on *Star Trek,* while the *Hunger Games* character Effie Trinket's pastel clothes and hair color toned down the hotter colors in style before the movies debuted. It's another example of one art inspiring another.

FIRE-MAKING

WE'VE ALL SEEN SOME DEPICTION of our ancient ancestors' discovery of fire: A bolt of lightning ignites a tree, scaring the ancient humans. But then they think, "Hey, I gotta get me some of that!" and work hard until they figure out how to start their own fires, so they can scare away beasts that want to eat them. Before long, they're roasting up some s'mores by the campfire. Except that's not how it happened. Anthropologists have discovered that it took people a long time to figure out how to make and control fire on their own— probably hundreds of thousands of years. Although our ancient ancestors understood fire more than 400,000 years ago, they probably only used it when they came across a natural wildfire. So when did they figure out how to make it? Probably closer to 50,000 years ago, when evidence shows humans regularly used fire.

FIRE-TAILED TITI MONKEY

YOU'D THINK THAT MONKEYS this adorable would be the mascots of every organization in the world. But the fire-tailed titi monkey, also known as Milton's titi monkey, was discovered only within the last decade. Sporting snazzy reddish brown sideburns and a fire red tail, these 3.3-pound (1.5-kg) monkeys live in the trees in the Amazon rainforest in Brazil. They hang with their families, sitting side by side on branches grooming each other, sometimes with their tails entwined—a monkey version of "holding hands."

FIRE WALKING

WALKING BAREFOOT OVER a bed of redhot, burning coals? Um, no thank you! But "fire walkers" in villages in northern Greece, Bulgaria, and Polynesia do it as part of religious festivals. Traditionally they believed it's a miracle they didn't get burned. But there's science backing it up. The people don't actually walk on fire; they walk on coal, which is a poor conductor of heat, so it takes longer for the heat to transfer to a person's skin—unlike, say, the metal wall of an oven. They may even cover their path with a layer of ash, which provides some insulation. So, does that mean coal-walking is safe? Nope. Sometimes a hunk of burning coal can stick to your foot. And don't even think about what would happen if you tripped.

FIRE WALKERS
IN THAILAND

FARMING

Picture a farm. Go on, close your eyes a second and really think about it. (No rush. We'll wait.) What did you see? Fields of corn or wheat? Tractors puttering around? Chickens strutting in a yard, or cows grazing in the field? All good. But did you imagine the rows and rows and rows of greenhouses? Or the drones flying over the fields? How about the veggies growing on the roof of a New York City warehouse?

We're not talking sci-fi. All of this describes farming today. Massive farms sprawl across hundreds of acres (hectares) of land in the United States and other countries. But in some places, innovative techniques produce more fruit, leafy greens, and other veggies per acre than the typical big American farm. And farms don't have to be big to be valued. More and more rooftop farms these days produce fresh veggies, greens, and honey for city dwellers.

In the Netherlands, a tiny country in Europe, farms are small, but they produce more fruit and vegetables 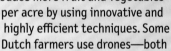 per acre by using innovative and highly efficient techniques. Some Dutch farmers use drones—both flying quadcopters and driverless tractors—to monitor everything from the nutrients and moisture in the soil to the growth of individual plants. Other farms grow crops entirely inside high-tech greenhouses, which create ideal growing conditions. An entire farm may be nothing but greenhouses.

Some farmers grow plants in nutrient-rich solutions instead of soil, a technique called hydroponic farming. This technique even allows farmers to grow plants top-down, hanging from fibers strung from ceilings or on walls. Using climate-controlled rooms and banks of LED lights, they make plants grow faster and bigger. We're talking tomato plants two to three times taller than the typical grown-up!

Urban farming, on the other hand, transforms spaces that otherwise would be wasted: vacant lots, patches of land between sidewalks and streets, and even rooftops. It's a growing movement (get it? growing!) that provides city dwellers with fresh leafy greens and other veggies. It also brings communities together (most urban farms use volunteers) and beautifies neighborhoods. The green cover of rooftop farms even provides insulation to the building below, reducing its air-conditioning costs. Win-win.

A FARMER PILOTS A DRONE OVER A WHEAT FIELD.

AND IF YOU LIKE FARM MYSTERIES, READ ABOUT CROP CIRCLES ON PAGE 27.

IMAGINING FARMS OF THE FUTURE
WE CAN'T EVEN CALL THIS SCIENCE FICTION. THESE IDEAS ARE BECOMING SCIENCE FACT.

- **A MASSIVE,** solar-powered, three-story floating farm, designed by Spanish architects based on existing technology, could grow a variety of fruits and vegetables in a hydroponic bay. Fish swimming below would live off the plants and fertilize them with their waste.

- **GREENHOUSES AND HYDROPONIC BAYS** could help us make a colony on Mars. They could use nutrient-rich solutions or water extracted from the Martian soil, which contains ice, to grow fresh greens and other veggies.

- **MEAT CAN BE GROWN** in laboratories—using way fewer resources than needed to raise whole animals for food. Technicians take actual cells from animals and grow them into the same kind of meat we usually eat.

NERD OF NOTE:
RON FINLEY

HE CALLS HIMSELF a "gangsta gardener," but Ron Finley is also an activist and a dreamer.

Ron grew up in a South-Central Los Angeles "food desert"—a neighborhood where it's hard to get good-quality fresh food. His neighbors suffered health problems from living where the only nearby food was fast food. He was tired of it, so he took action.

Ron planted a vegetable garden in front of his house ... the strip of dirt between the sidewalk and the street. He let neighbors come and take whatever they wanted to eat.

But somebody complained. Turns out, you couldn't grow fruit and veggies on those strips of city land. The city told Ron to remove the garden or else they'd arrest him. But Ron and his friends fought back, getting media attention, racking up 900 signatures on a petition, and winning over a city council member. They eventually got the law changed.

Ron and his friends planted gardens on other vacant plots owned by the city. He watched the gardens transform his neighborhood.

"Gardening is the most therapeutic and defiant act you can do, especially in the inner city," he says. "Plus you get strawberries."

 FAQ WHAT IS "FRANKENFOOD," AND SHOULD I BE SCARED OF IT?

"Frankenfood" may make you think of a monstrous, gigantic broccoli chasing after you, but it's not. It's a nickname given to food grown from GMOs, genetically modified organisms. GMOs are plants or seeds whose genetic makeup has been changed by scientists to give them qualities they wouldn't normally have. The plants may be able to grow in hotter places than normal or where the soil's not so good. Some GMO plants can fight off insects that would make them sick, while others produce food with more protein or vitamins than usual.

But as you can tell from the monster-like nickname, plenty of people don't like GMOs. They worry about the long-term effects of messing with nature—or the long-term effects on our health. Some people think GMOs increase food allergies or other health problems, so they eat organic food to avoid GMOs. But both the American Medical Association and the World Health Organization concluded that GMO foods are safe to eat, and the U.S. Food and Drug Administration regulates their safety like any other food.

47

FIREFLY SQUID

AS SQUID GO, THESE GUYS ARE TINY: only about three inches (8 cm) long. But they'll blow you away with their brilliance. Like their airborne namesakes, firefly squid glow. The end of their tentacles have special organs, called photophores, that light up in neon blue. Millions of the bioluminescent creatures live 1,200 feet (366 m) underwater in Toyama Bay, in the central Sea of Japan. But every year from March to June, they swim to the surface to look for mates, turning the water into an awesome light show.

FIREFLY SQUID OFF
TOYAMA BAY, JAPAN

FLATUS

SO ... IT'S, UH, one of those embarrassing things. You know, it makes your friends look at you accusingly, scrunch up their noses in disgust, and say things like "Really?" or "Eww, gross!" But, hey, it's not your fault. (Unless you gulped down a lot of air and didn't burp it back up. Then it's totally your fault.) Usually, though, you can blame it on the microbes in your gut. As they break down food to make energy, they produce gas. Just how much gas—and how stinky it is—varies from person to person depending on the type of food and the person's gut bacteria. The gas has to go somewhere, so ... you toot. Everyone does it—probably anywhere from six to 30 times a day.

FLOATING DECOR

TIRED OF ALL THE KNICKKNACKS sitting on your desk? Give them a lift—literally! Designers have figured out how to float lamps, plants, and whatnot a few inches up in the air. The secret is magnetic levitation, the same technology some superfast trains use. If you've ever had two magnets push apart—instead of clicking together—you know how it works. Magnets have different poles on each end—points where their magnetic force is strongest—and opposite poles attract each other while similar poles repel each other. Floating decor takes advantage of that force to stay in the air instead of crashing down because of the force of gravity.

FOLDING BUILDINGS

MAYBE YOU HAVE A FOLDING TABLE to seat the extra cousins who come for those big holiday meals. You swing the legs out, you stand it up, and you're set. A U.K. company has taken that idea to the extreme. They've designed entire buildings that fold and unfold, so you can put them anywhere you need them. Tired of living in the woods? Take your home to the beach! Like a huge, expanding accordion, the buildings unfold in only eight minutes to three times their transport size, and you can move in right away. All the fixtures are preinstalled and swing into place. You only have to push a button to make it work. It's even easier than setting up a folding table!

LA TOMATINA, BUÑOL, SPAIN

FOOD FIGHTS

WE'RE NOT TALKING ABOUT the occasional pea you flick at your best buddy across the school lunchroom. We're talking about epic food fights: thousands of people flinging fruit, veggies, or flour at each other. Spain reigns with three of the world's best food fights. The most popular might be La Tomatina, the last Wednesday in August, when people pelt each other with—you guessed it—tomatoes. Like your fruit fights sweeter? Around the same time, people celebrate the end of the grape harvest by throwing the fruit at each other during La Raima festival. And if you'd like a fluffier food fight, Els Enfarinats, or "the breaded ones," on December 28 is a day when people wear wacky military uniforms and launch flour bombs and eggs at each other.

ACCORDING TO OUR CALCULATIONS ...

The amount of ripe tomatoes thrown during La Tomatina festival—roughly 150 tons (136 t)—would make enough sauce for about 790,000 servings of pasta. (You might want to use fresh tomatoes, though.)

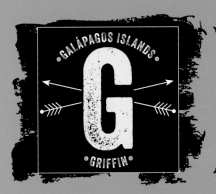

GALÁPAGOS ISLANDS

G

GRIFFIN

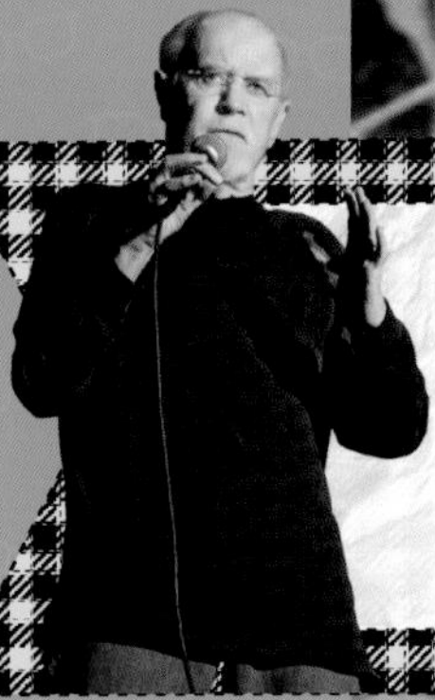

"Somewhere along the way, someone is going to tell you, 'There is no "I" in team.' What you should tell them is, 'Maybe not. But there is an "I" in independence, individuality, and integrity.'"

GEORGE CARLIN, stand-up comedian and social critic

GALÁPAGOS ISLANDS

"NOWHERE ELSE ON EARTH." That's a phrase you hear a lot when talking about the Galápagos Islands, located about 600 miles (1,000 km) off the coast of Ecuador in the Pacific Ocean. The islands' isolation, relatively recent volcanic activity, and location—where three oceans' currents come together—have created a world where unique and unusual animals and plants have flourished. Nowhere else can you find the odd iguanas that dive into the ocean for their meals, the sleek cormorant birds that can't fly, or the largest breeding population of blue-footed booby birds, which dance to find their mates. The Galápagos Islands are a treasure, a rare showcase of evolution—and the inspiration for Charles Darwin's theory of evolution.

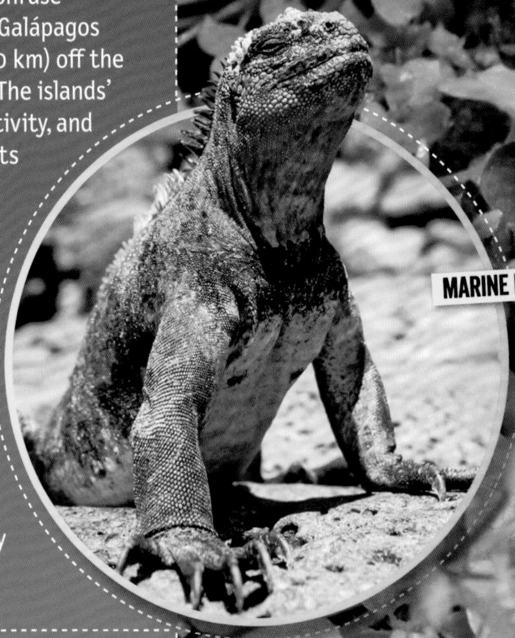

MARINE IGUANA

GARDEN GNOMES

GARDEN GNOMES AREN'T JUST STATUES of cute little humanlike dudes with long beards and pointy red hats. They're a phenomenon. People have been placing bizarre-looking beings in their gardens for centuries, but today's garden gnomes are rooted in German folklore from the mid-1800s. Ceramics artisans began making little statues based on magical gnomes who lived underground guarding treasure and only surfaced at night. If they were caught outside during daylight, they turned to stone. The statues' popularity spread worldwide, with the garden gnomes often seen as a whimsical piece of good luck.

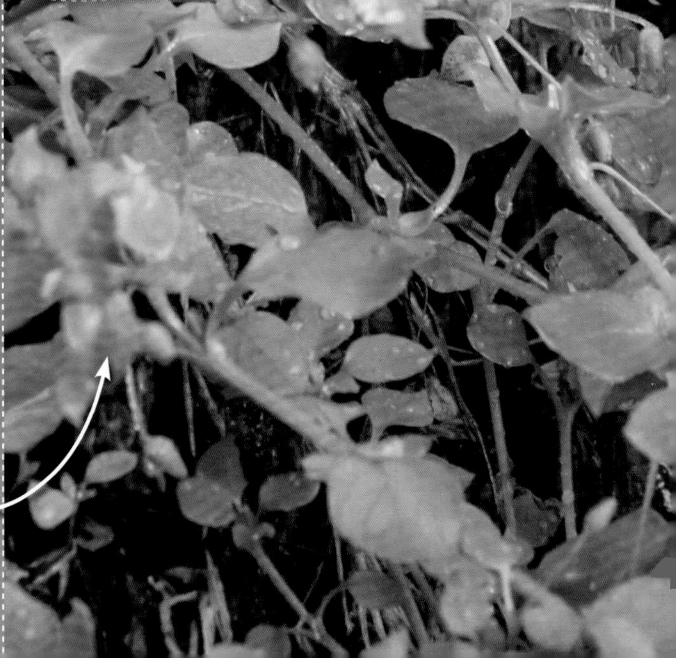

GENGHIS KHAN

A YOUNG MONGOL BOY NAMED TEMÜJIN, who was rejected by his own clan and attacked by rivals, grew up to create the largest empire in the world, expanding throughout Eurasia from present-day China to Russia and the Middle East. Known as Genghis Khan, which roughly translates as "universal ruler," he lived from about 1162 to 1227. Though his forces killed countless people and wreaked destruction during their invasions, the Mongol Empire went on to transform a large part of the world. The Mongols encouraged trade and the sharing of knowledge, modernized warfare, enacted environmental laws, abolished torture, and granted religious freedom to their subjects.

GEOGLYPHS

SOME OF THE MOST AWESOME and mysterious creations by ancient civilizations are geoglyphs, massive drawings on the ground created by removing or arranging stones or earth over a sprawling landscape—some longer than four football fields, others with lines stretching 30 miles (48 km). In Peru, the famous 500- to 2,000-year-old Nasca Lines include geometric shapes and the images of a monkey, a spider, and a hummingbird. In England, the 3,000-year-old Uffington White Horse stretches the length of a football field. Many geoglyphs were "discovered" relatively recently, when people flew over them in airplanes. But that makes them even more mysterious. Why did ancient civilizations create massive drawings that can be seen only from the sky? Were they messages to the gods?

GILGAMESH

THE 4,000-YEAR-OLD EPIC OF GILGAMESH is considered to be the world's first great work of literature. The epic poem tells the story of Gilgamesh, a king of ancient Mesopotamia—present-day Iraq and parts of Iran, Syria, and Turkey—who went in search of the secret of everlasting life. Written on clay tablets beginning around 2150 B.C., the epic has been pieced together like a jigsaw puzzle over the years.

GENETIC
Engineering

True or False:
1. Dinosaurs and woolly mammoths can be brought back to life.
2. Cells inside us can be changed to attack cancer.
3. Bunnies and kittens can be made to glow in the dark.
4. Humans can be given super senses and powers.

Tough quiz?

It should be. Scientists are making breakthroughs in genetic engineering all the time. It can be hard to tell what's fact and what's fiction! Before we sort it out, let's polish up our microscopes and take a closer look at what genetic engineering is all about.

Everything, including you and your pet, has a unique chemical blueprint. The instructions for all your traits—whether you're tall or short, boy or girl, brown-eyed or blue-eyed, and so on—are coded into a chemical called deoxyribonucleic acid, or DNA for short. Shaped like a long spiral staircase (but waaay smaller), DNA is in every cell in your body. It carries special codes, called genes, for making every part of

you, from how you look to how your body works. Each gene is like a recipe. But instead of being written with words, these recipes are written with four DNA chemicals in different patterns.

Scientists can read those recipes. And they can even change the ingredients! Using a technique called gene editing, they can "snip" a section out of a DNA strand and replace it with a different snippet. That way, they change the gene and change a trait linked to it. About 10,000 medical problems are linked to specific gene mutations—permanent changes in the DNA recipe—and gene editing someday may help get rid of them. But it's not without risks. What if, when we try to fix one gene, we accidentally

change other genes? And if we're able to change genes, it may be possible to create new life-forms. That raises a lot of questions about what's right and what's wrong. And it makes for a lot of great sci-fi stories!

As for the true-or-false quiz, you'll find the answers somewhere on these pages. Read on.

FUN FACT
Curing cancer is a huge goal of genetic engineering. Researchers are taking cancer patients' own healthy cells and changing them in hopes of getting them to destroy the cancer cells. That'd be even more awesome than Wolverine's healing power.

TO LEARN ABOUT OTHER WAYS TO FIGHT DISEASE, CHECK OUT NANODRILLERS ON PAGE 100.

FAQ CAN PEOPLE USE GENE EDITING TO BECOME SUPER STRONG OR SUPER SMART?

If you're hoping to become a superhero, you better find another way. Gene editing targets a trait or problem caused by one or a small number of genes. The thing is, most traits (and diseases) are nowhere near that simple. Lots and lots of ingredients go into those recipes. Take how tall you are. You'd think that would be pretty straightforward. Nope. Your height may be influenced by as many as 83 genetic variations! Turning a family of jockeys into basketball stars would be a tall order. And superpowers? Our spidey senses tell us you shouldn't hold your breath.

SO HOW ABOUT DINOSAURS AND WOOLLY MAMMOTHS— WILL WE BE SEEING THEM STOMPING AROUND SOON?

To bring them back to life—at least, Jurassic Park style—you'd need some of their DNA. But DNA starts to decay when creatures die, and there's not much hope of getting DNA from fossils any older than 6.8 million years.

Because dinos went extinct about 65 million years ago, the chances of finding dinosaur DNA is next to nil. The closest scientists could get to bringing a dinosaur to life is by re-creating one. They'd take modern DNA from a bird (birds are descended from dinosaurs!) and rearrange their genes to create a dino-looking animal, a "chickensaurus." Sounds silly? A little, but consider this: A "chickensaurus" would look like a Velociraptor. Awesome.

Mammoths are a different case. They went extinct about 4,000 years ago, and frozen mammoth carcasses have been found that contain DNA—but it's not in great shape. Scientists can still read it and figure out what traits make a mammoth a real mammoth. Then they can add those to an Asian elephant. It'd grow up to be a very furry elephant-like hybrid—not a true mammoth but a "mammophant."

FUN FACT

Yes, glowing bunnies and kitties are a thing. Scientists added sea jelly genes into some rabbits' and cats' genetic makeups so they'd glow under black light. The goal wasn't to make freaky pets but to let scientists check that their technique of transferring genes works. If you want your own glowing pet, glowing fish are widely available.

NERD OF NOTE: JENNIFER DOUDNA

JENNIFER DOUDNA has won countless prizes, fame, and fortune. But at her core, she's a science nerd—always has been, always will be.

Jennifer is an American biochemist and co-discoverer—with French microbiologist Emmanuelle Charpentier—of Crispr, a game-changing gene-editing technique.

Once, editing genes was really hard, like having to rewire an entire computer every time you tried it. With Crispr, it's more like using an app. Way more efficient. That means gene editing can be used someday to correct genetic mutations that cause serious health problems.

Jennifer has been fascinated with DNA ever since she was a kid and her dad gave her *The Double Helix*, the story of the discovery of the structure of DNA. "I think that was the beginning of starting to think, 'Wow, that could be an amazing thing to work on,'" she says.

Science is just as exciting to her now. One day, she was getting ready for a ritzy dinner—one of those special moments when you dress up fancy. But all she could think about was an experiment back in her lab. Forget dinner. She contacted the lab. "I was over here in my full evening gown, talking about the experiment. That's how nerdy I am."

GLADIATORS

FROM ABOUT 100 B.C. TO AT LEAST A.D. 400, gladiators were professional fighters who battled in large arenas to entertain the ancient Romans. Most gladiators were conquered peoples, slaves, or convicted criminals—but not all. The best gladiators became celebrities, and some free men and women—yes, women, too—volunteered to suit up and fight in hopes of earning fame or fortune. It was a gruesome pastime, but not all fights were to the death. The bouts usually had strict rules and sometimes were stopped when one fighter was seriously wounded. Either way, it was a rough life, and most gladiators didn't live beyond their 20s.

GLIDER RECORD

AN EXPERIMENTAL GLIDER, the Perlan 2, rides airwaves created by strong gusts of wind over mountains. The pilots used the waves to boost them high enough to set a new record, gliding more than 76,000 feet (23,165 m) in the air in 2018. At that height, the Perlan 2 gathers data about factors influencing climate change and radiation's effects on aircraft and pilots.

PERLAN 2

GLOWWORM CAVES

DEEP INSIDE A CAVE is the last place you'd expect to see a spectacular light show—unless you're exploring New Zealand's famous Waitomo Glowworm Caves. The caves are home to New Zealand glowworms—or *Arachnocampa luminosa,* if you want to get formal. They're actually a type of fungus gnat whose larvae have bioluminescent tails that glow blue-green. The light serves a purpose: attracting its prey to a trap of sticky threads. But to human explorers, all the little glowworms look like a night sky with twinkling stars.

GOTHIC

BLACK CLOTHES, black-dyed hair, black fingernails, black eyeliner—they're all part of the Gothic (or Goth) subculture. Not just about fashion, many Goths also like a range of alternative music styles and artistic expressions that draw on dark colors. The subculture started in England in the 1980s, growing out of the post-punk Gothic rock scene. But it took its inspiration from historical sources, too, including a genre of 18th- and 19th-century fiction that drew on spooky, mysterious, and horrific elements, including vampires and ghosts. (Think *Frankenstein* and *Dracula*.) But what about Gothic architecture, that style so popular with medieval churches? How do you go from towering cathedrals with pointed-arch ceilings, ornate stonework, and flying buttresses—features meant to let in light and show God's majesty—to heavy applications of black eyeliner? Some Goths say you can't. But imagine spooky churchyards and lonely footsteps echoing in a dark cathedral, and you'll see where gothic writers got some of their ideas. And those ideas inspired later movies and bands and ... you got it.

GRAFTING

MOST FRUIT TREES today are actually two trees in one. Orchards create them by grafting, attaching a tender shoot (called a scion) from the top of one tree to the bottom portion of another (called the rootstock). It gives the new tree the best traits of both—like making fruit trees shorter so it's easier to pick the fruit. Grafting isn't only for orchard keepers. An artist in New York State, U.S.A., got creative with grafting, attaching branches from 40 different fruit trees onto a single tree, so it would bloom in multiple colors and provide a feast of fruit.

ACCORDING TO OUR CALCULATIONS ...

One apple tree produces enough fruit in a year to make about 420 apple pies. Of course, those apples typically are all the same variety. For a true taste sensation, British horticulturist Paul Barnett may take the cake ... er, pie. He grafted 250 varieties of apples onto one tree over 25 years. During growing season, the branches become so heavy with fruit that he has to prop them up with extra supports.

GRIFFIN

WITH THE HEAD AND WINGS of an eagle and the body, hind legs, and tail of a lion, the griffin is one beast you definitely don't want to mess with. Lucky for you, that's not likely. The griffin is a legendary creature, a symbol of majesty and power. What else would you expect from combining the "king of birds" with the "king of the beasts"? Found in art dating back to the 15th century B.C., the griffin starred in the mythology of the ancient Greeks, Persians, and Egyptians. The Persians saw the griffin as a protector from evil and witchcraft.

"Do what you love. Know your own bone; gnaw at it, bury it, unearth it, and gnaw it still."
HENRY DAVID THOREAU, author and philosopher

HALLUCINATIONS

HALLUCINATIONS are when you see or hear something that isn't really there. Serious "uh oh" stuff, right? Maybe not. It turns out that anyone can be trained to hallucinate! Researchers found that hallucinations happen when our brains focus more on expectations and beliefs than on the actual information they're receiving through our senses. In an experiment, researchers played a sound every time they showed people a pattern. Even after researchers stopped playing the sound, most people still "heard" it whenever they saw the pattern— but it was a hallucination! Their brains focused on what they expected to hear, not what they heard in reality.

HAMILTON

LIN-MANUEL MIRANDA—the creator and star of *Hamilton*—didn't set out to make it a musical. He was on vacation, reading Ron Chernow's massive biography of Alexander Hamilton, and one scene jumped out at him: Hamilton was stranded on the island of St. Croix, which had been devastated by a hurricane, and he wrote a poem to get off the island. That, Lin-Manuel thought, was the essence of hip-hop: Artists write their way out of tough situations and envision a different future for themselves. Lin-Manuel was seriously inspired ... to write Hamilton's story in hip-hop. He planned to make a concept album. That's all. But as he wrote songs, he pictured his favorite rappers singing them. He saw them bring the story to life ... onstage. The cultural phenomenon was born.

HERPETOLOGY

SLIMY AND SCALY CRITTERS are seriously awe-some—just ask any herpetologist. Herpetology is the study of amphibians and reptiles, such as croco-diles, iguanas, snakes, turtles, and frogs. It's not just knowing why they're cool—like how geckos cling to ceilings or how snakes unhinge their jaws to eat huge meals. Herpetology also deals with the animals' behaviors and where they live. Many herpetologists work in conservation, keeping habitats safe for rep-tiles and amphibians.

HICCUPS

HIC ... HIC ... HIC. Embarrassing, annoying, uncontrol-lable. Yep, they're hiccups. Why do they happen? Your diaphragm, that usually well-behaved muscle that helps you breathe, gets irritated somehow and jerks downward. The jerk makes you suddenly suck in air, which hits your voice box, where your vocal chords snap shut, causing ... *hic!* Sometimes hiccups happen when you laugh a lot, drink fizzy drinks, or eat too much or too fast. But luckily, they hardly ever last more than a few minutes. There's no surefire way to end hiccups, but you can try putting a pinch of sugar under your tongue, holding your breath, pulling on your tongue, or having someone scare you.

ACCORDING TO OUR CALCULATIONS ...

Think you've had a bad case of hiccups? Well, they probably weren't this bad: Some people have reported suffering from hiccups for weeks, months, or even years. Charles Osborne, a farmer from Iowa, U.S.A, takes the cake. He had a spell of hiccups that lasted 68 years!

HIEROGLYPHS

HIEROGLYPHS WERE PICTURES, or symbols, used in ancient Egyptian writing, especially on monuments. Sometimes the hieroglyphs were pictures of the things they represented, but usually they stood for sounds. They're really different from our alphabet, but researchers figured out a simplified way of translating hieroglyphs to the sounds our letters make. For example, a horned viper stands for the sound "v," a foot for "b," and a ball of string for the sound "kh."

In 1918, during World War I, an army division's dog mascot, **STUBBY,** proved he really was MAN'S BEST FRIEND. When enemies launched a gas attack while the soldiers were sleeping, Stubby ran through the trenches waking them all—**and saving their lives.**

THREE LIONS CHASED OFF A GROUP OF KIDNAPPERS who had snatched a 12-year-old Ethiopian girl in 2005. **The lions stayed near the girl** but left when police arrived to take her back home.

When a man on a New York City sub-way platform fainted and fell onto the train tracks in 2007, **WESLEY JAMES AUTREY** didn't hesitate. He jumped down, **pulled the man into a bear hug,** and lay between the rails as a train rattled SAFELY OVER THEM.

DESMOND DOSS was a World War II medic. In 1945, his division came under fire on top of a cliff. Doss rigged up a stretcher on a rope and lowered all the wounded to safety, saving 50 to 75 lives.

Risking her life, abolitionist and civil rights activist **HARRIET TUBMAN**—who had escaped from slavery her-self—**led hundreds of family members and other slaves to freedom** on the UNDERGROUND RAILROAD during the U.S. Civil War.

A surfer was ATTACKED BY A GREAT WHITE SHARK off the coast of California, U.S.A., in 2007 and badly injured. But a **POD OF DOLPHINS** came to his **rescue.**

NELSON MANDELA led nonviolent acts of defiance against the South African government and its apart-heid policies, which denied the rights of black citizens. **After spending 27 years in prison for defying the regime,** he worked with white president F. W. de Klerk to change the system. In the country's first democratic elections, NELSON WAS ELECTED PRESIDENT.

It was 1956 and the roof of a mine had caved in, trapping a man. **JOHN W. BLAZEK, JR.** grabbed a shovel, **dug a small hole, and inched his way** under tons of unstable rock to reach the man and FREE HIM FROM THE SURROUNDING ROCK.

26 HEROES
TO HERALD

A SURVIVOR OF THE HOLOCAUST of World War II, **ELIE WIESEL** **spoke out against intolerance, indifference, and injustice around the world.** *Night,* his memoir of his time in a Nazi con-centration camp, is considered one of the most important works about the Holocaust and human dignity.

MALALA YOUSAFZAI was growing up in Pakistan, when the Taliban—a harsh, militant group—took control of the area where she lived and in 2008 **banned girls from going to school.** Malala spoke out about the IMPORTANCE OF GIRLS' EDUCATION and became famous around the world. The Taliban shot her, but she would not be silenced.

In 2008, a two-year-old in Nepal fell 60 feet (18 m) into a crevice—one so narrow that rescue workers couldn't reach her. **KAMAL NEPALI,** the 12-year-old brother of a rescuer, VOLUNTEERED TO CLIMB DOWN into the dark crack. He was gone for half an hour but finally emerged, **the little girl safely nestled in a bag** slung across his back.

Three mountain climbers were stranded 18,000 feet (5,500 m) up Canada's Mount Logan in 2007. With daylight fading and barely enough fuel, **JIM HOOD** FLEW HIS HELICOPTER ON THREE MISSIONS TO SAVE THEM.

The main leader of INDIA'S INDEPENDENCE MOVEMENT in the 1930s and 1940s, **MAHATMA GANDHI'S** nonviolent approach to civil disobedience **influenced the world.**

Born in Guatemala, **RIGOBERTA MENCHÚ TUM,** a member of the Maya K'iche' community, **grew up during a brutal civil war** waged by the military dictatorship and rich landowners against the Maya people. Rigoberta BROUGHT THE WORLD'S ATTENTION TO THE WAR.

Two women were biking in a California wilderness park in 2004, when a large mountain lion attacked one of them. The other woman, **DEBI NICHOLLS,** LEAPED INTO ACTION. **She grabbed her friend and held on,** slowing the mountain lion long enough for help to arrive.

A retired Korean racehorse named **RECKLESS** was TRAINED TO CARRY SUPPLIES TO SOLDIERS and transport the wounded. During a fierce battle in 1953, **she made 51 trips to resupply the front lines—** most by herself.

In 1910, the schooner *Merti B. Crowley* **ran aground in shallow water and thick fog** off the coast of Massachusetts, U.S.A. Four local fishermen, led by **LEVI JACKSON,** battled the sea for two hours, ROWING SMALL BOATS TO RESCUE THE CREW ONE AT A TIME.

In 1918, a woman carrying her baby and a suitcase was crossing a train track, with her other child following behind. They didn't see a train approaching, but **BEE LUSK** did. He ran down the track, **pushed the woman aside, and pulled the older child off the track.** HE SAVED THEIR LIVES with only seconds to spare.

THE FIRST WOMAN TO EARN A DOCTORATE in East and Central Africa, **WANGARI MUTA MAATHAI** worked to reduce poverty, advance democracy, and promote environmental conservation and sustainable development.

Swimming in high waves off the New Jersey shore one day in 1924, a man swam out too far—and couldn't get back. Only one person dove in to help: 14-year-old **CHESTER CONNOR.** HE TOWED THE MUCH BIGGER MAN 100 FEET (30 M) TO SHORE.

A pet pot-bellied pig named **LULU** **went for help** after her owner had a heart attack. The pig ran to a nearby road. A motorcyclist stopped and followed her. He found LuLu's owner lying on the floor and called for an ambulance, SAVING HER LIFE.

In 2011, **an earthquake and tsunami** caused a Japanese nuclear power plant to leak harmful radiation. **HUNDREDS OF RETIRED, OLDER MEN** VOLUNTEERED TO CLEAN UP so younger workers wouldn't be exposed to radiation.

During World War II, when the Nazis forced the Jewish population of Warsaw, Poland, into a walled ghetto, **IRENA SENDLER** pretended to be a nurse to get permission to care for them. She brought in supplies and smuggled out children, SAVING THOUSANDS.

SCARLETT, a homeless cat, was living in a garage with her four-week-old kittens when the garage caught fire. Burned and temporarily blinded, she made trip after trip into the blaze to RESCUE HER KITTENS.

A leader of the U.S. civil rights movement, **MARTIN LUTHER KING, JR.,** had a PROFOUND EFFECT ON RACE RELATIONS in America and abroad. **He encouraged nonviolent protest.**

ZOEY, a Chihuahua, was in a yard with her owner's one-year-old grandson in 2007. Suddenly, a rattlesnake slithered up behind the boy, **rattled, and struck.** But THE TINY DOG JUMPED IN FRONT OF THE BOY, taking the snake's bite herself. She got sick but recovered.

HIP-HOP

IN 1973, DJ KOOL HERC, who was born in Jamaica, was spinning records for his sister's party in their apartment building in the Bronx, New York City. He had been working on his technique, copying the style of Jamaican DJs who talked over the records they spun, and adding his own twist: using two turntables to extend parts of songs and add rhythm. His success at that party started the grassroots musical movement that became hip-hop. It quickly spread through the rest of the United States and, over the next two decades, other countries as well. With strong beats and rhythmic patterns, it featured a fresh style of delivering lyrics—not sung melodies and harmonies but hard-driving spoken or chanted expression, like rap. But hip-hop is more than a musical style. It's an entire subculture, which also features DJ scratching and break dancing, an athletic type of street dancing.

HOLOGRAMS

HATSUNE MIKU, a 16-year-old pop star from Japan, has opened for Lady Gaga and sung a "Happy" remix with Pharrell Williams. Not bad for a star who isn't even real! Hatsune is a Vocaloid hologram—a projection on a curved screen that creates an illusion of depth. She's seriously awesome. But she's not a real hologram. Holograms aren't projected onto screens, they're 3D images created by a special light technique. Holography uses a split laser beam to capture how much light bounces off an object (like regular photography does) and also how far the light traveled. When the two parts of the laser beams intersect, they create a special pattern (called an interference pattern) that records information about the 3D object and can be used to re-create it. Beaming moving holograms from another location is harder than it seems. In real life, those holograms are usually a series of stills that refresh frequently to make it look like they're moving.

HONKY-TONK

HONKY-TONK MEANS DIFFERENT THINGS, but it all comes down to music and having a good time. Honky-tonk often describes the classic sound of modern country music, with a swinging rhythm and lyrics focusing on rough times and lost love. Honky-tonk sprang up in taverns in southern and western towns in the United States and became really popular in the mid-1900s. But in the early 1900s, honky-tonk referred to a jazzy style of piano playing. What did they have in common? They both were played in rowdy music halls that didn't have the best reputations—and other places. Those dance joints also became known as honky-tonks.

HORSE HOOVES

LONG, LONG AGO—something like 50 million years ago—horses' ancestors were dog-size animals with three or four toes! As horses evolved and moved into new environments, they grew larger and larger—better suited to places where they'd have to tank up on a lot of grass instead of hide from predators in the bushes. But for a long time, why horses ended up with hooves was a mystery. It turns out that as horses grew larger, their middle toes got bigger and stronger to handle the stress of running and jumping. The outside toes, no longer needed, eventually shrank and disappeared, while the strong middle toes turned into hooves.

HUICHOL SPIRITUALITY

THE HUICHOL PEOPLE, indigenous people from the Sierra Nevada regions of Mexico, have kept their ancient traditions alive. Famous for their colorful artwork using beads and yarn, the Huichols' culture is deeply spiritual, celebrating their connection to nature. They have shamans, people who perform ceremonies to connect the human and spiritual worlds and heal people. Of the many Huichol ceremonies, one is the Dance of the Deer, when people dance their prayers to Mother Earth.

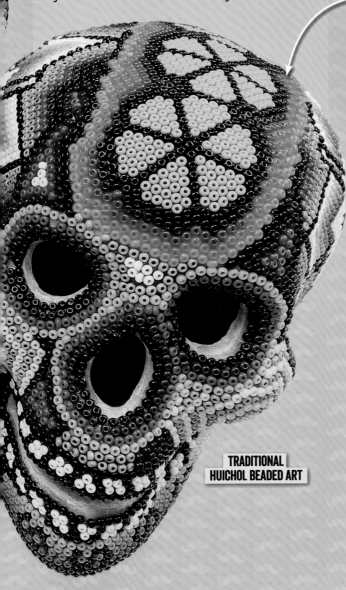

TRADITIONAL
HUICHOL BEADED ART

HUMMINGBIRDS

A BLUR. That's about all you see when a hummingbird flies by. These mini powerhouses are amazing athletes that can pull off feats that are impossible for other birds. They beat their wings 80 to 100 times a second or even more during courtship—so fast that it creates a soft hum. They can even hover in place or fly backward. For their size, they create more power with each stroke of their wings than birds typically do. Hummingbirds do it by rotating their wings when flapping down and up, creating swirls of air that lift them. There are about 340 recognized hummingbird species, all living in the Americas. Most are about the size of a grown-up's thumb and weigh about as much as three almonds, but the smallest weighs a little more than one almond.

HYPERLOOP

If zipping from one city to another in the blink of an eye sounds good to you, get ready to buy a ticket aboard the Hyperloop. The superfast transportation system will get you from Washington, D.C., to New York City, or from Los Angeles to San Francisco, California, in about half an hour—instead of the usual three to eight hours in a regular train. Yeah, it's that fast. We're talking about speeds of around 700 miles an hour (1,127 km/h). Inside the Hyperloop, futuristic passenger pods about the size of train cars will zoom through tubes at nearly the speed of sound. It doesn't take a rocket to move you that fast. Instead, the Hyperloop will be powered by electricity and magnets. You know how if you push the wrong ends of strong magnets toward each other, they bounce apart instead of snapping together? Engineers have figured out how to use that trick to move things. The pods will also float above the track on a pressurized cushion of air and the magnetic field, a technology called magnetic levitation, or maglev. The tubes won't just be oversize peashooters.

FUN FACT
The Hyperloop's speed, faster than 700 miles an hour (1,127 km/h), will blow away the competition. Airplanes average about 550 miles an hour (885 km/h), and high-speed trains in the U.S.A. can hit 250 miles an hour (402 km/h).

A lot of the air inside them will be sucked out to create extremely low air pressure inside. All those features work together to minimize friction and air drag, letting the pods speed along with little resistance. Better yet, using electromagnets instead of fossil fuels earns the Hyperloop some serious green cred.

Just one problem: The Hyperloop's not built yet. Companies have been working on the system for several years and figuring out where they'll build the first Hyperloops. But it'll be worth the wait.

REFERENCE · REFERENCE · REFERENCE · REFERENCE · REFERENCE · REFERENCE
WANT TO SEE SOME MORE WAYS TO "GO GREEN" WHEN YOU'RE ON THE GO? BUZZ OVER TO ELECTRIC CARS ON PAGE 38.

IMAGINING HIGH-SPEED TUBE TRANSPORTATION

IF THE HYPERLOOP SEEMS LIKE AN IDEA TAKEN STRAIGHT FROM SCIENCE FICTION, IT IS. SHOOTING PEOPLE THROUGH TUBES AT RIDICULOUSLY HIGH SPEEDS HAS BEEN A FAVORITE MODE OF TRANSPORTATION IN SCIENCE FICTION STORIES FOR MORE THAN A CENTURY.

- **IN HIS 1863 NOVEL *PARIS IN THE TWENTIETH CENTURY*,** science fiction writer Jules Verne envisioned tube trains, powered by magnetism and compressed air, running across the ocean. His son Michel Verne picked up the idea in an 1888 story, which featured passenger carriages pushed by "powerful currents of air" at speeds up to 1,120 miles an hour (1,800 km/h).

- **IN THE 1894 NOVEL *A JOURNEY IN OTHER WORLDS*,** by John Jacob Astor IV, travelers could "keep pace with the sun" by riding on a railway that used huge magnets to move train cars through tubes, which took advantage of a partial vacuum to reduce air resistance.

- **WHO NEEDS AN ELEVATOR?** In *The Jetsons* cartoon, created in the 1960s, George and his family pop up into their home through a pneumatic tube—a technology that usually uses compressed air or a partial vacuum to whisk objects on their way. George also crawls into a horizontal tube system to zip to work. No pod necessary.

NERD OF NOTE:
ELON MUSK

THE IDEA FOR TODAY'S Hyperloop came from Elon Musk, an inventor known for his big ideas. He's also come up with groundbreaking rockets, self-driving electric cars, new ways to store the sun's energy, and plans to colonize Mars.

When Elon sketched out the idea for the Hyperloop in 2013, he thought he was too busy to build it. He gave his plans to other engineers, who started companies to develop the Hyperloop. But Elon didn't keep out of the Hyperloop's development for long. He started yet another company to move forward on the idea.

Where does he get all that inspiration? Thinking and reading.

When Elon was a kid, he read from the moment he woke up until he went to sleep. He read anything he could get his hands on: comic books, science fiction, fantasy, even encyclopedias.

Elon wants to help create a future where clean energy powers our lives, so we don't keep harming Earth. In fact, he feels driven to do it—just like the characters in the books he loved as a kid, *The Lord of the Rings* and the *Foundation* series. Those heroes always felt a duty to save the world.

The same goes for Elon.

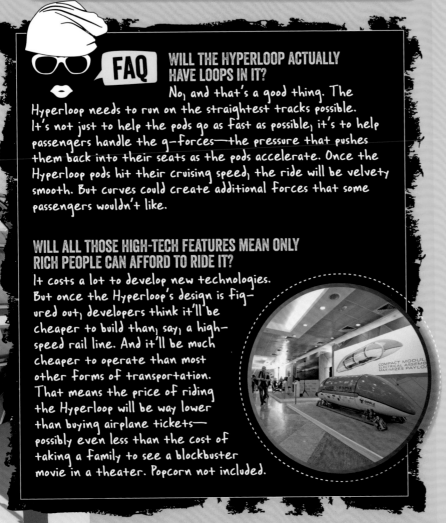

FAQ **WILL THE HYPERLOOP ACTUALLY HAVE LOOPS IN IT?**

No, and that's a good thing. The Hyperloop needs to run on the straightest tracks possible. It's not just to help the pods go as fast as possible, it's to help passengers handle the g-forces—the pressure that pushes them back into their seats as the pods accelerate. Once the Hyperloop pods hit their cruising speed, the ride will be velvety smooth. But curves could create additional forces that some passengers wouldn't like.

WILL ALL THOSE HIGH-TECH FEATURES MEAN ONLY RICH PEOPLE CAN AFFORD TO RIDE IT?

It costs a lot to develop new technologies. But once the Hyperloop's design is figured out, developers think it'll be cheaper to build than, say, a high-speed rail line. And it'll be much cheaper to operate than most other forms of transportation. That means the price of riding the Hyperloop will be way lower than buying airplane tickets—possibly even less than the cost of taking a family to see a blockbuster movie in a theater. Popcorn not included.

•ICE CAVES•

•INVASIVE SPECIES•

"I had great English teachers in high school who first piqued my interest in Shakespeare. Each year, we read a different play—Othello, Julius Caesar, Macbeth, Hamlet—and I was the nerd in class who would memorize soliloquies just for the fun of it."

IAN DOESCHER, author

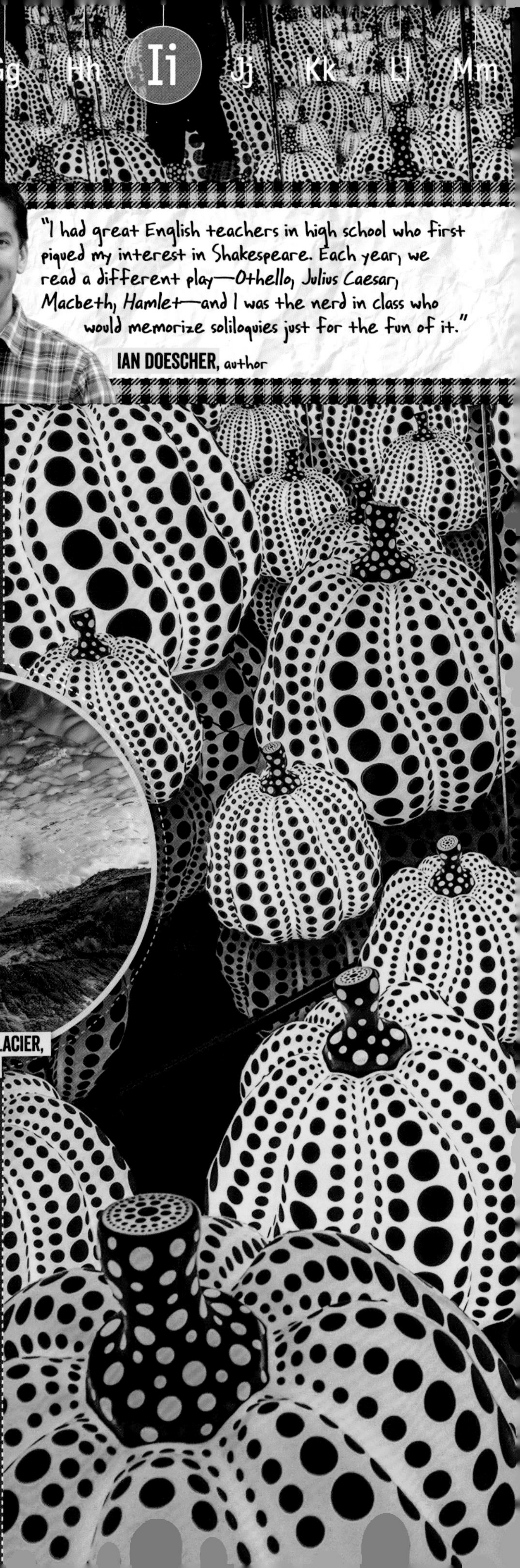

ICE CAVES

INSIDE A PARTIALLY HOLLOW GLACIER only 12 miles (19 km) from Juneau, Alaska, U.S.A., the Mendenhall Ice Caves surround you with shimmering blue walls and a ceiling made of ice. It's like a stunning, surreal crystal palace. The caves are not easy to reach. You paddle in a kayak and then ice-climb over the glacier. But it's totally worth it. The caves are called the "jewel" of Alaska's frozen landscape. If you want to tackle the journey, act fast—and bring along an experienced guide. Climate change is increasing the speed at which glaciers are melting.

MENDENHALL GLACIER, ALASKA

ICE ROADS

IN THE DEEPEST WINTER, the lakes and rivers in Alaska and Canada's Northwest Territories can freeze four feet (1.2 m) thick. Using heavy-duty plows and water sprayers, road crews transform these former waterways into smooth ice roads— more than 3,300 miles (5,300 km) of them in Canada alone. The ice roads connect remote communities and mines that at other times can be reached only by seaplane or barge. In the winter, residents rely on ice roads to stock up on a year's worth of supplies—or maybe to take a road trip.

IGUANAS

RANGING FROM ABOUT FIVE INCHES (12.7 CM) to seven feet (2 m) long, the 44 species of iguanas are definitely a diverse group. These stocky, saggy-skinned lizards are cold-blooded herbivores (vegetarians). They live in toasty climates—such as deserts, tropical and subtropical forests, and coastlines—in southern North America, Central and South America, the Galápagos Islands, some Caribbean islands, Madagascar, and Fiji. Though they have tough-looking spikes and sometimes lively colors, they're laid-back critters that enjoy lounging in the sun and hanging with their fellow iguanas. Many species make popular—but not very huggable—pets. But if you get one, plan to keep it or find it a good new home. Some iguanas have been released into the wild, and they've become invasive species, creating lots of problems in areas like Florida and Puerto Rico.

"INFINITY ROOMS"

THIS IS A WHOLE NEW WAY OF GETTING INTO ART. Japanese avant-garde artist Yayoi Kusama creates interactive rooms covered in mirrors on all sides. You step into the rooms and experience the art from the inside. True to their name, the rooms seem to go on forever. Polka dots, pinpricks of flashing lights, or stainless steel balls hanging from the ceiling or scattered across the floor make you feel like you're in a totally different world or traveling through space. When the Infinity Rooms exhibit comes to town, people line up for blocks just for a chance to get a ticket. Yeah, it's that cool.

ISS

THE INTERNATIONAL SPACE STATION (ISS) takes science to new heights. The most extreme science lab in our universe, the ISS is a partnership of space agencies from around the world, including the United States, Russia, Europe, Japan, and Canada. The station whips through space at 17,500 miles an hour (28,200 km/h) some 248 miles (400 km) above Earth. Scientists aboard the ISS perform lots of experiments, learning how microgravity—an extremely small force of gravity—affects people's health, plants' growth, and other things.

ENTOMOPHAGY sounds classy, like something you'd find in a fancy restaurant. The word is the formal term for "EATING INSECTS."

At least **TWO BILLION PEOPLE** around the world **eat insects**—both COOKED AND RAW—as part of their regular diets.

More than 1,900 species of **INSECTS** have found their way to dinner plates around the world—and they all taste like chicken. Just kidding. Some are SWEET, others SPICY. Some **taste like nuts.**

Animals and people aren't alone in eating insects. Some carnivorous plants, such as the **VENUS FLYTRAP** and **PITCHER PLANT,** feast on insects. They often live in WARM, MARSHY PLACES that contain little nitrogen—which they need to survive—so they supplement their diets with **nitrogen-rich insects.**

TERMITES might be pesky **wood eaters** that threaten our homes and fences. But pop them in your mouth, and you may want to become an aardvark. Termites have a MINTY TASTE.

Topping the list of tasty insects are **BEETLES.** With more **protein** than most any other insect, they make up nearly a third of the bugs that people eat. In Thailand, people like beetles FRIED CRISPY.

Here's a RECIPE for romance. When an insect lands in the web of a male **NURSERY WEB SPIDER,** the spider wraps it up tightly in **silk** and presents it, like a gift, to a female spider he's trying to woo.

26 INCREDIBLE EDIBLE INSECT FACTS

For the super brave, BEES, WASPS, and ANTS are popular snacks around the world. STINGLESS BEES (eaten before they mature) taste like **almonds** or **peanuts,** and wasps more like **pine nuts.** Ants are nutty and sweet.

Crawling into second place of insects most often eaten, around 18 percent of the total, are CATERPILLARS. They're TENDER, JUICY, and TASTY, and a great source of **protein** and **iron**—much liked by kids in southern and central Africa.

Want to get back at those pesky MOSQUITOES that BITE YOU? **Bite them back!** Mosquitoes aren't the most popular insect snack, but some people eat them. Lice, too.

Insects, of course, DON'T WANT TO BE EATEN. Some, such as the CINNABAR MOTH CATERPILLAR, protect themselves from predators by **eating plants that are toxic** to other animals and people.

Many insects are SUPER NUTRITIOUS. They have as much—or more—protein, fiber, minerals, and good fats as many other food sources. MEALWORMS, for example, are **as nutritious as fish and beef.**

INSECTS ARE EATEN in 36 countries in **Africa,** 29 countries in **Asia,** 23 countries in the **Americas,** and 11 countries in **Europe.**

People have been eating insects for THOUSANDS OF YEARS, according to the FOOD AND AGRICULTURE ORGANIZATION of the United Nations. The earliest mention of the practice is in the **Bible.**

Traditionally, EDIBLE INSECTS are gathered from forests, but people are beginning to FARM INSECTS, raising a lot in a small amount of space. One problem: How in the world are we going to add bugs to **"Old MacDonald Had a Farm"?**

Insects are a HEALTHFUL FOOD. But in a lot of Western countries, people may be a little **creeped** out by the thought. That may be changing soon. Several top chefs are offering edible insects—GRASSHOPPER TACOS, DEEP-FRIED CATERPILLARS, SILKWORM SOUP—on their menus.

You can have INSECTS YOUR WAY! Most people EAT THEM WHOLE, but they can also be **ground into grains or a paste.** Bug butter and jelly, anyone?

Eating insects is GOOD FOR THE ENVIRONMENT. Raising insects for food uses FEWER RESOURCES than livestock—a lot less. To get a pound (.45 kg) of **cricket meat,** it takes about two pounds (0.9 kg) of feed. To get a pound of beef, it takes about 10 pounds (4.5 kg)—five times as much! And, unlike cattle, crickets don't get so gassy that they add to our greenhouse gas problem.

The eggs of some WATER BUGS (backswimmers and water boatmen) are SO TASTY that in Mexico, they're served as **"Mexican caviar."** The dish, which tastes like shrimp, goes back to the time of the Aztec and was often prepared for ceremonies dedicated to Aztec gods.

GIANT ANTEATERS evolved to have LONG, SKINNY HEADS and even **longer sticky tongues**—perfect for scooping ants and termites out of their mounds. To lap up their dinner, giant anteaters flick their tongues in and out 150 times a minute! And they don't chew their food. It's soft—and they don't have teeth

It may seem like there's a NEVER-ENDING SUPPLY of insects, but ... no. Some insect species are **threatened** by POLLUTION, HABITAT DECLINE, and, yes, even OVERHARVESTING by people who want to eat them.

The NORTHERN SHRIKE, a **songbird** that lives in southern Canada and the northern United States, sometimes catches insects and then SKEWERS THEM ON THORNS or SPINY STALKS to eat later. It can even eat toxic bugs this way—waiting a few days for the toxins to break down and become safe to eat.

Think you'd NEVER EAT A BUG? Think again! Little pieces of insects are in some of our foods, including FRUIT JUICES, SPICES, and DATES. But, no worries. Food producers are required to keep them to an acceptably low limit. And, hey, they haven't **bugged** you yet!

LIKE SPICE? Then you'll want to scarf down a plate of RED AGAVE, or MAGUEY, WORMS. Among the edible insects, they're generally **seasoned with a spicy sauce.**

Hopping insects, such as CRICKETS and GRASSHOPPERS, are great protein sources. They don't have a STRONG TASTE, so they go well in all sorts of dishes. They're especially **yummy coated in chocolate.**

No one likes STINKBUGS—at least, when it comes to their FUNKY SMELL. But add them to a sauce, and that's a whole different matter. They add a nice **hint of apple flavor.**

INVASIVE
Species

Invasive species are animals and plants that are transported to a new ecosystem, where they can wreak destruction. Sometimes they hitch a ride on a boat or plane to their new homes. Sometimes people bring them as pets or exotic wonders. In these new homes, they don't have natural predators, and they spread quickly. They endanger native animals and plants that have no defense against them. They destroy habitats, and they spread diseases. Invasive species are to blame for one-fifth of all animal extinctions these days, and they create more than $120 billion worth of damage every year in the United States alone.

It's hard to know exactly how many invasive species there are, but they probably number more than 10,000. Check out the following animal invaders:

Burmese pythons from Southeast Asia, possibly former pets, have invaded the swampy Florida Everglades. Since 2002, the giant snakes have become top predators, eating everything from small mammals—such as marsh rabbits, possums, and raccoons—to deer and even bobcats. The snakes are so stealthy that even trained conservationists can barely spot them. That makes it really tough to control their numbers.

Kudzu, a fast-growing vine with large leaves and fragrant flowers, came to the United States in 1876 as part of an exhibit of Japanese plants. It was planted in gardens, along highways, and in other areas to prevent ground erosion. Unfortunately, it grows too well. It can cover entire trees and shrubs, preventing them from getting sun and nutrients and killing them.

Hunters imported wild pigs to the United States so they'd have something to hunt all year. Big mistake. The feral hogs have been sighted in 47 states, where they cause about $1.5 billion in damage and control costs every year. They are a nightmare for the environment because they eat turtle and wild turkey eggs, small birds that nest on the ground, and acorns and chestnuts that otherwise would grow into new trees.

Venomous brown tree snakes, native to Indonesia and Australia, were accidentally introduced on the island of Guam in the 1950s. And, yes, the "tree" in their name means they're great climbers. They've killed many native birds, which aren't used to climbing snakes. In fact, the snakes are so out of control on the island that they cause power outages by climbing utility poles.

BROWN TREE SNAKE

SOME OF OUR BEST FRIENDS HELP FIGHT INVASIVE SPECIES.
FIND OUT ABOUT DOGS DOING GOOD ON PAGE 34.

NERD OF NOTE:
ERIN SPENCER

FAQ

DO ALL PLANTS AND ANIMALS THAT COME TO A NEW AREA BECOME INVASIVE SPECIES?

Luckily, no! In the United States, a lot of food crops—including wheat, rice, and tomatoes—are not native to the region. If the plants are easily controlled, they won't become invasive. But if they grow unmanageably, harming property, land, and native plants and animals of the region, they're invasive. Even some animals we don't think of as invasive species can become problems in the wrong area. In 1949, for example, five cats were brought to Marion Island, part of South Africa, to control mice. But by 1977, the cats' numbers had grown to 3,400! They became a threat to local birds and had to be removed. Even pet cats that are allowed to roam outdoors in the United States are a threat to native birds, small mammals, and reptiles and amphibians, including some that are endangered.

PRICKLY PEAR CACTUS

IS THERE ANY WAY TO STOP INVASIVE SPECIES?

Yes, but it's usually hard work! Invasive plants can be pulled out, and animals can be caught. Conservation groups organize days when volunteers can work together to tackle invasive plants. Officials try not to use chemicals or poisons to kill invasive species, because they can also harm native plants and animals.

Sometimes officials will introduce other species to fight the invaders. In Australia, prickly pear cactus—a native of the Americas—was destroying rangeland where ranchers raised their livestock. So Australians brought in cactus moth caterpillars to eat the cactus. But introducing new species can be risky. They might become invasive species, too!

The best way to stop invasive species is to prevent them from coming. Be careful not to move animals, plants, or even firewood from one ecosystem to another—even clean your boots before hiking in a new area! Families should check that plants they're putting in gardens are native to their area, and fishing boats that travel far should wash their boats before returning home. And never, ever release a pet into the wild!

FUN FACT

A tiny bug called the Asian citrus psyllid carries bacteria that kill orange and lemon trees. It's so destructive that one of its nicknames is "yellow dragon disease."

A FISH CHANGED Erin Spencer's life.

She was 15 years old and scuba diving for the first time when she saw it: red-and-white zebra stripes, long spiky fins.

It was a lionfish, a native of the tropical waters of the Indo-Pacific, and it was in the wrong part of the world. Erin wasn't diving off the coast of Indonesia or Australia. She was in the waters off the Florida Keys, where lionfish are an invasive species.

Since lionfish were introduced off the coast of southern Florida in the mid-1980s, they've spread rapidly through the western Atlantic, Caribbean, and Gulf of Mexico, where they're threatening native fish populations. They eat about 70 species of fish and invertebrates, such as shrimp and crab, and destroy life on coral reefs, which are needed to provide habitats for thousands of other fish species.

Erin decided to do something about the problem. She became an ecologist and science communicator, using photos and stories to document how communities deal with invasive species. She shares their stories to inspire others to fight invasive species—and give them some ideas about what efforts work best.

JACKALOPE

JURASSIC FLYING MAMMALS

"What's cool about Spider-Man is that it's everybody ... you put on the suit, [and] anyone believes that you're Spider-Man. That's what's charming about the character. He's anyone. He's a huge nerd that ends up being this huge superhero."

JAKE EPSTEIN, actor and singer

JACKALOPE

BEWARE OF THE JACKALOPE. This rare, antlered species of rabbit is no ordinary fluffy bunny. A cross between antelopes and jackrabbits, the horned hares can be relentless fighters, using their pointy antlers to repel attacks. Brown like the remote areas of the American West where they live, they can bolt up to 90 miles an hour (145 km/h). Cowboys have sworn that jackalopes even have the ability to mimic human sounds! Does this all sound incredible? It should. Jackalopes are a popular myth, a hoax furthered by a Wyoming taxidermist who mounted a rabbit with horns on it. But here's the thing: There really are horned rabbits! There are pictures of them that date back to the 1500s. It turns out that rabbits can get a virus that makes them grow crusty horn-looking bumps made of keratin, the same stuff that animal horns—and our fingernails and hair—are made of.

JADE

WHEN YOU THINK OF JADE, you probably picture a deep-green gem. But "jade" actually refers to two different minerals—jadeite and nephrite—which come in a variety of colors. And jade wasn't always decorative. The strong material was once used for ax heads, weapons, and tools. But jade really shines as gemstones. For more than 5,000 years, Chinese artists have carved jade into jewelry, ornaments, and figurines. Long before geologists realized jade was two different minerals, these Chinese artisans figured out that jade from Burma (present-day Myanmar) was a richer, more beautiful stone, and it was easier to carve. They called it imperial jade, and only the emperor could own it. Even today, the best jades cost more than diamonds.

JAZZ

IT'S OFTEN CALLED "America's classical music"—and not just because it was born in the United States. In many ways, jazz reflects the ideals of American democracy. Different people come together to play a tune, but they can each give it their own individual spin. That freedom to express themselves musically, to give the tune their own interpretation, is called improvisation. It's the defining feature of jazz. Jazz originated in the late 1800s and early 1900s in African-American communities in the southern United States, especially New Orleans. But it spread throughout the country—and, eventually, the world—developing a variety of sounds and styles characteristic of different places.

DIZZY GILLESPIE, JAMES MOODY, AND HOWARD JOHNSON PLAY IN NEW YORK CITY IN 1947.

JEDI

YOU CAN'T SEE A *STAR WARS* movie without wishing you were a Jedi. But where did these Force-wielding guardians of galactic peace and justice come from? In the *Star Wars* universe, they've been around for thousands of years, but the Jedi are so rare that many people—Rey, Finn, and even Han Solo at first—think they're just legends. They're an order, bound by duty and shared knowledge known for their control over the Force. They're not the only beings that can harness the power of the Force or wield a lightsaber. (Just look at the Sith.) But Jedi have a deeper connection to the Force. Only Jedi can appear as Force spirits after they die. Though Jedi are an intergalactic force in the movies, *Star Wars* creators borrowed some Jedi concepts from earthly sources. "Jedi" comes from the Japanese work *jidaigeki*, a film genre that often featured samurai warriors and sword fights. "Padawan," the term used for a Jedi pupil, finds its origins in the Sanskrit word for "learner."

ACCORDING TO OUR CALCULATIONS ...

People's devotion to the ideals of the Jedi is growing. In the United Kingdom in recent years, 175,000 people listed their religion as "Jedi"—making it the seventh largest religion there—while 65,000 Australians, 9,000 Canadians, and 15,000 Czechs did the same. Some people may be joking, but others sincerely follow Jedi ideals.

It's pretty much everybody's fantasy: a **PERSONAL JETPACK** that lets you FLY THROUGH THE AIR. In 1965's *Thunderball,* when he lands, James Bond says, "No well-dressed man should be without one." The jetpack was actually the Bell Rocket Belt, which Bell Aerosystems was developing for the U.S. Army.

In 1989's *Licence to Kill,* Bond's cummerbund—the waist sash for his tuxedo—is not only dashing, it hides ropes that he uses to RAPPEL DOWN THE SIDE OF A BUILDING. **REAL SPIES** may hide their gadgets, too, but none pull it off with Bond's flair.

Bad guys better hope for sunny skies, because in the 1981 film *For Your Eyes Only,* **BOND'S UMBRELLA** can UNLEASH SPIKES and snap shut on them. Ouch.

In 1989's *Licence to Kill,* Bond needs to sneak HIGH-POWERED EXPLOSIVES into a building. Because he's dressed in a tuxedo, he can't exactly bring in sticks of dynamite. The solution? Explosives packed into a **TUBE OF TOOTHPASTE.**

The classic James Bond ride is a **SILVER ASTON MARTIN,** usually a model DB5. Like all cars, its features vary over the years, often sporting POP-OUT GUNS AND A BULLETPROOF SHIELD. A car collector in 2010 bought the car used in Bond movies for **$4.6 million**—even though the spy gear was really only movie props.

At the end of the 2002 movie *Die Another Day,* the BRITISH AGENT drives away in an **INVISIBLE VEHICLE.** (Cool trick, but we don't know why anyone would want to make an Aston Martin disappear.)

In the hands of the **INGENIOUS INVENTOR Q,** who designs Bond's gadgets, nothing is what it looks like. Sure, you can play a tune on a set of bagpipes, but you can also USE THEM TO SHOOT FIRE—at least in the 1999 film *The World Is Not Enough.*

In 1977's *The Spy Who Loved Me,* Bond is racing away from bad guys when he drives his car off a pier into the water. Lucky for him, his tricked-out **LOTUS ESPRIT** transforms into a submarine.

26 JAMES BOND GADGETS

Back in 1969, when *On Her Majesty's Secret Service* hit movie theaters, the idea of a **PORTABLE COPYING MACHINE** was mind-blowing. Of course, Bond's doesn't just copy secret documents, it also CRACKS SAFE COMBINATIONS.

An **UNDERCOVER BRITISH MI6 AGENT** definitely doesn't want to leave fingerprints behind. In 1971's *Diamonds Are Forever,* Agent 007 covers his own with a set of FAKE FINGERPRINTS.

Most of the tech in *Quantum of Solace,* which came out in 2008, is only a bit more advanced than what we have today. Still, it's seriously awesome to see M, the head of the SECRET INTELLIGENCE SERVICE MI6, flip through layers of intelligence documents displayed on a supercool, **TABLE-SIZE MULTI-TOUCH SCREEN.**

007 flicks his wrist back to SHOOT A DART—just in time to get out of a tough place. The handy **DART GUN** is in the 1979 movie *Moonraker.*

It's hard to top this way of SNAPPING A CANDID PICTURE of a crooked businessman: Bond uses a **CAMERA** concealed in a ring! In 1985's *A View to a Kill,* he lifts a glass of champagne, and click. Say "Cheese."

Among many cool James Bond watches, his **ROLEX SUBMARINER** in the 1973 *Live and Let Die* is one of the most awesome. Its magnetic face STOPS BULLETS and can turn into a miniature saw to free James when he's tied up.

If any watch is more impressive, it might be the **OMEGA SEAMASTER** that 007 wears in 1995's *GoldenEye.* It beams a laser, which Bond uses to CUT THROUGH THE FLOOR of a train compartment.

In 1997, when *Tomorrow Never Dies* came out, **MOBILE PHONES** were rare and the size of bricks. So when Bond pulls out a slimmer phone, it's pretty awesome—and that's even before he uses it to SCAN FINGERPRINTS and pick locks.

A **SCANNER** in 007's phone in 2008's *Quantum of Solace* creates an IMAGE OF SOMEONE'S FACE even when the person is looking to the side when scanned. It then links the image to MI6's database, so Bond gets all the info he needs.

In 1967's *You Only Live Twice,* Bond takes to the skies in "Little Nellie," a one-person autogyro **MINI-HELICOPTER.** Of course, because it's Bond's ride, it also has ROCKETS, FLAMETHROWERS, MISSILES, and the like.

In 1983's *Octopussy,* Bond tries to escape a villain's floating palace but gets GOBBLED UP BY A CROCODILE. Turns out, it's his ride out of trouble: a **CROCODILE-SHAPED SUBMARINE.**

In 1989's *Licence to Kill,* Q himself goes undercover. Posing as someone who sweeps up after others, he **RADIOS** ahead when he sees Bond approaching. So what high-tech gadget does he use as a radio? His broom, of course. Its BRISTLES HIDE AN ANTENNA.

A **SEABIRD** floating on water is the perfect camouflage for Bond in the 1964 movie *Goldfinger.* The seabird actually is like a hat on top of a full set of scuba gear that 007 uses to SNEAK THROUGH THE WATER. Of course, when he pulls off his wet suit, he's wearing a tuxedo.

Blink and you might miss this seriously cool tech from *A View to a Kill*: a **SUB** that LOOKS JUST LIKE AN ICEBERG.

Q puts the "boom" in **BOOM BOX** in the 1987 movie *The Living Daylights.* The music player can FIRE OFF A ROCKET.

In 1963's *From Russia With Love,* 007's **BRIEFCASE** is packed with AMMUNITION AND WEAPONS. But the really tricky part is getting it open. Anyone who does it wrong gets blasted with tear gas.

In 2015's *Spectre,* Q gives James a high-tech **WRISTWATCH** and warns him that the alarm is really loud. Yeah, like MAJOR BOOM LOUD. Turns out, it's explosive.

The remote-control **ROBOT DOG** that Q plays with in 1985's *A View to a Kill* was MIND-BLOWING back then, but it couldn't come close to matching the abilities of today's robotic pet dogs.

JELLYFISH

Long before dinosaurs roamed Earth, jellyfish swam the seas. For at least 500 million years, these alien-looking creatures have drifted through the oceans, their tentacles trailing behind them. As they move, their bodies pulse like heartbeats, flattening and then rounding again into a bell shape. They're awesome to watch—in an aquarium.

Most jellyfish are see-through. A lot of them are ghostly clear, but others are bright colors, like blues, oranges, or deep purples—sometimes with sporty stripes. Some even glow in the dark! Many jellyfish have long, skinny tentacles, and others have short, frilly ones. Most jellies range in size from less than half an inch (1 cm) to about 16 inches (40 cm) wide. But the largest is as wide as a car, and the smallest is only as wide as a penny's thickness.

Jellyfish are simple animals. No lungs, no stomachs, and usually no eyes. They also don't have brains! Instead, they have a network of nerve cells—a "nerve net"—that lets them feel the touch of another animal, the nearness of food, and the light of the sun. Made of a soft jellylike substance, jellyfish are 95 percent water and tear easily. They're so fragile, they can be ripped apart in a strong wave. And if they're washed up on a beach, they evaporate in the sun, leaving behind just their gooey cores.

Jellyfish may be delicate, but most pack a powerful weapon: stingers. Their tentacles are lined with mini harpoons full of venom. Whenever something touches them, zing. The tip shoots into the poor fish (or human) and injects toxin. That's how they get their dinner. The toxin paralyzes their prey. For us, it's usually just a painful souvenir of our beach vacation!

It's not just jellyfish stings we need to worry about. Sometimes swarms of jellyfish, called blooms, invade areas, endangering swimmers, clogging power-plant machinery, and wreaking havoc on fishing. Until recently, jellyfish's predators—sea turtles, seabirds, some fish, marine mammals, and even other jellyfish—have eaten jellyfish and their food sources, keeping jellyfish populations under control. But overfishing and pollution have made the predators' numbers decline. Add to that the jellyfish's ability to adapt to all kinds of water conditions, and jellyfish are on the rise. Blooms are a red flag that the ocean's ecosystem is out of whack—too warm, too polluted, or overfished. And that's not the jellyfish's fault.

REFERENCE • REFERENCE • REFERENCE • REFERENCE • REFERENCE •

SOME JELLYFISH ARE INVASIVE SPECIES, MOVING INTO NEW OCEAN ECOSYSTEMS. TO FIND OUT WHY THAT'S A PROBLEM, READ ABOUT INVASIVE SPECIES ON PAGE 68.

FAQ

CAN A JELLYFISH STING KILL YOU?

Not usually. We'd like to tell you never—really, we would—but we can't. The amount of pain you experience after a jellyfish sting depends on the species of jellyfish. Most times, the sting may hurt (like a bee sting) and leave you with a red welt, but it isn't too dangerous. Some jellyfish stings don't hurt people at all. But a small number of jellyfish are very, very toxic to people.

The Australian box jellyfish (Chironex fleckeri), which is about 10 inches (25 cm) wide with tentacles that can trail 10 feet (3 m), has some of the deadliest venom in the world. Even the sting of the chickpea–size Irukandji (Carukia barnesi), a type of tiny box jellyfish, makes people really, really sick and in rare cases, can kill them. Portuguese man-of-wars—which aren't jellyfish but are related to them—also pack a really painful punch, which can be deadly in rare cases. They can even sting after they've been washed up on the beach.

To have a relaxing beach vacation, find out what kinds of jellyfish are in the waters there and obey any signs about closed beaches. And, above all, keep this in mind: You don't have to fear most jellyfish any more than you do bees at a picnic. Be a little careful, and you'll be fine.

BOX JELLYFISH

WHAT DO YOU DO IF YOU GET STUNG?

First, don't panic. Most jellyfish stings are not deadly. They just hurt. Here's how to make them less painful. Keep still (moving can release more venom), and remove any tentacles that are still on the skin. Rinse the skin with seawater. If you planned ahead, pour vinegar on the sting. It deadens the stinging cells of most jellyfish. So does heat, so a warm bath can help. If anyone has signs of an allergic reaction, such as trouble breathing or breaking out in hives, call 911 emergency services.

Here's what not to do: Pour fresh water, urine, or meat tenderizer on it. If any tentacles are still on the skin, they'll fire more toxins.

PORTUGUESE MAN-OF-WAR

NERD OF NOTE:
LISA-ANN GERSHWIN

LISA-ANN GERSHWIN is a true jellyfish expert. She's made a career studying, naming, and classifying them.

The first species she named and classified turned out to be the largest invertebrate discovered in the 20th century. It's the black sea nettle (Chrysaora achlyos), whose bell can grow more than three feet (1 m) wide.

During her career, Lisa-ann has named and classified hundreds of new species of jellyfish. "To actually discover a whole new type of creature that's never been seen before. Wow. It's just the most incredible, unbelievable rush you can imagine."

But no matter how much she loves jellyfish, she hates to see the damage their increasing numbers do to an ocean ecosystem. "Jellyfish, in many ways, are the perfect weed," Lisa-ann says. "They grow really fast, and if they can't find food, they don't need food. They just de-grow real slowly, and then when they find food, they just re-grow again—no harm, no foul."

They can thrive in some waters that have become too polluted for other organisms. "Well, it's awesome in the oh-my-god kind of way, but there's nothing beautiful about it. It's incredibly damaging to have this happening in the ecosystem."

JET LAG

IF YOU TRAVEL FAR ENOUGH, you'll cross different time zones, regions of the globe where everyone sets their clocks and watches to the same standard time. Crossing time zones quickly can throw off your "body clock"—your natural tendency to do certain things, like sleep or eat, at particular times of the day. Until you adjust to the new time zone, you can have trouble sleeping or you may even feel disoriented or dizzy. It's called jet lag, and it can make you goof up more than usual. Take the example of baseball. Researchers studied 20 years of data on baseball players, who have to zip across the country a lot, and discovered that jet-lagged teams allowed their rivals to get more home runs than usual. They also found what many travelers already knew: Jet lag is worse when you travel toward the east. For most of us, it's harder to advance our body clocks than to delay them. Flying west adds time to our days, giving our bodies more time to adjust.

JUMPING BEANS

OK, JUMPING BEANS don't really jump—at least, not very high. And they're not actually beans. But they're still really awesome. Jumping beans, also called Mexican jumping beans, are the seedpods of a shrub that grows in rocky deserts in northern Mexico and the southwestern United States. Hold them in your hand and they wiggle around! The secret to this action is found burrowed inside: the larva of a small gray moth that is feasting on the insides of the seed pod. When the larva gets too hot—and it may only take the warmth of your hand to get it there—it moves around inside the pod, making it roll around.

JUGGLING

IT'S HARD TO JUGGLE, but that hasn't stopped people from doing it for centuries. It turns out that juggling is an ancient form of entertainment, documented in societies around the world and as far back as 4,000 years ago. And it wasn't just fun and games. In ancient China, some warriors juggled to impress their foes. As legend has it, one warrior, Xiong Yiliao, was so skilled at juggling that when he kept nine balls up in the air one day on a battlefield, the opposing troops fled without a fight! More recently, jugglers wow crowds by throwing and catching all sorts of things, including knives, flaming torches, and chain saws. (Don't try that at home. For now, stick with scarves and tennis balls.)

JUNO MISSION

IN GREEK AND ROMAN MYTHOLOGY, the goddess Juno peered through a veil of clouds that Jupiter drew around himself to hide his mischief. In doing so, she saw Jupiter's true nature. It's no surprise then that NASA's Juno mission seeks to reveal the mysteries of the giant planet Jupiter. Launched in 2011, Juno arrived at Jupiter in 2016. The spacecraft orbits the planet and sends back information about its composition, atmosphere, temperature, and magnetic fields. The information will help us understand how the giant planet originated and evolved and even how our solar system began.

JUPITER'S AURORAS

MASSIVE AMOUNTS OF ENERGY swirl over the polar regions of the planet Jupiter. They help create the giant planet's amazing auroras, dazzling light shows ringing the polar regions. But they don't do it the way scientists expected. Jupiter has the most powerful auroras in the solar system, and scientists figured it'd take a lot more energy to produce them than it takes to make Earth's northern and southern lights. And, indeed, scientists observed energy fields on Jupiter that are 10 to 30 times stronger than those on Earth. But the energy alone is not enough to make Jupiter's most intense auroras—a fact that puzzled researchers. On Jupiter, the high energy has to somehow speed up or get turbulent—a process scientists are still trying to figure out—to create the bright auroras.

JURASSIC FLYING MAMMALS

IF YOU KNOW YOUR dino history, you'll know that freaky-looking flying reptiles called pterosaurs ruled the Jurassic skies some 199.6 million to 145.5 million years ago (and beyond). What you may not know is that much cuddlier creatures also took wing. (And, no, we're not talking about bats. They entered the picture tens of millions of years later.) These furry Jurassic fliers were mammals that glided from tree to tree in an area that's now eastern China. Thanks to skin membranes that stretched down to their wrists and ankles, they parachuted from perch to perch. One of the species, named the *Maiopatagium* (it means "mother with skin membrane"), was about the size of today's flying squirrels, while the other, *Vilevolodon* ("toothed glider") was more mouse size.

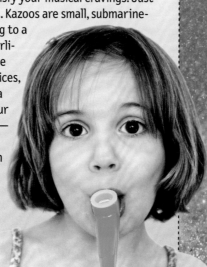

"When I was in high school, I was certain that being an astronaut was my goal. It was a very important time—Sally Ride was making her first flight into space and she had a real impact on me. Those 'firsts' kind of stick in your head and really become inspirations for you."

KAREN NYBERG, astronaut

KARAOKE

IF YOU ALWAYS WANTED TO LEAD A BAND but find your musical performances don't really go beyond singing in the shower, you might want to try karaoke. You get a real microphone and a real chance to show off your talent (or lack of) in front of a crowd of adoring (or not) fans. In karaoke, you sing along with recorded music—usually popular songs without the lead singer's part—so you can polish your favorite tune before you take it live. Karaoke is a lot of fun. So who came up with the idea? A Japanese drummer and keyboard player who in 1969 taped some songs as a favor for a guy who was going to have to sing for some business pals. The system worked, and the musician came up with a way of making it better: jukebox-type machines with recorded music and microphones that anyone could use. By the early 1970s, karaoke was a craze in Japan, and it went on to become a worldwide phenomenon.

KAZOO

IF SINGING ISN'T YOUR STYLE and you never learned to play an instrument, you can still satisfy your musical cravings. Just pick up a kazoo and hum into it. Kazoos are small, submarine-shaped instruments that belong to a family of instruments called mirlitons or membranophones. Those are fancy names for simple devices, created in the 1800s, that use a vibrating membrane to give your voice a different sound quality—granted, one that sounds a bit like buzzing. By humming, which creates the vibration necessary for sound, you actually provide the different notes and sounds that make a kazoo play.

KELPIE

A KELPIE IS A WATER HORSE. Notice: water horse, not seahorse. Seahorses are cool little fish with horse-shaped heads. They hang on to coral reefs with their curly tails and look adorable. Kelpies, on the other hand, are mischievous, sometimes destructive, shape-shifting spirits that stir up waters so badly that no sailor can cross safely. They've been said to spook regular horses just for fun or they even take over boats—unless the captain soothes them by completing rhymes. Lucky for us (unless you're Scottish), kelpies hang out mainly in Scotland. Even more lucky for us, they're mythological creatures. Whew.

KINESIOLOGY

IF YOU'RE ONE OF THOSE PEOPLE WHO'S CONSTANTLY on the move, have we got a career for you! You can become an expert on physical activity. Kinesiology is the study of movement, performance, and body function—usually human, but some kinesiologists focus on animals, instead. Kinesiology combines aspects of a lot of other sciences that study the mechanics and health of movement and everything that goes into it, from the functioning of muscles to the thought processes that power it. Kinesiologists work in a variety of roles: physical education teachers, researchers, therapists who help you recover from injuries, and more. Some study further and become doctors.

KINGFISHER

SOMETIMES ALL YOU SEE OF A KINGFISHER is a flash of blue as they streak from the air into the water to catch fish. The kingfisher's brilliant blue isn't from coloring, or pigment, but from tiny structures in their feathers that reflect light like a finely carved jewel. But their beautiful color isn't the only spectacular thing about these birds. When they dive at high speeds into the water, they barely make a splash, thanks to their long, pointy beaks, which slice into the water. Kingfishers got their name from their amazing ability to dive into water and catch fish. But some species of kingfishers rarely go near water—and don't eat fish.

KITES

You may think of them as nothing more than colorful playthings dancing on the wind. But kites can perform daring acrobatics and solve scientific mysteries. Some even have had godlike powers in stories. Seriously. If you need proof, look to the myths and folklore of Asia and Polynesia. You'll find legends that go something like this:

Long, long ago, a man looked up to the skies in wonder. What would it be like to fly among the clouds and stars? He would not rest until he knew. He built himself a marvelous kite, one with wings so big it carried him into the heavens. He flew so high, he became immortal. He became a god.

Yes, a god. You'll find variations of that story in the legends of many native peoples. In the mythology of the Māori, the indigenous people of New Zealand, a man-god actually becomes a kite. In Hawaiian legend, the demigod Maui flies a powerful kite the size of a home. Throughout Asian and Polynesian tradition, kites provided a link between humans and gods.

A MAN HOLDS A TRADITIONAL KITE IN KELANTAN, MALAYSIA.

They also provided meals. Since prehistoric times, kites have been used for fishing—and still are today. Fishing kites dangle a line along the water, tricking fish into thinking it's an insect.

When kites became popular in Europe in the 1500s, they were just for fun. But it didn't take long before scientists realized it'd be really handy to have something that flies. In the 1700s, they started using kites to study weather conditions, and engineers later used them to study aerodynamics.

Over the years, different cultures adapted kites for many uses, including various sports. One of the more thrilling is kite fighting, a sport that may have started in China but spread throughout Asia and the Middle East. People fly fighter kites in aerial battles, trying to force down competing kites.

REFERENCE • REFERENCE • REFERENCE • REFERENCE • REFERENCE • REFERENCE

INTERESTED IN OTHER HIGHFLIERS?
CHECK OUT THE X-PLANE ON PAGE 159 AND THE GLIDER ON PAGE 54.

IMAGINING KITE FLYING

IF ANYTHING IS BETTER THAN FLYING A KITE, IT HAS TO BE RIDING A KITE. JUST LOOK AT WHERE THAT CAN GET YOU.

- **IN A QUEST TO RETURN TO HIS HUMAN FRIEND ANDY,** Woody escapes Sunnyside Daycare by flying on a kite over the playground and wall in *Toy Story 3*. It looks like a perfect flight ... right until the end.

- **AMONG THE VILLAINS IN THE BATMAN COMICS,** Kite Man is a joke. Or is he? The minor villain—an aerodynamics engineer who commits crimes by swooping in on a variety of kites—becomes a key figure in a supervillain brawl.

- ***STAR WARS* MOVIES ARE KNOWN FOR THEIR COOL TECH.** But in *Return of the Jedi*, the good guys are helped by a fearless, fuzzy Ewok who flies through the forest on a kite to drop rocks on the evil Imperial stormtroopers.

NERD OF NOTE: JOSÉ SAINZ

JOSÉ SAINZ DIDN'T FLY KITES until he was a grown-up, but he's made up for lost time. He jumped into competitive kite sports and even started making his own kites. Within only a few years, José was winning awards and became a master kite builder.

It started when José watched one of his friends fly a stunt kite, a kite with two strings that let you precisely control its flight, making it swoop and loop, climb and dive. José knew he had to try it. He bought his own stunt kite, practiced a lot, and got so good he was asked to join a competitive team.

José took to kite making as fast as he mastered kite flying. With a lifelong passion for art, he was a natural at designing kites. "I credit my mother for giving me the love and inspiration for sewing," he says. "I remember as a child growing up, standing next to my mother's sewing machine, watching her create beautiful bridal gowns."

José drew on his Mexican heritage, too. He decorated his kites with bold, bright colors and designs from the Aztec people, whose culture flourished in Mexico from the 1300s to 1500s. People loved it—and José was thrilled to share the culture of the Aztec.

FAQ

CAN A KITE LIFT YOU OFF THE GROUND?
Definitely! But probably not the one you take out on a windy day. Writings going back to ancient times describe using kites to lift people, but it wasn't until the late 1800s that people got serious about riding kites. Many inventors made large kites—often several layers of connected kites—to lift people above the ground. In the early 1900s, Samuel Cody, who made several people-lifting kites, put a small engine on an untethered kite and flew it.

These days, of course, people take to the sky on hang gliders, large wing-shaped kites that you launch either by running off a high spot or by being towed by a boat or vehicle before detaching. But get some lessons first!

WHAT'S THE BEST SHAPE FOR A KITE?

It depends on what you want to do. The popular diamond-shaped kite—the one that pops into our heads when we picture a kite—is easy to fly in a variety of winds. So is the delta kite, which is shaped kind of like a bat. It flies great in gentle winds or stronger, smooth breezes, but it gets kind of crazy in gusty winds. In general, single-line kites are easier to fly, but you can do more stunts with multi-line kites, the ones with two or more strings that you use to control them.

ADELAIDE INTERNATIONAL KITE FESTIVAL, AUSTRALIA

KNIGHTS TEMPLAR

IN THE EARLY 1100s, the Knights Templar formed to protect Christian pilgrims, but they soon became a powerful, brave, and mysterious order. Dressed in white habits with red crosses on them, the knights took an oath of poverty and obedience, swearing never to gamble, drink alcohol, or even use bad language. But they fought—fiercely and without retreating—and built castles and even a banking system. Religious and secular leaders grew worried about the knights' power and wealth. In the 1300s, they forced the knights to disband. But some people think the knights became a secret order that still guards religious artifacts today.

KNUCKLEBALL

IT'S ONE OF THE HARDEST PITCHES FOR A BATTER TO HIT, but of about 360 pitchers in major-league baseball, there's usually only one or two who can throw a knuckleball. Knuckleballs aren't fast pitches. They travel 60 to 80 miles an hour (97 to 129 km/h)—far slower than fastballs, which can top 100 miles an hour (161 km/h). But knuckleballs are hard to throw. Pitchers hold the baseball in their hand and kind of push it toward home plate. They try not to put spin on the ball—a fast rotation that makes most pitches move a certain direction—so a knuckleball can be affected by the wind or any loose stitching or scuffs on the leather. That makes its path unpredictable and hard to hit. It's sometimes considered a trick pitch, and that's another reason it's unpopular. No matter how you feel about them, knuckleballs take skill to get right.

KOALA

KOALAS MIGHT LOOK LIKE THE cuddliest teddy bears in the whole wide world. But they're not bears. These fuzzy-eared mammals are members of the marsupial family, animals with pouches, like kangaroos, wallabies, and possums. When a baby koala—called a joey—is born, it's only the size of a large jelly bean. The first thing a joey does is climb into mom's pouch, where it stays for six months, growing and drinking milk. When the joey is too large for the pouch, it climbs onto its mom's back and rides piggyback style. Native to Australia, koalas hang out in eucalyptus trees, munching their leaves when they're not sleeping.

KRAKEN

TRUST US, YOU DON'T WANT TO TANGLE WITH A KRAKEN. These giant sea creatures are so big—often a mile (1.6 km) long—that sailors mistake them for islands. They can also be grumpy, causing whirlpools and attacking ships. A member of the cephalopod family, which includes the squid and octopus, the kraken was first mentioned in scientific literature in 1735, soon described as a "monster" with "dreadful nostrils." But the scientists who wrote those books admitted they had never actually seen one. In fact, probably no one has. Sailors may have seen giant squid, which average around 33 feet (10 m) and may get close to 60 feet (18 m). But the kraken? It's just a myth.

KREMLIN

IF YOU'VE EVER HEARD PEOPLE talk about "the Kremlin," they're probably referring to Russia's leader. It's like saying "White House" when you're talking about the U.S. president. But like the White House, the Kremlin is an actual place—and one of the most important and impressive in the world. It's the historic and geographic heart of Moscow, an entire fortress built between the 14th and 17th centuries. For centuries, the Kremlin was the center of both political power and religious life, and it contains cathedrals and palaces in addition to government and military buildings inside its walls. Along its side are the famous Red Square and Russia's most famous cathedral, St. Basil's, with its brightly colored, onion-domed steeples. The fortified complex is considered a masterpiece of architecture.

ACCORDING TO OUR CALCULATIONS ...

The Kremlin Clock, a symbol of Moscow, is one pricey timepiece. Over the years, parts of the clock—the hands, rim, and figures—have been covered in gold. In 1932, the Soviet Union used nearly 62 pounds (28 kg) of gold to regild those parts. That amount of gold would cost around $1.2 million dollars today. The parts that make the clock work, its chimes, and clock face would be much more.

WHAT KIND OF GEOGRAPHY GENIUS ARE YOU?

START HERE

WHEN YOU TRAVEL, DO YOU LOOK OUT THE WINDOW?

- Yes, it's cool to see what's around. → FIND PEOPLE FASCINATING?
- No, I can keep myself entertained. → LIKE COMPUTERS?
- If it helps me know where I am. → THINK YOU CAN CREATE A MAP?

FIND PEOPLE FASCINATING?

- Definitely! → WHAT DO YOU WANT TO KNOW ABOUT THEM?
- Not so much. → HOW ABOUT NATURE?

WHAT DO YOU WANT TO KNOW ABOUT THEM?

- Everything! What they're like, who's in their family, you name it!
- Why they live where they do.
- How their lives affect Earth.

HOW ABOUT NATURE?

- Now you're talking! → LIKE ANIMALS?
- I'm more into shiny metal things. → LIKE COMPUTERS?

LIKE COMPUTERS?

- Duh! Who doesn't? → THINK YOU CAN CREATE A MAP?
- I'm more of a bookworm. → THINK YOU CAN CREATE A MAP?

LIKE ANIMALS?

THINK YOU CAN CREATE A MAP?

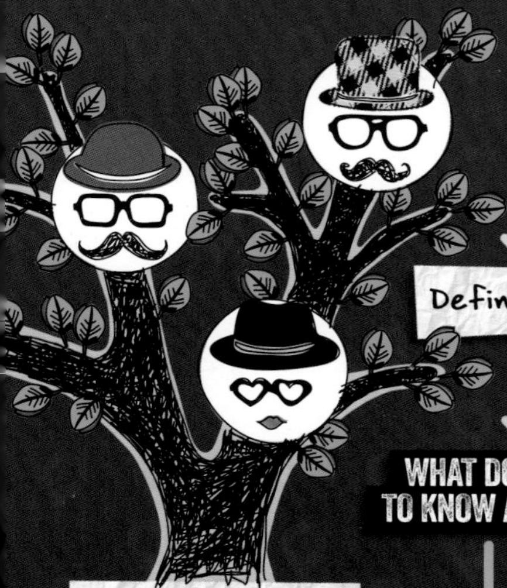

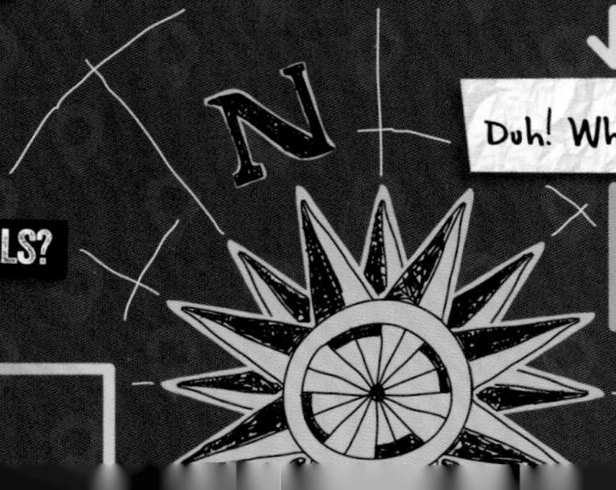

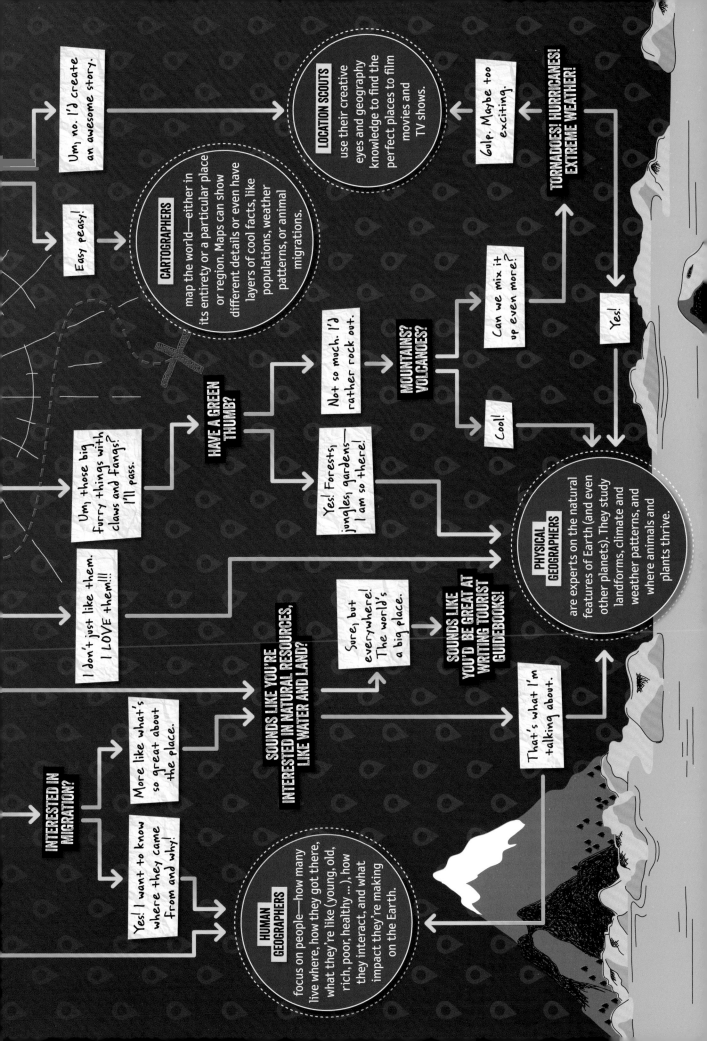

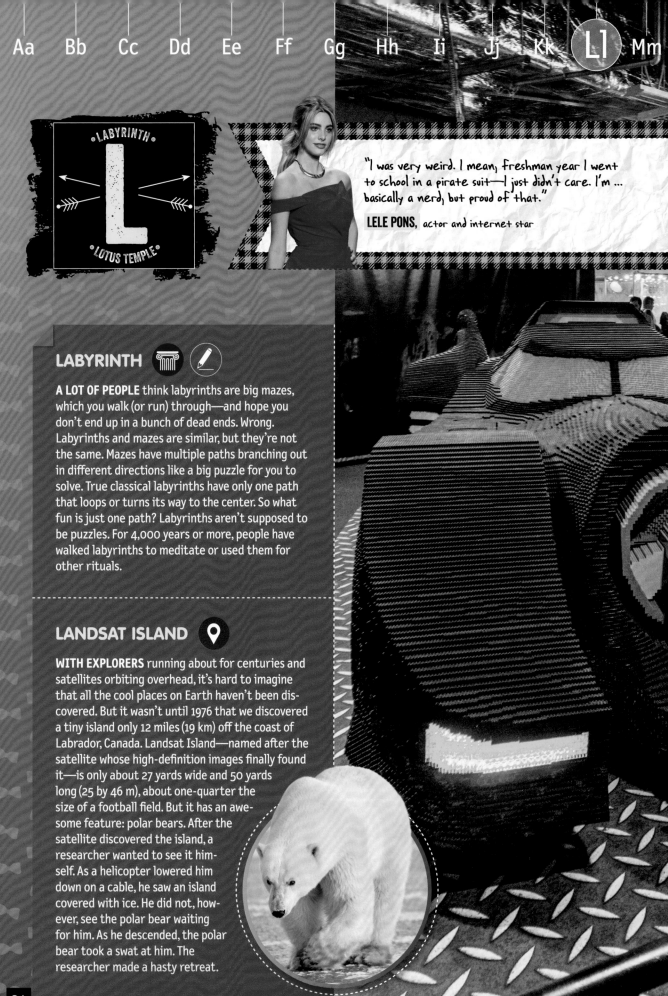

LABYRINTH

LOTUS TEMPLE

"I was very weird. I mean, freshman year I went to school in a pirate suit—I just didn't care. I'm ... basically a nerd, but proud of that."

LELE PONS, actor and internet star

LABYRINTH

A LOT OF PEOPLE think labyrinths are big mazes, which you walk (or run) through—and hope you don't end up in a bunch of dead ends. Wrong. Labyrinths and mazes are similar, but they're not the same. Mazes have multiple paths branching out in different directions like a big puzzle for you to solve. True classical labyrinths have only one path that loops or turns its way to the center. So what fun is just one path? Labyrinths aren't supposed to be puzzles. For 4,000 years or more, people have walked labyrinths to meditate or used them for other rituals.

LANDSAT ISLAND

WITH EXPLORERS running about for centuries and satellites orbiting overhead, it's hard to imagine that all the cool places on Earth haven't been discovered. But it wasn't until 1976 that we discovered a tiny island only 12 miles (19 km) off the coast of Labrador, Canada. Landsat Island—named after the satellite whose high-definition images finally found it—is only about 27 yards wide and 50 yards long (25 by 46 m), about one-quarter the size of a football field. But it has an awesome feature: polar bears. After the satellite discovered the island, a researcher wanted to see it himself. As a helicopter lowered him down on a cable, he saw an island covered with ice. He did not, however, see the polar bear waiting for him. As he descended, the polar bear took a swat at him. The researcher made a hasty retreat.

LASERS

LASERS ARE SUPERPOWERFUL light beams that can shine for miles (kilometers) into the sky (great for light shows), help doctors perform surgery, or cut through all sorts of materials. But they're not just flashlights with superpowers. They use light in a totally different way. Light travels in waves of energy. Most light waves—like from the sun or a flashlight—vibrate every which way. A laser beam is different. Its light is polarized, meaning it vibrates in just one direction. It makes one tight, narrow beam.

LEGO MASTER BUILDERS

YES, there really are Lego master builders—not just in the movies. Lego employs artists (sorry, only about half a dozen or so) to design and build amazing sculptures from the tiny plastic bricks. The artists' creations include a 17-foot (5-m)-long, 7-foot (2-m)-tall Batmobile and a life-size *Star Wars* X-wing fighter. Erik Varszegi, one of the artists, explained it to *Popular Science* this way: "For me, a rough day at the office is one where I run out of the yellow bricks." Best. Job. Ever.

LEGO BRICK BATMOBILE AND BATMAN

LEMMINGS

LEMMINGS ARE SMALL, furry rodents that look like mice or hamsters. They live in far northern areas of North America and Europe, and they have a peculiar reputation. Their populations rise and fall dramatically, and sometimes huge numbers are found washed up on beaches. For years, people believed that packs of lemmings ran off cliffs, plunging to their deaths—for no reason. In 1958, a Disney nature documentary, *White Wilderness,* showed that behavior on film. But the filmmakers actually faked the scenes, supposedly to replicate lemming behavior. The thing is, the lemmings' population swings aren't because of some mindless self-destructive act. The swings actually depend on the availability of food (and the lemmings' inability to swim far when they look for it). Still, the reputation sticks. In fact, people who blindly follow others who do self-harming things are often called lemmings.

LEPRECHAUNS

DON'T EXPECT LEPRECHAUNS to give you a wink and hand over their pot of gold. These mythical Irish fairies—the best known of several varieties of fairies—actually like to keep to themselves, making shoes for other fairies (which evidently pays really well). But if you cross leprechauns, they can be quite mean, so you'd better be on your best behavior. Unfortunately, that won't help you get their gold. They'll give up their treasure only if you trap them and demand the gold in exchange for their freedom. Even then, they're likely to trick you to get away—and you won't end up any richer.

LIP PRINTS

IT TURNS OUT THAT YOUR LIP PRINTS are just as individual as your fingerprints. Some people have grooves that go straight up and down, others have branches that spread out like tree roots. Some lips have swirly whorls, and others have crosshatches. Our lip grooves form when we're still in our mothers' wombs, and they stay the same throughout our lives. Though it's not likely that police detectives will identify any criminals by their lip prints soon, researchers are making connections between lip patterns and genetic traits linked to health. Pucker up.

LIVE-ACTION ROLE-PLAY

WANT TO TAKE YOUR GAME PLAY to the next level? Maybe experience your favorite fantasy movie for real? If so, become your favorite character! LARP lets you do it. LARP stands for "live-action role-play." Players physically portray their characters, inhabiting the fantasy world of their game or story—but in real life. LARP-ers meet in an actual location that best represents the world they're imagining. They dress up and stay in character the whole time, working with others to achieve goals and following the rules of play. Many LARP events feature large battles, with orcs, elves, and dwarves clashing on a large field. But others are more thematic. Potterheads may meet in a castle to study potion-making or play a game of Quidditch (unfortunately, without brooms). It's a ton of fun and a great way to meet friends who share your passions.

LOCH NESS MONSTER

ONE OF THE MOST MYSTERIOUS CREATURES is said to live in a lake in the Highlands of Scotland. The Loch Ness monster—named for the lake where it supposedly lives—was first seen by a monk in the seventh century. Ever since, a handful of people claim to see "Nessie" every year. But the scientific community has never found evidence of the monster's existence. In 1933, a famous photograph claimed to prove the existence of Nessie, but it turned out to be fake. The photo was actually of a toy submarine with a sea-monster head attached. Or was it? Some people say the confession about the photo was, itself, fake.

LOCOMOTIVES

LOCOMOTIVES, the awesome powerhouses that pull trains, changed the world. When the first steam locomotives began to ride the rails in the early 1800s, they pulled people and stuff from place to place faster than ever before possible—though early locomotives were really slow by today's standards. (A good bicyclist today could pass them.) Still, trains let businesses send their products farther, and people could settle in more places. They could get what they needed—even food, if harvests were bad—by train deliveries. In the next several decades, railroads gave a boost to the industrial revolution, when factories produced more goods faster and cheaper than ever before.

LOTUS TEMPLE

IN NEW DELHI, INDIA, a religious temple appears to bloom like a lotus flower. It has 27 marble "petals" that cluster in groups of three. If you know your division, that makes nine sides to this flowery temple. And that's important, because in the Baha'i faith, houses of worship must include nine sides arranged in a circular shape. Most Baha'i temples pull that off by building a dome on top of the nine sides. But the architect of the Lotus Temple—which is big enough that 2,500 worshippers can gather inside—looked to nature for a new and beautiful approach. It's an example of biomimicry ("bio" meaning living things, and "mimic" meaning to copy)—taking a design from nature.

LAUGHTER

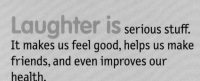

JUST FUN

How does NASA organize a party?

They planet.

Laughter is serious stuff. It makes us feel good, helps us make friends, and even improves our health.

"Laughter is probably one of the most complex and nuanced things we do," neuroscientist Sophie Scott says. Adrenalin—that "fight-or-flight" hormone related to being scared or stressed—decreases, and your brain releases feel-good hormones. That leaves you happy and relaxed. If you laugh hard enough, you might even lose a little control over your muscles. "You become a bit floppier and a bit weaker," Sophie says. "And that's why we literally become helpless with laughter."

And then there's the weird sound. It's caused when the muscles that help you breathe contract really fast and push air out through your windpipe and voice box. Laughs are more like animal sounds than human—and there's a good reason for that.

We humans actually have two types of laughter. One kind comes naturally, like when we're tickled or find something so funny we can't help but laugh. That helpless, involuntary laughter seems to be wired deep into our primal, mammal selves.

Then there's

the other social kind of laughter that we do when we interact with other people. Think about a time when a friend told you a joke that wasn't very funny, but you laughed anyway. When you choose to laugh like that, it sounds a bit different—more like a shorter, lower-pitched heh-heh. It's different, but it's not fake. It's a social laugh. It's like saying, "You're important to me." And it helps build friendships.

In fact, researchers found that you're 30 times more likely to laugh if you're with

JUST FUN

Why aren't koalas actual bears?

They don't meet the koala-fications.

someone else than if you're alone. No joke!

REFERENCE • REFERENCE • REFERENCE • REFERENCE • REFERENCE • REFERENCE

FOR OTHER AMAZING THINGS OUR BODIES DO, READ UP ON NEUROPLASTICITY ON PAGE 102. INTERESTED IN OTHER FORMS OF COMMUNICATION? FIND OUT ABOUT WEIRD WORDS ON PAGE 153.

FAQ CAN PEOPLE TELL WHEN YOU'RE DOING A SOCIAL LAUGH INSTEAD OF A NATURAL LAUGH?

Telling them apart is a skill you learn as you get older. Six-year-olds usually can't tell the difference, but all through your childhood and young adult life, you get better and better at recognizing which is which. By the time you hit your 30s or 40s, you're pretty much an expert at telling social laughs apart from natural laughs.

That's not the only funny thing that changes as you get older. The younger you are, the easier it is to start laughing when other people are doing it. Laughter gets less contagious the older you get. It's not just that everyone gets grumpy as they get older (at least, we don't think so!). It's probably because the social aspects of laughter become more important to older people.

WHY ARE YOU MAKING SUCH A BIG DEAL ABOUT NATURAL LAUGHTER BEING PART OF OUR "PRIMAL, MAMMAL SELVES"?

Because laughter is a mammal thing, not just a human thing! That's right—other animals laugh, too. Mammals like to play, and they often laugh while playing—especially if they get tickled. Our primate cousins, chimpanzees and apes, laugh a lot—but so do rats! They don't necessarily sound like us when they laugh (because their vocal chords didn't evolve to allow speech like ours). Chimp laughter sounds more like a cross between screeching and panting, while rat laughter sounds more like chirps.

When dog laughter—a type of panting varied in length—is played around other dogs in an animal shelter, they wag their tails more and act more sociable and playful. Dolphins also keep things friendly with a special type of communication: a short burst of pulses followed by a whistle. They do it only when they're play fighting, so researchers believe it's a way to keep the interaction fun—much like a human laugh.

JUST FUN

A boy stayed up all night trying to figure out where the sun had gone. Then it dawned on him.

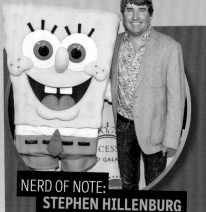

NERD OF NOTE:
STEPHEN HILLENBURG

YOU MAY NOT KNOW Stephen Hillenburg, but he's probably made you laugh.

Stephen was the mastermind behind SpongeBob SquarePants. The cartoon isn't just popular. It's a phenomenon—the most-watched television cartoon for a dozen years—with fans all over the world.

How'd this worldwide phenomenon get started? Ever since he was a kid, Stephen loved to draw. But art wasn't Stephen's only passion. He also found the sea fascinating. In high school, he became a scuba diver to see the underwater world up close.

So he became a marine biologist and worked at the Marine Institute in California—where he got to teach kids and work as a staff artist. After a few years, he realized he wanted to do art full-time. He studied animation, made some short cartoons, and landed a job working at the Nickelodeon television network.

One day, a work friend got excited about a comic book Stephen had created to teach kids about tide pools. "It started me thinking," Stephen said. "If I'm going to do a show, I would do it about invertebrates and these crazy animals that exist in the ocean."

SpongeBob was born.

"That's the beauty of creativity: Any one of us can have an imagination to rethink what assumptions are."

MAYA LIN, designer and artist

MAGNETIC RESONANCE IMAGING

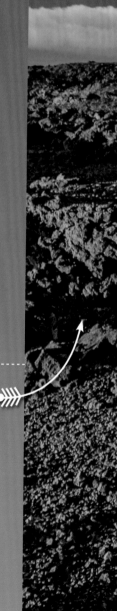

JUST CALL IT AN MRI—even doctors and technicians do. An MRI is an amazing piece of technology that lets you see the details of your insides. The MRI machine is a doughnut-shaped magnet. You lie down on a movable table that slides into the tunnel (the doughnut hole). Then the machine uses a magnetic field and radio waves, which interact with and track the position of atoms in your body, to make detailed pictures of every layer of your insides. MRIs see some things, such as muscle tears or spinal cord injuries, better than other types of imaging, like x-rays. They're noisy, so you have to wear earplugs, but they're completely painless.

MARS SIMULATION SITE

YOU DON'T HAVE TO TRAVEL six months in space to experience life on Mars. On the Big Island of Hawaii, an isolated site on the side of a volcano is a lot like Mars—rocky and barren. It's a good place to practice experiments for Mars or to see what it would be like to live there. The site, called HI-SEAS (short for the Hawai'i Space Exploration Analog and Simulation), has a 1,200-square-foot (112-sq-m) domed habitat where NASA has studied how a group of six "astronaut-like" strangers handle living together for a year. It's so real that one participant wrote that she missed Earth.

MCKINLEY CLIMATIC LAB

IT'S WHERE AIRCRAFT GO TO TEST THEIR STUFF. At Eglin Air Force Base in Florida, the McKinley Climatic Lab is the largest indoor weather-testing facility in the world. The facility's various chambers can create ice- and snowstorms, temperatures ranging from minus 65°F to 165°F (–54°C to 74°C), 40-mile-an-hour (64-km/h) sand-storms, pelting rainstorms, and other awful conditions. Some aircraft actually fly, chained in place, during the tests. The tests make sure the aircraft can handle any situation they may face during real flights.

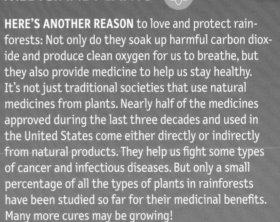

AN AIRCRAFT GOES THROUGH COLD WEATHER TESTING.

MEDICINAL PLANTS

HERE'S ANOTHER REASON to love and protect rain-forests: Not only do they soak up harmful carbon diox-ide and produce clean oxygen for us to breathe, but they also provide medicine to help us stay healthy. It's not just traditional societies that use natural medicines from plants. Nearly half of the medicines approved during the last three decades and used in the United States come either directly or indirectly from natural products. They help us fight some types of cancer and infectious diseases. But only a small percentage of all the types of plants in rainforests have been studied so far for their medicinal benefits. Many more cures may be growing!

MEDITATION

WHEN YOU MEDITATE, you turn your attention away from distracting thoughts and focus on something—maybe your breathing, bodily sensations, or a repeated word or phrase—that's happening right now. Meditating trains your brain and makes it strong and more able to think clearly. It also helps you keep calm and feel for others. Meditating every day has big payoffs in every aspect of your life. Try it: Sit comfort-ably in a quiet place, close your eyes, and focus on your breathing—nothing else. Think breathing in, breath-ing out. Start with only five minutes a day, and you'll be well on your way.

93

Starting in the mid-1500s, maps of Southeast Asia showed THE SOURCE OF THE REGION'S FIVE GREAT RIVER SYSTEMS to be LAKE CHIAMAY. European mapmakers probably goofed by using **mythical descriptions** from Hindu-Buddhist accounts of the rivers' spiritual center, but the mistake showed up for nearly four centuries.

In 1558, Nicolò Zeno, a wealthy resident of the city-state of Venice, **claimed his ancestors had discovered the New World** a century before Columbus. His proof included a map of FRISLAND, an island in the North Atlantic Ocean they passed on their journey. FRISLAND DIDN'T ACTUALLY EXIST but was included on maps for the next century.

In 1683, sailor William Ambrose Cowley DISCOVERED AN ISLAND north of the Falkland Islands in the South Atlantic. He named it PEPYS ISLAND, but his sailing companion believed it was **really part of the Falklands.** Turns out, the companion was right and Cowley had made a mistake—one that, you guessed it, showed up on maps.

26 MONUMENTAL (AND MISLEADING) MAP MISTAKES

In the 1850s, the United States claimed SARAH ANN ISLAND, A SMALL ISLAND in the Pacific Ocean, thanks to a law that allowed countries to claim islands covered in bird poop. **But no one can actually find it.**

The borders of the United States, defined in a treaty after the Revolutionary War, used ISLE PHELIPEAUX in Lake Superior as the country's **northern border.** Trouble is, surveyors in the 1820s DISCOVERED NO SUCH ISLAND EXISTS. It was created by an explorer trying to please Jean-Frédéric Phélypeaux, a French official who decided which explorers' voyages should be funded.

THE INTERNATIONAL DATE LINE, a line put on maps to separate two calendar dates, HAD TO BE REDRAWN IN 1910 after it was discovered that **Byres Island** and **Morrell Island** didn't really exist. They were another creation of Benjamin Morrell, the 19th-century captain with an overactive imagination. The international date line originally was diverted around the fictional islands, supposedly located northwest of Hawaii.

The LEGENDARY lost city of EL DORADO, a city of gold and riches, is rumored to lie deep in South America but has never been found. That didn't stop it from being mentioned on a mid-19th-century map.

The philosopher Plato told of ATLANTIS, an island that SANK IN THE ATLANTIC OCEAN some 9,000 years ago. Though he **made up the story** to prove a point, people have believed it to be true for nearly 2,400 years. And why not? Maps in the late 1800s included its possible location.

Several 19th-century explorers told of their daring adventures in the **MOUNTAINS OF KONG, AFRICA,** earning the mountains a place on several maps—even though THEY DON'T EXIST. Turns out, the first explorer **made up his adventurous story.** The others were too embarrassed to admit they couldn't find a mountain range, so they pretended they had great adventures there, too.

University of Michigan fan Peter Fletcher put **BEATOSU AND GOBLU, OHIO,** on a 1978 Michigan State Highway road map. Ohio State University fans realized the fake towns meant "BEAT OSU" and "GO, BLUE" and **demanded they be removed.**

A mid-18th-century map of North America shows a massive **SEA OR BAY OF THE WEST,** COVERING MUCH OF THE AMERICAN/CANADIAN WEST and opening into the Pacific Ocean.

ST. BRENDAN'S ISLE showed up on maps from the 1400s through 1600s. Said to be discovered by Christian monk and explorer St. Brendan—who also supposedly HELD A MASS ON THE BACK OF A WHALE—it's actually **only mythical.**

One of the BIGGEST CARTOGRAPHIC BLUNDERS showed **CALIFORNIA** as **an island, not connected to continental North America.** The error started in 1510 but, despite proof to the contrary (and correct maps), was revived again in the 1600s.

From the 1930s through the 1980s, the **SOVIET UNION FALSIFIED ITS PUBLIC MAPS**—misplacing rivers and streets and LEAVING OFF GEOGRAPHICAL FEATURES—**to fool spies and would-be invaders.**

After setting sail in 1524, Giovanni da Verrazzano DECLARED HE'D FINALLY FOUND the **NORTHWEST PASSAGE** through North America. He actually sailed into an inlet on the East Coast.

In the 1930s, General Drafting mapmakers put the fake town of **AGLOE, NEW YORK,** on a map TO CATCH COPYCATS. Too bad for them, someone had seen their map and built the "Agloe General Store" on the spot, **creating an actual town.**

A map mistake may have contributed to French emperor Napoleon Bonaparte's infamous 1815 defeat at the BATTLE OF WATERLOO, in present-day **BELGIUM.** Napoleon **used an incorrect map** when planning his battle strategy.

In 1591, a **French mapmaker** put a lake on a map of southeastern America, where Florida now is. THE LAKE DIDN'T EXIST, but a Dutch cartographer added it to his 1606 map—after making it bigger and moving it into the Appalachian Mountains. **LAKE APALACHY** showed up on maps until the early 1700s.

In the 1820s, British explorers sighted AN ISLAND BETWEEN NEW ZEALAND AND ANTARCTICA. Eventually known as **EMERALD ISLAND,** explorers searching for it only saw it now and then. Historians suspect **it was a mirage**—but it remained on maps until 1987.

Maps from 1325 to the 1800s showed **HY-BRASIL,** an island off the west coast of Ireland. It was believed to be A PARADISE WITH AN ADVANCED CIVILIZATION. It was said to be clouded in mist—only visible one day every seven years. **It exists only in Irish mythology.**

In 1823, Benjamin Morrell declared he had discovered **NEW SOUTH GREENLAND,** a mountainous land stretching 400 miles (644 km) **just off the Antarctic Peninsula.** It showed up on maps until around 1915, EVEN THOUGH IT DIDN'T EXIST … and despite Morrell's reputation for exaggerating.

According to legend, a French woman was abandoned in the mid-1500s on the **ISLE OF DEMONS,** off the coast of Newfoundland, but was rescued two years later. The island appeared on maps from the 16th and 17th centuries.

European mapmakers included **TERRA AUSTRALIS INCOGNITA** (unknown land of the south) on maps through the 1400s. NO ONE HAD EVER SEEN IT, but people imagined **mermaids and griffins** lived there.

SANDY ISLAND, New Caledonia, was discovered off the coast of Australia by James Cook in 1772. Other navigators **confirmed its existence,** and it was even on U.S. military maps. But in 2012 a surveyor found nothing but water.

An 1862 map of south-central Africa shows the **ZAMBEZI RIVER.** But the mapmakers guessed at how parts of it flowed—resulting in **a river that ran in a circle.** Oops.

First described in 330 B.C. by Greek explorer Pytheas, the island of **THULE** represented the FAR NORTHERN ENDS OF THE EARTH, as imagined back then. **Despite being mythical,** it showed up on maps until the 1700s.

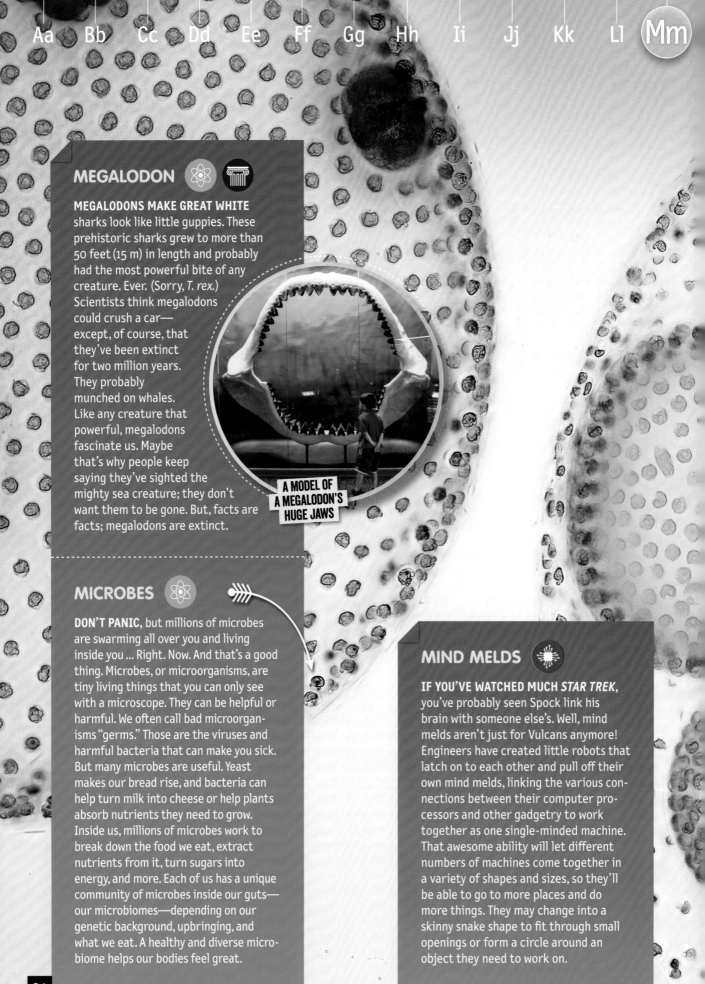

MEGALODON

MEGALODONS MAKE GREAT WHITE sharks look like little guppies. These prehistoric sharks grew to more than 50 feet (15 m) in length and probably had the most powerful bite of any creature. Ever. (Sorry, *T. rex.*) Scientists think megalodons could crush a car— except, of course, that they've been extinct for two million years. They probably munched on whales. Like any creature that powerful, megalodons fascinate us. Maybe that's why people keep saying they've sighted the mighty sea creature; they don't want them to be gone. But, facts are facts; megalodons are extinct.

A MODEL OF A MEGALODON'S HUGE JAWS

MICROBES

DON'T PANIC, but millions of microbes are swarming all over you and living inside you ... Right. Now. And that's a good thing. Microbes, or microorganisms, are tiny living things that you can only see with a microscope. They can be helpful or harmful. We often call bad microorganisms "germs." Those are the viruses and harmful bacteria that can make you sick. But many microbes are useful. Yeast makes our bread rise, and bacteria can help turn milk into cheese or help plants absorb nutrients they need to grow. Inside us, millions of microbes work to break down the food we eat, extract nutrients from it, turn sugars into energy, and more. Each of us has a unique community of microbes inside our guts— our microbiomes—depending on our genetic background, upbringing, and what we eat. A healthy and diverse microbiome helps our bodies feel great.

MIND MELDS

IF YOU'VE WATCHED MUCH *STAR TREK*, you've probably seen Spock link his brain with someone else's. Well, mind melds aren't just for Vulcans anymore! Engineers have created little robots that latch on to each other and pull off their own mind melds, linking the various connections between their computer processors and other gadgetry to work together as one single-minded machine. That awesome ability will let different numbers of machines come together in a variety of shapes and sizes, so they'll be able to go to more places and do more things. They may change into a skinny snake shape to fit through small openings or form a circle around an object they need to work on.

MUMMIES

THE ANCIENT EGYPTIANS believed that people who died passed into an afterlife, which was pretty similar to the one they'd just left. So they were buried with things they'd need on the journey to the afterlife, and their bodies were preserved—because they'd need those, too. The ancient Egyptians preserved bodies by making them mummies, a process that took up to 70 days. They'd wash and purify a body, remove all the organs (except the heart), and stuff the body to make it look normal. Then they'd dry out the body, stuff it anew, and wrap it in layers of cloth. The finished mummy was put in a container called a sarcophagus. The removed organs were sealed in containers and also put in the burial tomb. Except for the brain. The ancient Egyptians didn't think it did anything important. (Oops.)

MINIATURES

THE WORLD at your fingertips. Miniatures stoke your imagination, letting you experience something you love through tiny replicas of characters or places. Since the 1600s, when miniature houses (what we now call dollhouses) were first made, people have collected amazing, highly detailed miniature objects. In the 1700s, people re-created epic military battles using tin soldiers. Fast-forward a couple of centuries, and miniature figures—or "mini-figs"—of metal, plastic, or paper represent characters from history, mythology, games, and popular culture. Many people make, or at least paint, their own miniatures. Role-playing gamers and strategy gamers both use miniatures and enter them in competitions. A lot of artistry can go into mini-figs, and many become valuable pieces.

MUSIC CHILLS

HAVE YOU EVER BEEN LISTENING to some music and a chill runs up your spine even though you're not cold (or scared)? Getting chills from music may mean you have a special brain. Researchers found that the brains of people who get music chills—maybe from a favorite song or when music builds up to a dramatic moment—are wired differently. They have more connections between the parts of their brain that process sound and the parts that process emotions. The extra connections mean they feel the emotions more intensely.

ACCORDING TO OUR CALCULATIONS ...

Miniatures don't just make the Dungeons & Dragons experience more awesome; they can also be worth a lot as collectibles. Just check this out: The Huge Gold Dragon miniature is worth $40 as a collectible—even if it doesn't get a lot of game time. The popular Huge Red Dragon miniature can net $55 for collectors. But that's nothing compared to the not-so-miniature Colossal Red Dragon, which can fetch around $600 or more.

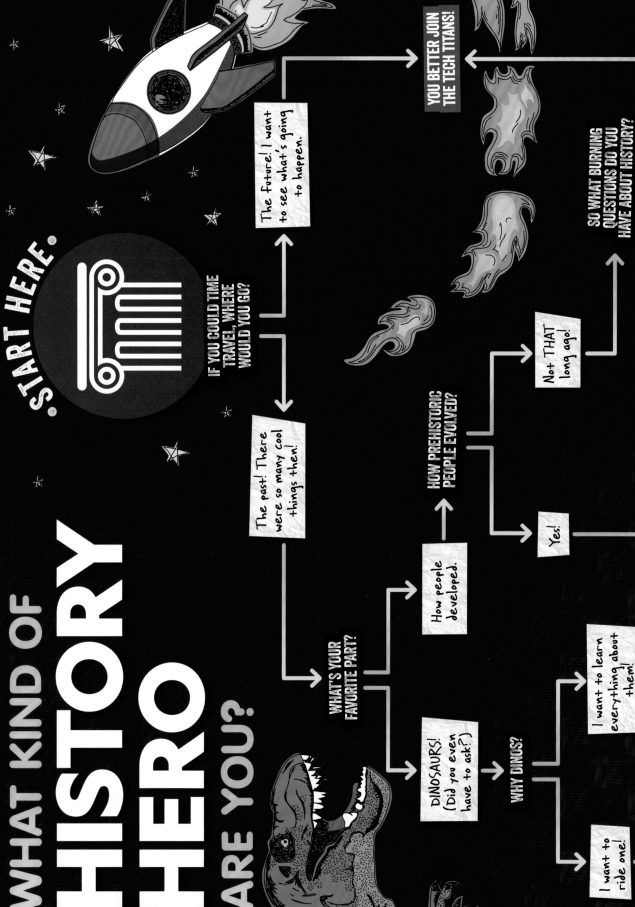

WHAT KIND OF
HISTORY HERO
ARE YOU?

START HERE

IF YOU COULD TIME TRAVEL, WHERE WOULD YOU GO?

The Future! I want to see what's going to happen.

YOU BETTER JOIN THE TECH TITANS!

The past! There were so many cool things then!

WHAT'S YOUR FAVORITE PART?

How people developed.

HOW PREHISTORIC PEOPLE EVOLVED?

Not THAT long ago!

Yes!

SO WHAT BURNING QUESTIONS DO YOU HAVE ABOUT HISTORY?

DINOSAURS! (Did you even have to ask?)

WHY DINOS?

I want to learn everything about them!

I want to ride one!

How many grandparents managed to live without smartphones when they were kids.

HISTORIANS OF SCIENCE AND TECHNOLOGY study innovation over the ages.

If it mattered who was the leader of a country.

What it was really like living in a castle.

POLITICAL HISTORIANS study the role of political leaders, states, and empires in history.

CULTURAL HISTORIANS are experts in the beliefs, rituals, and artistic expressions of people over the centuries.

I live for books.

That'll come in handy! So will an interest in other artifacts, like photos, coins, or diaries.

Cool. How about art and music? I'm interested in how that changed over the years.

HOW DO YOU WANT TO STUDY THEM?

I want to dig up evidence!

ARCHAEOLOGISTS dig into human history and prehistory by studying human remains and artifacts.

PALEONTOLOGISTS study the record of animal, plant, and other life on Earth left as fossils.

That would be **SO AWESOME.** But, we hate to break it to you, dinos were gone long before people arrived.

NANOBIONICS
N
NOVEL WORDS

"Science is not a boy's game, it's not a girl's game. It's everyone's game. It's about where we are and where we're going. Space travel benefits us here on Earth. And we ain't stopped yet. There's more exploration to come."

NICHELLE NICHOLS, actor and former NASA ambassador

NANOBIONICS

HERE'S ANOTHER REASON TO LIKE SPINACH:
Not only is it a superfood—packed full of nutritious stuff—but it also can have superpowers! Engineers have turned spinach and other kinds of plants into sensors that can alert people to trouble. They call their technique "plant nanobionics." They embed nanoparticles—little bits waaaay too small to see without a microscope—into the plant's leaves so they can detect something dangerous, such as pollution or chemicals used in land mines and other explosives. When one of those things is in the groundwater that the plant sucks up, it gives out a fluorescent signal that an infrared camera can see. The camera is attached to a small computer, which emails people the alert.

NANODRILLERS

IN THE FUTURE, one of our most powerful protectors might be machines so tiny that it'd take 50,000 of them to equal the width of one of your hairs. These nanomachines could fight cancer by drilling into cancer cells—a very effective way of killing them. Don't picture super-tiny versions of machines you see drilling into streets. These nanodrillers are actually molecules strung together by chemists. When ultraviolet light hits them, they kick into action. They grasp cancer cells then rings of atoms spin around, kind of like a chain saw, and rip through the cells' walls. So long, cells!

A CANCER CELL UNDER NANODRILLER ATTACK

NATURE'S HEALING POWER

SPENDING TIME IN NATURE—going on long kayak trips, hiking in the woods, camping out for a while—makes you feel better. And not just because you're getting good exercise. Being surrounded by nature actually reduces your stress and helps your body fight off illness. Studies show that simply looking at a beautiful view improves your heart and blood pressure, and listening to nature sounds—waves splashing, wind rustling, birds chirping—helps people recover from high levels of stress. Some researchers even discovered that plant smells, like some pine trees, help boost our immunity and lower high blood pressure.

NAUTILUS

THE IMAGINATION of the great 19th-century science fiction writer Jules Verne inspired many scientific advancements in real life. One of his most inspiring creations was the Nautilus, the fictional submarine from *20,000 Leagues Under the Sea*. When the story was published in 1870, there were no real submarines anything like the Nautilus. Verne's submarine was big—roughly three-quarters the length of a football field—and powered by electricity drawn from batteries. It could stay underwater for days at a time, purifying seawater (which is saltwater) to make drinking water—much like subs do today. Though Verne got some facts about the ocean wrong, his story got people excited about exploring it.

NEANDERTHALS

WITH THEIR STOCKY BUILDS, JUTTING BROWS, AND WIDE NOSES, Neanderthals—our closest extinct human relatives—often are portrayed as dumb brutes. But that wasn't the case at all. Neanderthals (*Homo neanderthalensis*, if you want to be formal) lived during the Ice Age 400,000 to 40,000 years ago in Europe and in southwestern to Central Asia. Their stocky bodies were adapted to the cold environment, and they had brains as large as ours and sometimes even larger. They lived in shelters, wore clothing, and warmed themselves by fires. Not only were they skilled hunters, but they also ate their veggies. They fashioned and used a variety of tools and sometimes even ornamental objects. Most amazingly, Neanderthals buried their dead and may have marked graves with offerings, such as flowers. No one else at the time did that—not even our *Homo sapien* ancestors! No one's figured out—yet—why Neanderthals went extinct.

NEURO-
plasticity ⚛

Neuroplasticity is also called brain plasticity. And, no, it doesn't mean your brain is made of plastic. But if you think about how plastic can be molded into new and different forms you'll start to get the picture. Neuroplasticity is about how our brains change throughout our lives.

We're not just talking about how you go from a babbling baby to a brainiac as you grow up. Of course, your brain changes a lot then. The thing is, for the longest time, we thought that was the only time our brains changed. Like they were totally hardwired and fixed by the time we became adults. Turns out we were wrong. Thanks to recent scientific research, we now know our brains change throughout our lives and in different ways—that they're "plastic." Not only that, we can change them on purpose.

Here's how it works: Your brain is kind of like a power grid, with billions of connections, or pathways, running every which way. Every time you do something, think, or feel an emotion, your brain fires messages from neuron to neuron (microscopic nerve cells) along certain pathways. If you do the same thing over and over, those pathways get stronger, and it gets easier and easier for your brain to use them. It's like a bunch of people following the footsteps of someone who trudged through deep snow before them. Each time someone goes the same way, the path gets better and easier to walk on.

But if you learn a new task, do something differently, or choose a different emotion, you start creating a new pathway—like walking through fresh snow. If you keep doing it, your brain gets used to sending messages along the new pathway, and it gets stronger. So something that starts out as a challenge becomes easy-peasy. You just rewired your brain.

It's not only your choices—like taking on a challenge—that change your brain. If someone's brain is damaged, the brain can reorganize and form new connections to undamaged regions, shifting brain functions over to the undamaged part. It's an amazing ability, all thanks to neuroplasticity.

> **FUN FACT**
> Neurons that fire together, wire together. That means if you keep doing the same thing, you'll strengthen the neural connections related to it. Not good if you get stuck in a rut, but great if you're learning to play piano.

TO BECOME AN EVEN BIGGER BRAINIAC, LEARN ABOUT MEDITATION ON PAGE 93, THE PLACEBO EFFECT ON PAGE 111, AND THE UNCONSCIOUS MIND ON PAGE 142.

FAQ

CAN I MAKE MY BRAIN GROW STRONGER?

Yes! Just like you can beef up your muscles by lifting weights, you can train your brain. Any time you challenge yourself to learn a new skill, you're growing new pathways in your brain. In fact, when you become expert at something, the areas in your brain that work on that skill grow and change.

Researchers have found that musicians grow thicker outer layers of brain than non-musicians. That doesn't just help them play music, it also boosts their attention and helps them manage their emotions. Researchers also compared the brains of taxi drivers and bus drivers in London and found that the part of the brain that works on navigation was more developed in taxi drivers. Why? They had to figure out the best way to get places, but the bus drivers drove the same route day after day.

CAN A BRAIN ALWAYS REPAIR ITSELF?

Brains are probably better at healing than we realize. They don't necessarily "repair" damage. They rewire themselves to use undamaged parts to carry out functions. But can they always do it? If we're talking 100 percent recovery for every problem, then the answer is no. Some injuries may be too severe. For other problems, we may not have discovered how to trigger the brain's neuroplastic powers. Scientists and doctors have to do a lot more research!

But there already are remarkable cases of brains healing. Take, for example, the case of a man who suffered a stroke—when blood flow to part of the brain is cut off and the brain is damaged. The part of the brain that controlled the man's left arm was damaged, and he couldn't move his arm anymore. So how did doctors and scientists help the man? They strapped his right arm so he couldn't use it and told him to clean a table! At first, it was impossible. But he kept trying and slowly his brain rewired itself. After a while, he could move his left arm again—and not just to clean tables. He wrote with it and even played tennis.

FUN FACT

Stay chill—it's good for your brain! Learning healthy ways, like meditation or exercise, to handle tough, stressful situations helps keep your brain happy and "plastic."

FUN FACT

Our brains are power hungry. They make up only about 2 percent of our total body weight, but they use 20 percent of our body's energy.

NERD OF NOTE:
NORMAN DOIDGE

NORMAN DOIDGE is deeply fascinated with people. Not like that's a huge surprise. After all, he's a psychiatrist and psychoanalyst, a type of doctor who helps people improve their mental health.

When he was in medical school, people still believed that our brains were hardwired by the time we reached adulthood and couldn't change. Norman didn't buy that idea. So he went on to become a psychiatrist so he could focus more on people's minds. He learned about how the brain can change, reorganize itself, and sculpt itself into something new. "Somehow or other, thought itself can do that work," he says. "It became apparent that this link between mind, brain, and energy really is central to who we are and what we do."

Norman became an expert on neuroplasticity. He's written books about people whose lives have been changed by treatments that draw on their brains' ability to rewire themselves. "I still have to pinch myself about what is possible," he says.

Neuroplasticity can help all of us. "Personally I realized that one can develop new kinds of circuitry at any point, I found a reason to expose myself to many new experiences!"

NEFERTITI

ONE OF THE MOST INTRIGUING WOMEN IN ANCIENT EGYPT, Nefertiti was also one of the most powerful. She ruled alongside Pharaoh Akhenaten from 1353 to 1336 B.C. and may have taken over after he died. Artwork from the time shows Nefertiti in roles usually only performed by pharaohs: leading religious worship, driving chariots, and smacking enemies with a mace, a ceremonial staff. Nefertiti also was known throughout Egypt—and even today—for her beauty. She wore makeup of her own creation and long gold beads called nefers. And, yes, it's no coincidence that the beads sound like her name.

ACCORDING TO OUR CALCULATIONS ...

A famous painted sandstone bust of Nefertiti, created more than 3,000 years ago and rediscovered in 1912 or 1913, is one of the most copied works of ancient Egypt—and one of the reasons Nefertiti is known for her great beauty. But in 2009, scans of the sculpture revealed a covered-up limestone carving of another woman, and she looked seriously different. Was it someone else—or a more realistic portrayal of Nefertiti?

NEW URBANISM

THREE DECADES AGO, a lot of cities in the United States were pretty dead at night. People worked there but at the end of the business day, they hopped in their cars and drove home farther and farther to sprawling suburbs. But city designers—and people who hate spending a lot of time driving—wanted to breathe life back into city living. In a movement called new urbanism, they worked to create an enjoyable, sustainable, and convenient lifestyle where people would have everything they needed—shops, restaurants, entertainment, schools, parks, and workplaces—within a short walk of where they live. The movement transformed many cities. And even suburbs are replacing big shopping malls with new town centers, where people can walk to restaurants and shops. It's not only convenient, but replacing car trips with walking is good for our health and the environment.

TOKYO, JAPAN

NGOZI

WATCH OUT WONDER WOMAN, there's a new superheroine in town. Ngozi, a teenage Nigerian girl, fights evil in Lagos, the capital of her country. Debuting in Marvel Comics' "Blessing in Disguise," part of the Venomverse series in 2017, Ngozi is wheelchair-bound until she is transformed by a Venom Symbiote—an alien that bonds with human hosts—into a superbeing. She not only regains the use of her legs but also many other powers, including the ability to jump like a grasshopper. Moments after her first transformation, she must face down a terrible villain. But never fear: She's up to it. The story, created by Nigerian-American author Nnedi Okorafor, is the first Marvel story set in Africa.

NORTH YUNGAS ROAD

IT'S NICKNAME IS "DEATH ROAD," and if that doesn't scare you enough, the actual drive might. The North Yungas Road may be the most terrifying stretch of pavement in the world. It starts in La Paz, Bolivia, and winds its way 43 miles (69 km) through the mountains to the Yungas region of the Amazon rainforest. On one side of the road is a wall of solid rock; on the other, a 2,000-foot (610-m) drop. For most of its existence, there was nothing keeping you from plunging off the side—no guardrails, no yellow stripes, nothing. Even after being "modernized" with better pavement, drainage systems, and some guardrails, the road remains dangerous. If that's not bad enough, warm winds from the Amazon rainforest often bring fog and torrential rain, and mudslides and falling rocks are a constant threat. But if you survive the drive, you'll see some of the most amazing scenery in the world.

NOVEL WORDS

FICTION AUTHORS, especially ones who write for kids, sometimes make up novel words. And many become part of everyday language. Muggles stuck in traffic jams wish they could apparate. People chortle at ridiculous things. If you think you've won a golden ticket, you hope there isn't a catch-22. Your friends may want a bite of your scrumdiddlyumptious dessert, and you hand it over because you're such a Hufflepuff. Authors often base new words on linguistic roots common in our language or give them sounds that make their meanings clear. Thank Lewis Carroll for "chortle" ("snort" plus "chuckle"); Joseph Heller for turning "catch-22" into the supreme gotcha; Roald Dahl for "golden ticket" and "scrumdiddlyumptious"; and J. K. Rowling for "muggle," "apparate," "Hufflepuff," and other novel words.

"Being a nerd or a geek means having passion, power, intelligence. Being a nerd just means there is something in the world that you care deeply about—be it 12-sided dice, a favorite sports team, your new laptop, or Knight Rider."

OLIVIA MUNN, actor and author

OLINGUITO

IF YOU HAVEN'T HEARD OF THIS FUZZY, reddish mammal, don't feel bad. The two-pound (0.9-kg) olinguito was undiscovered by scientists until relatively recently. But thousands of the little, large-eyed creatures—the smallest members of the raccoon family—scamper through the trees of cloud forests in Colombia and Ecuador. Trouble is, they stay by themselves and come out at night, when dense fog hides them. And for years, they were mistaken for their cousins, the olingos. The olinguito's discovery excited scientists and animal lovers everywhere because it's rare to find a new mammal, especially a carnivore (meat-eater)— not to mention, one so cute!

OP ART

OPTICAL ILLUSIONS and art go together like peanut butter and chocolate. An awesome combo. Of course, artists have always been interested in the nature of what we perceive. But in the 1950s, optical art—or op art—started to become a serious art movement, which became a big deal in the mid-1960s. Artists used abstract patterns, usually with stark contrasts between the background and foreground, to produce effects that excite our eyes and trick our brains.

ORGANOIDS

SCIENTISTS HAVE DISCOVERED how to grow miniature versions of human organs, such as lungs, intestines, and livers. These organoids aren't big enough to take the place of our real organs. They're only the size of a pencil tip! But they're helpful in many other ways. Scientists study them to learn how tissues and cells—even cancer—develop and to test if new medicines are effective. A Dutch biologist figured out how to grow organoids from a special type of mother cell, called a stem cell, that can create all other kinds of cells the organs need to function.

ORGANS ON A CHIP

HAVEN'T HAD YOUR fill of tiny human organs? Scientists have figured out how to re-create the parts of a living organ on a chip that's about 1.4 inches (36 mm) long and half an inch (13 mm) wide. It has channels lined with thousands of living organ cells. Blood or other nutrients are pumped through the channels, and the cells function just like they do in a person's body. Why's this so great? It's a way to research actual, living human organs—studying diseases and testing new medicines—with no risk to people. Someday, scientists think they'll be able to make chips that match an individual, so medicine can be tailor-made to that person.

OREO VINYL

A COOKIE YOU CAN DANCE TO? Yes, please! In China, some Oreo cookies were made to play music when you put them on a tiny record player. Like vinyl records—those big, black music discs that are becoming popular again—these cookies were engraved with grooves on their surfaces. As they spun on a mini-record player, the turntable's arm ran over the grooves, producing musical notes. Unfortunately, the cookies only played one song—the "Oreo anthem"—but they played it in four musical styles. And, yes, you could eat them when

ORIGAMI-INSPIRED CLOTHES

REMEMBER YOUR FAVORITE T-SHIRT? You know, the one you outgrew waaaay too fast? Wouldn't it be cool if your clothes could grow with you? Well, a London-based designer thought so, too. An aeronautical engineer by training, the designer was frustrated by how fast his niece and nephew outgrew the clothes he bought them. So, inspired by origami—the Japanese art of paper folding—he designed kids' clothes made from durable, pleated fabric that expands as the kids grow. The origami-inspired garments target the three-month- to three-year-old group. Kids grow by

OCTOPOLIS
and Octlantis

Octopuses

may be amazing creatures—
with their suckered tentacles, ink
squirting, complex brains, and so on—but
they aren't exactly party animals. In fact, they
have reputations as serious loners.

"We do tend to think of octopuses as solitary," marine biologist David Scheel says. "If they're going to get together, it's either
for mating or the big one's going to eat the little one."

You'd definitely expect that solitary behavior from a species called
gloomy octopuses—like they'd be off by themselves sulking all the time
(probably about their name). But it turns out, these animals aren't loners at all.
In the subtropical waters off eastern Australia, gloomy octopuses live clus-
tered together in places researchers dubbed Octopolis and Octlantis.
More than a dozen octopuses have been seen in each place.

"We think that's because this is a little bit of shelter and a big
sea of food, and so it's a great place to hang out," David says. "But
in order to do so, they have to tolerate each other."

Of course, tolerating each other doesn't necessarily mean
they've become best buddies. The male octopuses spend a lot of
time chasing each other out of their dens. Sometimes they squirt
water, kicking sand into each other's faces, and researchers even saw
one throw a shell at another.

But the most amazing thing about the octopuses at Octopolis and
Octlantis is that they communicate among themselves—even when they're
fighting. Because they can't speak, they use body language, signaling each other by changing shape and even color.

But life isn't always a brawl. Most of the time the octopuses just hang out together.

When researchers found Octopolis in 2009, they wondered if it was just a one-of-a-kind
happening. They noticed the octopuses had built dens around a sunken human-made object
possibly made of metal. But several years later, they discovered Octlantis not too far away and
not near any sunken human object. Both octopus cities are in Jervis Bay, whose floor is pretty
flat and featureless—except for the sunken object at Octopolis and a rock outcropping at
Octlantis. Both are ideal for building dens.

FUN FACT

Octopuses have awesome
defenses. Not only can they
jet away, but they also squirt
ink to hide their getaway and
to confuse their opponent. In
fact, you might say they're
well armed. (Sorry,
couldn't resist.)

TO FIND OUT ABOUT OTHER AMAZING UNDERWATER CREATURES,
READ ABOUT JELLYFISH ON PAGE 74 AND SEA ANGELS ON PAGE 126.

FAQ IS IT TRUE OCTOPUS ARMS CAN LIVE IF THEY'RE CHOPPED OFF?

Not forever! But they do react to things for a while even after they've been severed—for example, jerking away from pain. The reason they can do that is because two-thirds of the octopus's brainy nerve cells are in its arms, not its head. That means (when they're all attached) an individual arm can figure out how to do things, like breaking into a shellfish, while the animal does something else, like looking for the next snack. It's like octopus arms have minds of their own.

HOW SMART ARE OCTOPUSES?

Octopuses are super smart and even have distinct personalities. The cephalopods have brains similar to mammals in terms of their relative size and complexity. Octopuses can solve problems, like how to open a jar to get to the food inside or, in one case, even escape from their aquarium tanks. They also can learn to recognize shapes and navigate mazes. Like brainy mammals, octopuses are curious animals. They need to keep their minds occupied or they'll grow unhappy. They may even enjoy playing. In one aquarium, an octopus pushed a plastic bottle into the stream of water flowing into its tank—over and over and over, like it was dribbling a ball.

IMAGINING OCTOPUSES
IN ANIMATED FEATURES AND CARTOONS, OCTOPUSES HAVE ALMOST AS MANY PERSONALITIES AS ARMS.

• IN *FINDING NEMO*, one of Nemo's classmates is a young pink octopus named Pearl. When startled, she releases her ink—even if she doesn't want to: "Aw, you made me ink!"

• THE SPLASHY SEA WITCH URSULA, who tricks innocent merfolk in *The Little Mermaid*, is a human-octopus hybrid. She actually only has six tentacles, so you'd have to count her humanlike arms to truly call her an octopus.

NERD OF NOTE:
DAVID SCHEEL

YOU MIGHT CALL David Scheel the Dr. Doolittle of octopuses. OK, David doesn't actually "speak octopus," but he's learning their language.

David has found that octopuses have a surprisingly complex social life. They interact and communicate in a variety of wordless ways.

"They're kind of flashy actually," he says. "The octopuses turn dark, stand up very tall, spread their arms and web very wide, and then they raise their mantle—which is sort of the body sack behind the eyes—they raise that up above their eyes. And then sometimes they will even seek out high ground to do that display on top of."

What are they trying to say? "We think it means, 'I'm not going to back down. I'm this big, and I'm here, so watch out.'" If other octopuses don't heed the warning, the big, flashy ones might chase them away.

How does David know all of this? He spends hours studying octopuses. And, yes, that means he has to go swimming in the ocean, scuba diving with exotic sea creatures, and zipping around in submersible vessels. Yeah, it's a tough job. But, you know, he puts up with it for the sake of advancing scientific knowledge.

• PANGAEA •

P

• PYRAMIDS OF GIZA •

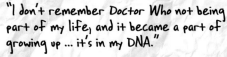

"I don't remember Doctor Who not being part of my life, and it became a part of growing up ... it's in my DNA."

PETER CAPALDI, actor

PANGAEA

FOR ANYONE STRUGGLING to remember the names of Earth's seven continents, this bit of science may make you yearn for the old days. The really, really old days. Nearly 300 million years ago, all of Earth's landmasses were part of a supercontinent, Pangaea. It was formed from earlier paleocontinents that collided with each other. But about 200 million years ago, Pangaea began to break apart into the continents we have today. We weren't around when that happened, but geographers and other scientists have found geographic and fossil evidence that connects the dots.

PELE

THIS IS ONE GODDESS you don't want to dis. Pele, the Hawaiian goddess of fire and volcanoes, has the power and fiery temper fitting her role. According to legend, she wanders through the island chain, sometimes appearing as a long-haired woman (young or old). To stay on her good side—very helpful for avoiding lava flows—you need to greet her with "aloha," offer help, and maybe give her some food or flowers. And don't take any lava rocks home from Hawaii as souvenirs. Not only is it illegal, but according to folklore, Pele will curse you. Every year, Hawaiian park and postal officials receive packages containing lava rocks that people want returned to their origin.

AN OFFERING TO PELE, CALLED A PU'OLO

PHOENIX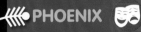

FEW LEGENDARY CREATURES are as amazing as the magical phoenix, a long-lived and brilliantly colored bird the size of an eagle or peacock. It lives hundreds of years, but when it feels the end of its life is near, it dies by bursting into flames. Then it rises from the ashes, reborn, to start a new life. Its name comes from the Greeks, but similar magical birds are found in mythologies around the world: the Native American thunderbird, the Russian firebird, the Egyptian Bennu, the Chinese fèng huáng, and the Japanese ho-o. Because of their powers of renewal, phoenix birds show up in stories throughout the ages—like Fawkes, the magical phoenix in J. K. Rowling's Harry Potter series, whose tears heal wounds—lucky for Harry.

PIEZOELECTRICITY

A SOCCER BALL gets kicked around during the day, then powers a light in the evening. A dance floor produces enough electricity to power the DJ's booth. What's going on? The soccer ball and the dance floor are specially designed to harness piezoelectricity (pronounced pee-AY-zo-electricity), the charge created when certain crystals, such as quartz, are squeezed together. The special crystals, circuitry, and maybe batteries are placed inside things that move. When the crystals are stressed—when the ball is kicked or the floor danced on—the electricity flows. It can be stored in a battery or used to power all sorts of gadgets.

PLACEBO EFFECT

YOUR BRAIN CAN TRICK YOU into getting better. It's called the placebo effect, and experiments have shown how it works: A doctor gave volunteers some medicine. The volunteers thought it was real medicine, but some of the volunteers got fake look-alikes, called placebos. Logic would tell you placebos are not going to do anything, right? But they often do because people believe they will! Our minds are so powerful that they help our bodies heal. Yes, even with fake medicine.

111

PIRATES

Swashbuckling seamen with patches over their eyes and parrots perched on their shoulders. Massive frigates flying the Jolly Roger and sailing the seven seas in search of treasure. Cannons firing, swords clashing, and captives walking the gangplank. Arr, we're talking pirates, matey!

Or are we? Many common beliefs about pirates are more Hollywood than history. But that doesn't mean pirates were boring—anything but! Throughout history (and even today), wherever people moved goods on long, unprotected trade routes, pirates have been happy to relieve them of their valuables. But one era, from the mid-17th through the early 18th centuries, stands out as the Golden Age of Piracy, when more than 2,000 pirates terrorized the seas. Large sailing ships transported more valuable cargo than ever, especially across the Atlantic Ocean, and major colonial empires were too busy fighting wars to protect them. Perfect pickings for pirates.

Pirates even created their own settlements at Tortuga, an island off Hispaniola (now part of Haiti); Nassau in the Bahamas; Port Royal in Jamaica; and Madagascar.

Pirates had little respect for government authority. They raided and plundered other ships for a living, often killing their crews or stranding them on islands without food or water. But most pirates otherwise were regular seamen (and, rarely women). For the crew, working conditions were usually much better on a pirate ship than on a merchant ship or military vessel, where the captain's authority was supreme.

Some pirate captains were cruel to their crews, but most were not. In fact, at a time when royal governmental powers were exploiting colonies, plundering ancient civilizations, and profiting from the slave trade, many pirate ships were amazingly democratic. Before a pirate ship set sail, all the crew members got together to decide where to go, what rules to have on the ship, how to divide up the booty—and even who would be captain! No wonder, then, that some seamen decided, "a pirate's life for me."

READ ABOUT OTHER SEAFARING WARRIORS, THE VIKINGS, ON PAGE 148. IF YOU'RE MORE OF A LANDLUBBER, CHECK OUT GLADIATORS ON PAGE 54.

IMAGINING PIRATES
FICTION, MORE THAN HISTORICAL FACT, HAS SHAPED OUR IMAGES OF PIRATES. BUT WHO CAN RESIST THESE SWASH-BUCKLING SCALAWAGS?

● **IN ROBERT LOUIS STEVENSON'S 1883** adventure novel *Treasure Island*, Long John Silver is the cunning leader of a band of pirates seeking buried treasure. With a pet parrot named Captain Flint, the character helped create the popular perception of pirates as one-legged seafarers with parrots perched on their shoulders.

● **CAPTAIN HOOK,** the captain of the pirate ship *Jolly Roger*, seeks revenge against Peter Pan for cutting off his left hand and feeding it to Tick-Tock, the crocodile. Captain Hook is one of the most popular Disney villains and a key character in Disney's 1953 animated film *Peter Pan*.

NERD OF NOTE:
CHING SHIH

CHING SHIH (or Zheng Shi) terrorized the South China Sea during the early 19th century and was probably the most successful pirate of all time.

She—yes, she—was a rarity in many ways, and not just because she was a female pirate. She didn't set out to be a pirate. But in 1801, Zhèng Yi, commander of a fleet of pirate ships called the Red Flag Fleet, was struck by her beauty and wanted to make her his wife. Some historians say he had his pirates capture her. Others say he proposed.

What's more certain is that Ching Shih soon began to run the Red Flag Fleet together with her husband. When her husband died suddenly, Ching Shih took over.

Ching Shih grew her fleet until she commanded more than 1,800 pirate vessels and about 80,000 pirates. A brilliant strategist, she ran her fleet with a strict code of laws. For example, any ship that captured loot got to keep a good chunk of it, while the rest was split among the fleet. Ching Shih also did not allow captives to be mistreated.

Ching Shih's fleet was unstoppable, easily defeating the Chinese navy. The Chinese government finally offered to forgive her crimes—if she would just stop being a pirate!

FAQ WAS CAPTAIN JACK SPARROW REAL?
Jack Sparrow has to be fiction, right? Not totally! Actor Johnny Depp definitely put his own spin on the character of Captain Jack in the *Pirates of the Caribbean*, which was set in the 1700s. But his character was inspired by a pirate named John Ward.

Here are the details: John Ward terrorized ships in the eastern Mediterranean Sea in the early 1600s. He was described as short and almost bald. OK, doesn't sound much like Jack Sparrow—wrong name, wrong place, wrong date, wrong looks. But read on. John Ward also was described as a flashy dresser who acted foolish but really was very smart tactically. Getting warmer. Still not convinced? His nickname was Sparrow. Oh, and he was referred to as "Jack" instead of "John." Bingo!

DID PIRATES REALLY MAKE CAPTIVES WALK THE PLANK?
We've all heard of this horrible practice: pirates forcing their captives—or crewmen who tried to mutiny—to walk off a wooden plank extending over the side of the pirate ship. Splash. Goodbye. Oh, and in case the cold water or sharks didn't get them, the poor victims' hands were often tied up to make sure they couldn't swim.

Walking the plank pops up in a lot of pirates stories—but it doesn't show up in history. Some pirates were definitely brutal, but many pirate ships had codes of conduct that included how captives would be treated. Historians can't find evidence that pirates forced anyone to walk the plank. Looks like this pirate "fact" is really fiction.

PLANETS

TALK ABOUT A DIVERSE GROUP! Planets, those big worlds that circle their suns, range from rocky to gaseous, blisteringly hot to frigid, and large to small. Just in our solar system, we've got hard, rocky terrestrial planets, like Earth and its closest neighbors: Mars, Venus, and Mercury. But farther from the sun, there are larger planets, including the gas giants Jupiter and Saturn and the more distant icy giants Uranus and Neptune. Based on other spacey evidence, scientists suspect our solar system has an additional, faraway planet, dubbed Planet 9 or … George. (Yes, really.) But they haven't set eyes on it yet. And that's just our solar system! Almost every star has a planet orbiting it. With as many as hundreds of billions of stars in our galaxy and hundreds of billions of other galaxies on top of that, there are countless planets.

ACCORDING TO OUR CALCULATIONS …

Pluto, once considered the ninth planet in our solar system until it was demoted to "dwarf planet" status in 2006, is one weird traveler. Its orbit, which takes 248 Earth years to circle the sun, is extremely elliptical—like a circle got seriously smushed. Sometimes, Pluto is more than 49 times farther from the sun than Earth is. But for 20 Earth years of its orbit, Pluto is closer to the sun than Neptune is. Neptune is usually the eighth planet in our solar system.

POP ART

POPULAR CULTURE, MEDIA STARS, and everyday objects took front and center in the pop art movement, which did away with the idea that art was a lofty pursuit that should focus only on "high art" themes of history, morality, or mythology. From the mid-1950s to 1970s, pop art—whether Andy Warhol's paintings of soup cans or colorful pop stars or Roy Lichtenstein's comic strip-inspired work—celebrated the commonplace, lifting it to the level of fine art.

A CUPCAKE STYLE INSPIRED BY ANDY WARHOL

PREHISTORIC ART

PEOPLE HAVE A TRADITION OF MAKING ART that goes back to about 100,000 B.C., when the first human artists ground clay to make reddish pigments that they used to draw on rock. Some of the most impressive prehistoric art was made at least 38,000 years ago in caves and rock shelters. Besides geometric shapes, animals were the most popular subjects: including horses, lions, rhinos, bison, turtles, crocodiles, and many more. It shows that animals were really important to our ancestors from long ago—and that humans have been showing their creative sides for a really, really long time.

ANCIENT ART IN UTAH, U.S.A.

PYRAMID INTERNATIONAL LABORATORY

AT THE NOSEBLEED HEIGHT OF 16,568 FEET (5,050 M) above sea level, the Pyramid International Laboratory, at the base of the Nepali side of Mount Everest, is the world's highest land-based science lab. Its design is as seriously awesome as its setting. The research center is self-sufficient, powered by solar energy. Researchers there study the fragile environment, climate change, geology of mountains ... and how well humans handle living at such a high elevation, where the oxygen is thin.

PYRAMIDS OF GIZA

TOWERING 21 TO 45 STORIES TALL, the three pyramids, built more than 4,000 years ago to be tombs for Egyptian pharaohs, took an estimated 10,000 workers to erect. Huge stone blocks cut from quarries were carried up the Nile River to Giza, where they were loaded onto large sledges—sledlike platforms—that workers pushed or pulled to the construction site. They poured water on the sand in front of the sledges, reducing the friction so only half as many workers were needed to move them. To haul the stones up the pyramid, workers used a system of ramps. Researchers are scanning the pyramids to find out how exactly they worked—and to find any hidden chambers inside.

"I really don't know how to be anyone else, and whenever I try to be anyone else, I fail miserably."

QUEEN LATIFAH, actor and musician

QUAGMIRE

YOU DON'T WANT TO GET STUCK IN A QUAGMIRE. In the real world, quagmire is squishy, mushy wetlands—like bogs, swamps, or marshes—that sinks when you walk on it. It's really hard to walk around when the ground is sinking underneath you. So hard, that "quagmire" has become a term that means anything that you can get stuck in, like a difficult situation full of problems or other kind of predicament.

QUANTUM COMMUNICATION

QUANTUM COMMUNICATION—also called teleportation—happens on the level of particles, the microscopic atoms and molecules that make up matter. Teleportation is like scanning something in one place and then sending the instructions for assembling it somewhere else using different atoms and molecules. It sounds like you're making a copy or clone, but you're not. During teleportation, the thing doesn't exist any more in its original state. It'll be a while before you can say, "Beam me up, Scotty!" Scientists have used quantum communication to send little particles of light or messages vast distances through space and water. But we're nowhere close to teleporting people. Yet.

QUEST

A QUEST IS A DIFFICULT, challenging adventure someone goes on, usually confronting and overcoming many obstacles to gain something from the experience—whether it's learning something new, acquiring skills, or finding a treasure. Quests of some sort are part of many fictional stories, but they're part of real cultures, too. Native Americans sometimes go on a vision quest, a difficult ritual that varies from tribe to tribe, to find their life's purpose.

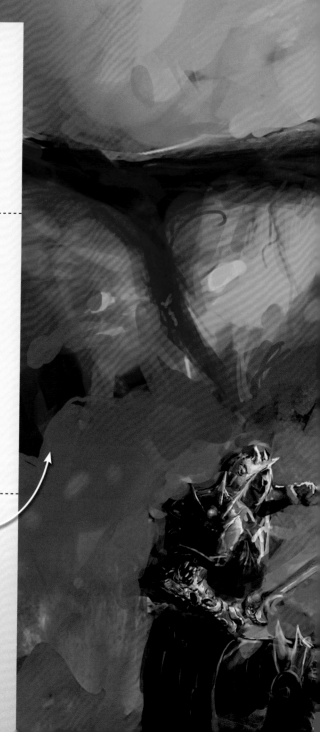

QUICKSAND

IT'S A CLASSIC MOVIE SCENE: Someone steps onto a patch of innocent-looking ground and starts to sink. He's just stepped onto quicksand. The more he struggles, the faster he gets sucked down, until ... death by quicksand. Is it just Hollywood, or is it really possible? Quicksand is a mix of sand, clay, and water. When it's not disturbed, it thickens. But put a little pressure on it, and it gets soupy really fast. If you thrash about, you'll sink. But, relax, you'll only sink to about your waist. People aren't as dense as quicksand, so we end up floating! But it's still hard to get out. After you sink partway, the quicksand thickens. To get out, wiggle your legs to create a space between them where water can flow and loosen the sand. Little by little, you can wiggle your way free.

QUILL

JOHN HANCOCK DIDN'T MAKE HIS FANCY SIGNATURE on the U.S. Declaration of Independence with a ballpoint pen. Like people had been doing for 1,500 years, he used a quill, a pen made from the flight feather of a large bird, which he dipped into a little pot of ink. These feathers have strong, hollow shafts—ideal for flying—which can also hold ink. Their tips were cut to make a fine writing point. When John dipped his quill into the ink, it rose up the shaft, thanks to a process called capillary action. Capillary action draws liquids up in something solid, even with gravity pulling against it. But when the point touched the paper, a little ink flowed down. People used quills until the mid-1800s, when steel tips started replacing them.

QUIRKS

A QUIRK IS AN ODD OR UNIQUE HABIT SOMEONE HAS. One person always eats M&M's in even numbers (so one side of your mouth doesn't get jealous if the other side has one). Another always sets an alarm clock to odd numbers to wake up at 8:01, not 8:00. A guy always wears bow ties (never straight ties) for special occasions. A lot of quirks are fun and harmless things we start doing to express ourselves or stand out as individuals. They're part of our personality.

·RADAR·
R
·ROCKETS·

"I'm proud to be a railway modeler. It means more to me to be on the cover of *Model Railroader* than to be on the cover of a music magazine."

ROD STEWART, rock star

RADAR

RADAR—RAdio **De**tecting **A**nd **R**anging—is a way of locating something by picking up its echo. Radar sends out short pulses of electromagnetic, or radio, waves that bounce off objects and come back to the radar's receiver. How long it takes for the waves to bounce back tells the radar apparatus how close something is. Radar was first developed in World War II to detect enemy aircraft, but now it's used in all sorts of ways—to track airplanes, forecast weather (yes, it can bounce off raindrops), and to see if cars are speeding on the highway.

RAT NIGHTMARES

DREAMING ABOUT RATS might give you the creeps. Well, rats may actually know how you feel. It turns out that rats may be as likely to have bad dreams as we are. Researchers let some rats run around a maze and at a certain corner, the researchers blasted the rats in the face with air. (It didn't hurt them, but it scared the bejeebers out of them.) Then the researchers monitored the rats' sleep using high-tech computers. They could see the rats' brains lighting up in patterns corresponding to their mental maps of the maze. When the rats' brains recalled the corner where they got the scary air puff, the part of their brains that processes emotion fired up big time! So, it turns out that people give rats nightmares, too.

RATTLESNAKES

THE SOUND OF A RATTLESNAKE shaking its tail in warning is some people's worst fear. All of the more than 24 rattlesnake species have rattles at the tip of their tails. When they shake their tails, hollow, doughnut-like segments bang together, making the rattly sound. Rattlesnakes grow new rattle segments when they molt, or shed their skin. Though a rattler's sound scares us, the snakes themselves can't hear it the way we do. Like other snakes, rattlesnakes don't have ears and don't hear most sounds. Instead, they feel vibrations.

RECYCLING

WONDER WHAT HAPPENS to the plastic water bottle you toss into the recycling bin? Trucks haul wannabe-recyclables to facilities where the stuff is piled on conveyor belts and sorted by machines, including metal detectors, and people—so your plastic bottle ends up with other plastic. Then your water bottle and many, many others are smushed into 1,000-pound (454-kg) bales that are sold to recyclers, sometimes in other countries. At the recycling facility, the bottle bales are broken up and dumped on conveyor belts. The smushed bottles are washed, sorted by color, and washed again in a hot goop that makes their labels and caps fall off. After that, they're ground into small flakes, washed and dried yet again, and heated to get rid of anything that might contaminate them. Then the clean plastic flakes are off to companies that melt them and mold them into new products, such as carpets, fabric, or even the stuffing for your favorite teddy bear. To become a new bottle requires a little more work. The plastic flakes go through a process to sterilize them, so they can be used to hold food.

REENACTMENTS

REENACTMENTS ARE YOUR CHANCE to live through a famous historical event. They're re-creations of earlier events, staged like theatrical performances, and sometimes where the event originally happened. Sure, you know how it's going to turn out, but experiencing the drama firsthand is awesome. Reenactments range over history and include ancient Roman battles, Viking combat, and more. Reenactments aren't a new thing. Back in the Middle Ages, from the fifth to 15th centuries, actors staged tournaments with ancient Roman themes. Reenactors these days are often amateurs who have a passion for the historical event.

REGALIA

REGALIA ARE THE FANCY (and sometimes weird) clothes that people wear to show off their status. That includes stuff like the crowns, cloaks, and scepter of royalty. Schools have regalia too: During graduations, students and teachers wear long robes and funny hats with tassels. It's a tradition that goes back to the 12th and 13th centuries in Europe, where scholars (who were usually clergy) wore gowns and hoods. Students adopted the same garb, partly to stay warm in unheated buildings and also to set themselves apart from others. Regalia vary depending on a person's education level. If you're getting a four-year college degree, you wear a gown with pointed sleeves. But if you go on to get a master's degree, you'll get oblong sleeves and a hood. Stay in school even longer to get a doctoral degree, and you'll have serious bling: long velvet stripes on the front and back of your gown, velvet crossbars on the sleeves, and a fancier hat.

ACCORDING TO OUR CALCULATIONS ...

Plastic lasts about 500 years, so every bottle you've ever used exists somewhere, in some form, on Earth. Worldwide, we use about 100 billion pounds (45 billion kg) of the type of plastic (polyethylene terephthalate, or PET) that makes plastic bottles— every year! The good news is that PET plastic can be recycled over and over, so we don't need to use more natural resources (crude oil and natural gas) to make new plastic. Making bottles from recycled PET plastic uses less energy and less water—so it's a lot better for Earth. It's not always the cheapest way to make things, but it's kindest to our Earth.

OCTOBOT, the first TOTALLY SOFT-BODIED ROBOT, can squeeze and squish itself in and out of tight places, **like a real octopus.** Plus, a chemical reaction makes its arms flex, propelling it through the water. Someday, it may help study oceans.

The seriously ADORABLE ROBOTIC DOG **AIBO,** first released two decades ago, is new and improved with super-advanced tech that makes it **act like a real puppy.** It can recognize and respond to you by playing, wagging its tail, and learning what you like.

Sleek and cute to boot, **AQUA-PENGUINS** SWIM LIKE NATURAL PENGUINS, propelling themselves underwater with their wings and rudderlike tails.

The **CHEETAH 2** robot can FLEX ITS "BACKBONE" to increase its strides and **speed and leap over obstacles** in its way. It's fast, but not as fast as real cheetahs.

26 RAD AND RIDICULOUS ROBOTS

3D-printed **BIONIC ANTS** are six-legged robots with ELECTRONIC INNARDS, SENSORS, AND CAMERA EYES. They use wireless technology to communicate, so they can **work together like real ants.**

IT CRAWLS LIKE A WORM! IT ROLLS LIKE A LOG! It's **SNAKEBOT!** The tube-shaped robot is made from a series of disc-shaped flexible chambers. Equipped with suction cups, **it can pick things up and climb walls.**

Here's an unusual way for a robot to move: A tiny, **DUMBBELL-SHAPED ROBOT,** smaller than the head of a pin, TUMBLES END OVER END OR SIDEWAYS. That may help it **maneuver in places where legs are not practical,** like to deliver medicine to exactly where a body needs it.

SPOTMINI, a nimble, PET-SIZE ROBOT developed by Boston Dynamics, **can move around a home or yard,** even climbing stairs, using advanced sensors and gyroscopes.

Designed to GRIP FRAGILE AND DELICATE THINGS, one robot is covered with soft, grippy elastomer (elastic polymer). Trouble is, soft coverings can rip easily. But this **robot** can **HEAL ITSELF!**

These robots may be tiny, but they're serious warriors. **NANO-ROBOTS** made from genetic material can be PROGRAMMED TO FIGHT CANCER. In lab experiments, they block the blood supply to a cancer tumor, making its tissue die and the tumor shrink. **Robots 1, Cancer 0.**

ROBONAUT 2—he goes by the nickname "R2"—HELPS ASTRONAUTS on the International Space Station. Designed to handle the boring tasks (he doesn't mind), **he frees up astronauts to do more important stuff.** With hands as agile as humans, R2 may someday handle repairs on the ISS.

A **ROBOTIC SPIDER,** created on a 3D printer, is the SIZE OF YOUR HEAD. You can use a remote control to let it **creep along** on its eight flexible legs.

SPIRULINA, an algae, can be used as a robot that one day may SWIM INSIDE HUMAN BODIES, moved by a magnetic field. It degrades after a few days, releasing a compound that is safe for most cells—but not cancer cells. **Robots 2, Cancer 0.**

Big, blue **BUTTERFLY ROBOTS**—we're talking 20-inch (51-cm) wingspans—FLY LIKE THEIR NATURAL COUSINS, thanks to GPS and sensors that keep them right-side up and help them **"see" obstacles** in their way.

Need a STEALTHY UNDERWATER ROBOT to do your bidding? A five-foot (1.5-m)-long **ROBOT SHARK** can swim deep in the ocean or skim along the top with only its fin visible. **Like real sharks, it uses its tail to control its movement.** It could be used to spy on other ships or to bring repair supplies.

EVER NEEDED A HELPING HAND? Just strap on the **AUCTO ROBOTIC ARM,** an extra limb that **extends your reach.**

A **ROBOTIC FISH,** which swims by swishing its tail back and forth like the real deal, isn't just a fun toy. IT HELPS FIGHT WATER POLLUTION. The fish is packed with sensors that help it **check the purity of water and recognize pollutants.**

Hungry? Have a **ROBOTIC COOK** whip you up a little dinner! The robot is just two arms and hands suspended from a track in a kitchen, but it can COOK LIKE A PROFESSIONAL CHEF. Controlled by a smartphone, the robot **even loads the dishwasher.**

ASIMO has been around for two decades, but the HUMANOID BOT is more agile than ever. It adjusts its center of gravity with every step, so it can **climb stairs, run at a jogging pace, hop on one foot, or kick a soccer ball.**

A soft robot that LENGTHENS AND CONTRACTS, bends this way and that, and twists around was **inspired by an origami twisted tower** made of multiple origami parts. The **TWISTER ROBOT** may be of use someday in surgery, on assembly lines, or even in outer space.

The **LOOMO** robot, FROM THE FOLKS WHO MAKE SEGWAYS, is called an **"advanced personal robot."** It can follow you around like a pet, check to see who's at the front door and, yes, even give you a lift somewhere.

When you need to repair something underwater, call an underwater **SNAKE ROBOT!** Its sleek shape lets it SLIP INTO TIGHT PLACES, like on the base of an oil platform, that other robots can't reach. These robots are **perfect at making repairs** and doing routine maintenance on the seabed.

A **BIONIC KANGAROO?** Why not? The 3-foot (1-m) -tall **engineering marvel** uses the power of one jump to launch into the next, thanks to springs that recover the mechanical energy of landing.

Oh, great, just what we need: ROBOTS THAT SCURRY AROUND like **COCKROACHES!** Researchers studied them to make a roach-inspired, **multi-legged robot that scurries past bumps and over gaps.** Researchers hope the technology will help robots handle different kinds of terrain.

Robotic **EXOSKELETONS** are PUSHING THE BOUNDARIES OF HUMAN MOBILITY. One exoskeleton helps stroke victims regain use of their legs by **automatically pulling cords to move their joints** more naturally. Others help people carry heavy loads, such as welders and industrial tools.

Like the roots of a plant or fungus, one **SOFT ROBOT** grows ever longer, WORKING ITS WAY INTO NARROW PLACES AND AROUND OBSTACLES. Once it gets to its destination, it can turn levers or twist itself into whatever shape is needed. It may **help in search-and-rescue operations** or by bringing water to fight fires in hazardous areas.

121

REGGAE

REGGAE IS ONE OF Jamaica's gifts to the world. This genre of music, which started in the late 1960s, combined other styles, including popular forms of Jamaican music and American jazz and rhythm and blues, into a new sound. It uses a strong four-beat rhythm driven mainly by drums and guitars. Lyrics often speak of love, or rebellion against negative things, like poverty, violence, racism, and government oppression. Reggae quickly became Jamaica's dominant music and soon spread throughout the world, where it was especially popular in the United States, United Kingdom, and Africa.

RETROFUTURISM

IF YOU'VE EVER SPENT TIME wondering what the future will look like (flying cars? personal robots?), you're not alone. Throughout the ages, people have dreamed of the future. The 1930s, during the Great Depression, were a particularly rich time for imagining the future because people were eager for a better life. They imagined us speeding along in monorail trains driven by airplane propellers, driving cars with ball-shaped tires, and wearing clothes made of unusual materials, including glass! Retrofuturism is going back to the past (the "retro" part) to discover visions of the future—and it's a blast. The futuristic art from way back then inspires artists and designers today, and many use the style in their work now, like steampunk, which features sci-fi inventions made of old technology, like steam-driven machines.

RIPTIDE

A RIPTIDE IS A STRONG ocean current that quickly pulls you farther and farther from the shore. To understand how it works, think about regular ocean waves. When waves break on the shore, the water from earlier waves runs back under them, creating a gentle current along the bottom of the ocean that pulls things, like shells, back into the water. It's not strong enough to be a problem for most people. But when there's heavy wave action, the water from early waves builds up and then rushes out to sea more strongly, creating a rip current. If you get caught in one, don't try to fight your way back. If you try, you can get exhausted—and that's really dangerous. Instead, swim parallel to the shore until you get beyond the riptide (which is usually less than 100 feet, or 30 meters, wide) or float on your back until you're beyond the current's pull (usually 50 to 100 yards [45 to 90 m] from shore), then swim back.

PEOPLE OF THE FUTURE, IMAGINED IN THE 1950S

ROBBER CRABS

FORGET ABOUT THE CUTE little hermit crabs you see on the beach or pet shop. Robber crabs—frequently known as coconut crabs—are ginormous creatures that grow up to a yard (meter) long and weigh more than a Yorkshire terrier. They're a type of hermit crab, but supersize. They are the largest land-living arthropods—a group of animals that include scorpions, spiders, insects, and crabs. They're strong enough to crack into coconuts, but they'll also eat other fruit, dead animals, and even their own discarded body parts. (As they grow, they molt their tough outer layer.) So where do they get their name? Robber crabs do, indeed, steal. They'll snatch anything that smells like food, including forks and spoons, and carry loot off to their burrows. They live on islands in the Indian and southern Pacific Oceans.

ROCKETS

BREAKING FREE OF EARTH'S GRAVITY is an amazing feat, and rockets are perfectly engineered to do it. To get off the ground, they create a massive amount of thrust—the force it takes to move away from Earth's gravity—through the gas, flames, and smoke that shoot out of their engines. That force creates a push in the opposite direction, launching the rocket into the sky. Rockets actually are more like two or more rockets stacked on top of each other. The bottom rocket, called the core stage, lifts the spacecraft off the launchpad but then drops off when it runs out of fuel or reaches a target speed or height. The upper rocket continues the journey into space.

United States

Discovery

WHAT KIND OF TECH TITAN ARE YOU?

START HERE.

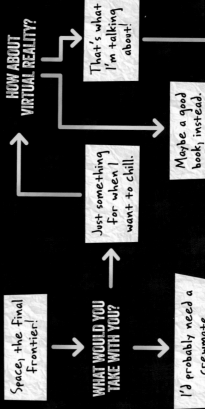

IF YOU WERE AN EXPLORER WHERE WOULD YOU GO?

Someplace that exists only in dreams.

Space, the final frontier!

I don't know, but somewhere really, really unusual.

The place doesn't matter. I'd just enjoy traveling there.

HOW ABOUT VIRTUAL REALITY?

That's what I'm talking about!

Just something for when I want to chill.

Maybe a good book, instead.

SOUNDS LIKE YOU'RE A CULTURE CONNOISSEUR!

WHAT WOULD YOU TAKE WITH YOU?

I'd probably need a crewmate.

WHAT ABOUT TAKING A REAL PLUNGE—LIKE TO THE OCEAN FLOOR?

I'm up for even more of an adventure.

In a submarine? Awesome!

WOULD YOU GO BY LAND OR SEA?

I love the ocean!

Actually, I'd fly. Planes are cool.

It'd be awesome to go on a train.

WHAT'S THE BEST THING ABOUT TRAIN TRAVEL?

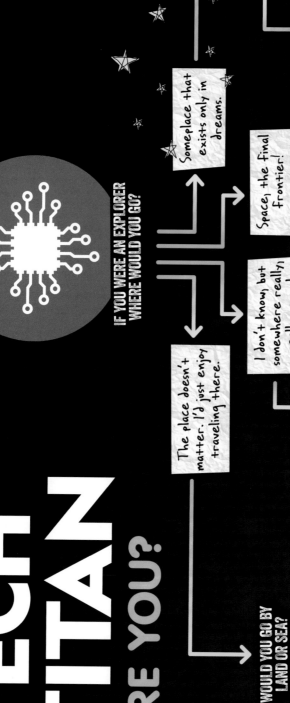

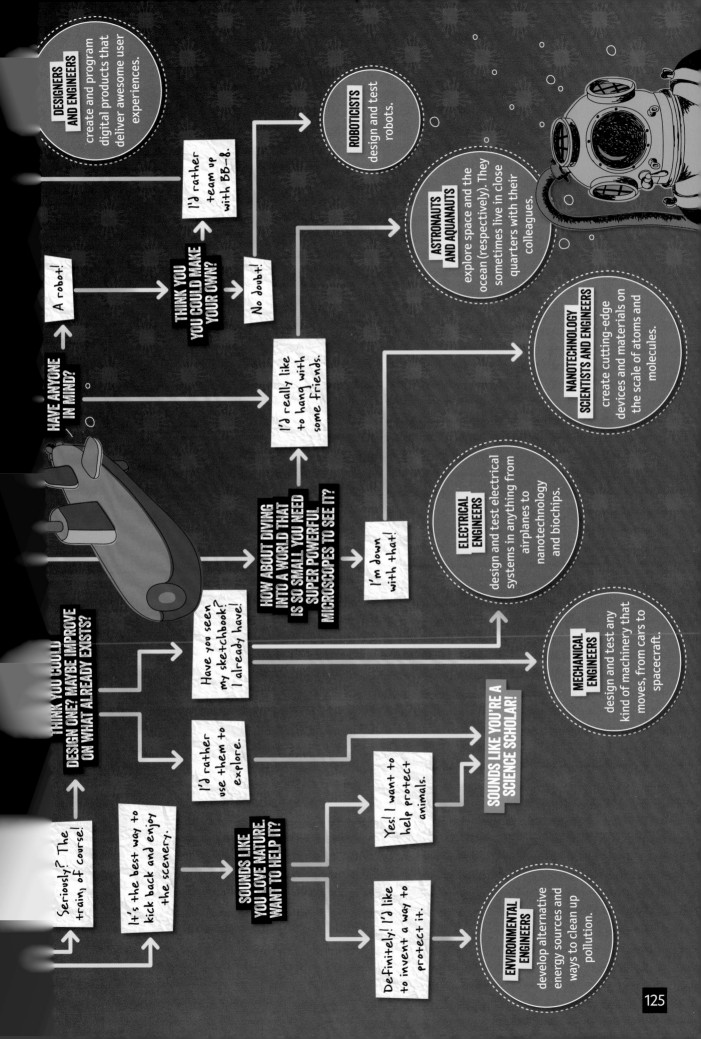

DESIGNERS AND ENGINEERS create and program digital products that deliver awesome user experiences.

ROBOTICISTS design and test robots.

ASTRONAUTS AND AQUANAUTS explore space and the ocean (respectively). They sometimes live in close quarters with their colleagues.

NANOTECHNOLOGY SCIENTISTS AND ENGINEERS create cutting-edge devices and materials on the scale of atoms and molecules.

ELECTRICAL ENGINEERS design and test electrical systems in anything from airplanes to nanotechnology and biochips.

MECHANICAL ENGINEERS design and test any kind of machinery that moves, from cars to spacecraft.

ENVIRONMENTAL ENGINEERS develop alternative energy sources and ways to clean up pollution.

I'd rather team up with BB-8.

A robot!

No doubt!

THINK YOU YOU COULD MAKE YOUR OWN?

HAVE ANYONE IN MIND?

I'd really like to hang with some friends.

HOW ABOUT DIVING INTO A WORLD THAT IS SO SMALL YOU NEED SUPER POWERFUL MICROSCOPES TO SEE IT?

I'm down with that!

THINK YOU COULD DESIGN ONE? MAYBE IMPROVE ON WHAT ALREADY EXISTS?

Have you seen my sketchbook? I already have.

I'd rather use them to explore.

Seriously? The train, of course!

It's the best way to kick back and enjoy the scenery.

SOUNDS LIKE YOU LOVE NATURE. WANT TO HELP IT?

Yes! I want to help protect animals.

SOUNDS LIKE YOU'RE A SCIENCE SCHOLAR!

Definitely! I'd like to invent a way to protect it.

·SAMHAIN·
S
·SURREALISM·

"Indiana Jones inspired a whole generation of scholars because we saw the excitement, and the passion, and the drama. What's amazing to me about archaeology is the stories are even better than what you see in a Hollywood movie."

SARAH PARCAK, archaeologist

SAMHAIN

DO YOU LIKE TRICK-OR-TREATING on Halloween? If so, thank the Irish! Halloween has its origins in Samhain (pronounced SAH-win), an ancient Celtic festival—celebrated also in Scotland and the Isle of Man—marking the beginning of winter. According to Irish legend, the spirits of the mythological otherworld crossed over to our world and killed the vegetation with their breath so that the next day, nothing would be growing. On Samhain, the boundary between the two worlds was at its thinnest, allowing spirits and fairies to easily cross into our world, where some would visit their old haunts. Some people would set out a favorite meal for the visiting spirits.

SEA ANGELS

SEA ANGELS ARE ALSO KNOWN AS sea slugs, but they're way too awesome to have that name. They look like the snow angels you make by lying down in a fresh patch of the fluffy cold stuff and flapping your arms. Except they're see-through, only two inches (5 cm) long at most, and swim in the frigid waters of the Arctic, subarctic Atlantic, and northern Pacific Oceans. When sea angels find a mate, they seem to dance together, flapping their wings and twirling through the water—pausing now and then to eat. Sea angels are also remarkable because each one is both male and female at the same time.

SECRET FLOORS

BUILDINGS WITH SECRET FLOORS aren't just in spy thrillers. The famous Empire State Building, in New York City, has 102 floors—officially. But in reality, there's a sealed-off 103rd floor with a narrow out-door walkway, intended to be a dock for airships. The luxurious Greenbrier Resort, in West Virginia, has a huge, hidden underground bunker, code-named Project Greek Island. The top-secret site was built in the 1950s to hold the entire U.S. Congress in case of an attack by the then Soviet Union. Plymouth Church of the Pilgrims, in Brooklyn, New York, has a secret door behind its organ. It leads to a hidden floor and tunnels, part of the Underground Railroad in the mid-1800s.

SEMI-INTELLIGENT SLIME

WE'RE NOT TALKING ABOUT THE GOOPY stuff you play with. There's a gooey type of simple, living organism that people call slime mold. Slime mold has no brain or central nervous system, but it can learn, remember, and even solve simple problems. It's a single-celled organism that joins with others to explore its environment and look for food. It communicates by sending pulsing wiggles through its vine-like structure. Researchers put it in a maze, where it repeatedly found the shortest route to food. They did experiments where it learned to anticipate blasts of cold air (which it doesn't like). It's like a biological computer.

SHIPWRECK CAPITAL

IN A 17-SQUARE-MILE (44-square-km) stretch off the coast of Fourni, Greece, archaeologists have found buried treasure: the wrecks of more than 50 ships dating from 525 B.C. to the early 19th century. The number of shipwrecks blows away previous dis-coveries, and the area has been dubbed the "ship-wreck capital of the world." The Fourni archipelago, a group of 13 tiny islands, was an important stop-ping point for trading ships traveling between the Black, Aegean, and Mediterranean Seas. Ships may have sought shelter from violent storms in the area, but it wasn't the safest spot. Pirates also liked hanging out there.

ACCORDING TO OUR CALCULATIONS ...

China is getting serious about cleaning up its energy act. The world's biggest carbon emissions polluter, China has an infamous smog problem. But China also has been building solar installations like crazy.

SMOG-VACUUMING TOWER

THE SMOG IN BEIJING, CHINA, can get so thick that you can't see a block away. But there may be hope. A 23-foot (7-m)-tall tower was built to suck up polluted air, clean it, and release it, so that people nearby can breathe clean air. As the tower sucks in the air, an electrical current charges dirty particles in the air, trapping them inside the tower—kind of like how you can rub a balloon on your hair and make it cling. Built to go in parks and playgrounds, the smog-vacuuming tower produces air that is 55 to 75 percent cleaner than in the rest of the city.

SNOLAB

SCIENTISTS ARE KNOWN for being deep thinkers—especially the ones working at SNOLAB near Ontario, Canada. Or, we should say, under Ontario. SNOLAB is buried in a mine about 1.2 miles (2 km) under the ground, making it the world's deepest science lab. Being deep underground, the lab is shielded from most of the radiation, a type of energy, from cosmic rays that stream from space to Earth. Its unique position lets SNOLAB scientists study the creation of stars and galaxies, the makeup of the universe, and the origins of earthquakes.

SPIDER STEALTH

SPIDERS ARE SNEAKY. You almost never see them coming until they're hanging from a little string right in front of your face. Well, researchers have figured out the secret to spider stealth. When they descend on their silk threads—their draglines—the lines barely move or spin. That's because, unlike other fibers that spring back into shape after they're stretched, dragline silk actually changes in a way that steadies the spider. It has a unique arrangement of molecules that is both rigid and soft. The rigid structure helps the dragline silk keep its shape, and the soft structures work like a cushion to absorb motion. Seriously sneaky.

SPORTS

WONDER HOW LONG PEOPLE have played sports? At least 3,000 to 4,000 years! The Olympic Games started with one event in 776 B.C.: a 200-yard (183-m) footrace. Within years, Olympians added longer races and other sports. But these sports aren't the only ones with deep roots. Gymnastic tumbling was depicted in ancient Egyptian hieroglyphs and was an art form in ancient China. Polo, a game like hockey on horseback, goes back to the sixth century B.C. in the Persian Empire (present-day Iran). In Mesoamerica and South America (present-day Mexico and farther south), a brutal ball game—kind of like rugby, Quidditch, and basketball combined—was invented sometime between 2500 to 100 B.C. Competing for "oldest game ever" honor is Ireland's national pastime, hurling— a fast-paced stick-and-ball game that combines aspects of lacrosse, baseball, and field hockey. Irish legends mention a mythical hurling match that supposedly took place in 1072 B.C.

SOLAR BIKE PATH

IN THE NETHERLANDS, a small country, space is in short supply. They can't just put large installations of solar panels out in fields. So they need to look elsewhere, such as the roofs of homes and businesses or even out at sea. In 2014, engineers came up with a really creative solution: Because the country has large numbers of biking enthusiasts, they turned a bike path into a solar installation. They embedded sturdy, non-slippery solar panels into a stretch of bike path about the length of three-quarters of a football field. Within the first year, 300,000 cyclists and scooters rode on the path—casting their shadows on it—but the amount of energy the path generated still surpassed their hopes. It was a success. The short stretch produced enough electricity to power three homes for a year.

SPYING

Spying—or to be fancy, espionage—is all about secrets. Someone has secrets, and somebody else secretly tries to get those secrets.

The "someone" is often a government that wants to collect information about other countries: their plans, what their leaders think, if they're developing any new technologies or weapons, or if any dangers are brewing. And that's if the two countries get along! If they don't, especially if they're in a conflict, the countries will try to find out each other's strengths and weaknesses, military strategies, locations of troops, and more.

It's not just countries that spy on each other. Other organizations, such as big companies, try to collect any kind of information about their competitors that can give them an advantage. They may even try to steal plans for new inventions or other technological secrets.

Information that spies gather is called intelligence, or intel. Spies try to get this info in lots of ways. Governments can snoop using satellites and huge antennas to intercept phone, email, text, and radio communications. That kind of information is called signals intelligence—or SIGINT in the trade. Supercomputers sort through the SIGINT to flag any info of value.

When intel is gathered straight from human sources, it's called HUMINT. Some of it may be collected openly, or overtly, like when spy agencies interview foreign spies or scientists who defected from, or abandoned, their country. But a lot of it is gathered covertly, when agents secretly get people to give them important information. The spies often have to spend a lot of time buddying up to those people to gain their trust. Sometimes spies convince people to hand over information, but other times they trick them into spilling secrets. Some spies also go completely undercover, pretending to be someone else to get close to a person of interest or to gain access to a place.

If it's too dangerous to meet in person, spies or their assets—people who provide information—leave messages in hiding places, called dead drops. Or they might leave coded messages on websites or in draft email messages that others can access.

Spying may be all about secrets, but it's no secret that espionage happens. Governments work hard to keep foreign spies from snooping on them. But sometimes they let foreign spies steal secrets on purpose. In that case, they feed them fake secrets—a perfect way to trick other countries or to catch the spies.

> **FUN FACT**
>
> Spies plant "bugs"— tiny listening devices consisting of a microphone and radio transmitter—in all sorts of hiding places, like decorations inside houses, light fixtures, or the heels of shoes.

MOST OF THE TIME, SPIES RELY ON THEIR SMARTS TO COLLECT INTEL. BUT SOMETIMES THEY USE TOOLS. NONE ARE MORE AMAZING THAN THE GADGETS OF THE FICTIONAL BRITISH AGENT 007, ON PAGES 72 & 73.

IMAGING ESPIONAGE
SOME OF THE BEST SPIES EVER COME FROM STORIES, BUT EVEN THEY GET CAUGHT!

- **IN THE POPULAR NOVEL *HARRIET THE SPY,*** budding writer Harriet practices her observation skills by spying on friends and neighbors and recording her detailed thoughts about them in a notebook. And she carries the notebook with her all the time. What could go wrong?

- **RECRUITED BY BRITAIN'S MI6 SPY AGENCY,** teenager Alex Rider, hero of a book series also called *Alex Rider,* goes on a series of missions, following mysterious leads, hunting down bad guys, and narrowly escaping death. James Bond himself couldn't do better.

- **A WILD RIDE OF ACTION AND AMAZING GADGETRY,** the *Mission: Impossible* movie series focuses on agent Ethan Hunt and his Impossible Missions Force (IMF) teammates, who take on the missions that no one else can handle.

- **STEPBROTHERS PHINEAS AND FERB** invent and scheme and pull off crazy stunts—but none as amazing as those of their pet platypus, Perry. Unknown to the boys, Perry goes undercover as a secret agent to fight the evil Dr. Doofenshmirtz.

NERD OF NOTE:
MARY BOWSER

DURING THE U.S. CIVIL WAR, 1861 to 1865, few people knew the South's plans like Mary Bowser.

Mary was born into slavery on a Richmond, Virginia, plantation owned by John Van Lew. Though the family freed their slaves after John died, Mary worked for them through her teen years. Mary was really smart, and with the help of the Van Lews' daughter, Elizabeth ("Bet"), she got an education in Philadelphia, Pennsylvania.

After the war started, Bet helped run a secret spy network in the capital of the Confederacy. Mary and Bet hatched a plan. Mary pretended to be a servant who worked for a member of Richmond's high society. She helped at events held by Jefferson Davis's wife, Varina. She was so good at her job that Varina hired her to work in the Davis household.

No one suspected a servant could read and write. But Mary listened to Jefferson Davis's conversations and read all the documents he left on his desk.

When she finally came under suspicion she fled the Davis home. As she left, she tried—unsuccessfully—to set it on fire.

Mary Bowser survived the war and went on to lecture about her experiences and to teach former slaves.

FAQ **HOW DO YOU TELL IF SOMEONE'S A SPY?**
If they're really good, you can't! Undercover spies assume aliases, pretending to be someone else. At a minimum, they'll use a fake name and memorize some details. But if they have a long-term mission, spy agencies will create entirely new identities for undercover spies—complete with an entire life history, called a legend. Only about 10 percent of spies are involved in secret missions, or ops (operations). It's the riskiest type of espionage, and the spies have to be excellent actors to pull it off. One slipup—like if they forget the year their made-up sibling was supposedly born—and the spy might be caught.

Spies also get caught when they send info they gathered back to their home agencies. Sometimes they get caught in the act of passing it. But they also get discovered when information only they could know gets back to the people they spy on—especially if it was fake secrets planted to catch spies.

SPRITE SATELLITES

IF "SATELLITE" MAKES you think of gigantic spacecraft, prepare to be amazed. A program to launch robots into space has sent the smallest-ever satellites into orbit. Called Sprites, the nanosatellites are the size of a postage stamp and weigh less than a nickel. But they contain all the parts that satellites need: computers, sensors, radios, and solar panels. In the future they may help us explore space. The creators hope the satellites will be able to fly at 20 percent the speed of light, reaching our nearest star system, Alpha Centauri, in a bit more than 20 years.

STONEHENGE

STONEHENGE HAS AMAZED and mystified people for ages. And they've come up with a lot of theories about how it was built and used. Was it a Druid temple? An astronomical computer for predicting eclipses? Built by space aliens? Archaeologists today think it was probably used as a temple and was aligned with the movements of the sun. What's more certain is that it was a feat of engineering genius when it was erected around 2,500 B.C. Researchers still don't know how the huge stones were brought to the site, but just lifting them into place took a lot of steps. Teams of people slid a stone into a large hole with a sloping side. Then they pulled it upright using ropes tied around the stones and probably slung over large frames. They packed the base with rubble to hold the stones in place. To put the vertical pieces on top, people built towering wooden platforms.

STRANDBEESTS

DUTCH PHYSICIST turned artist Theo Jansen doesn't think small. He creates enormous moving sculptures called strandbeests—Dutch for "beach animals"—that seem to be alive. Amazing works of artistry and engineering, the beasts are both complex and simply lifelike. They're taller than a grown-up and built mainly from lightweight PVC pipes. Powered by wind, they trot along the sand on multiple legs, with some flapping winglike sails. They're like something out of a dream.

A WALKING SCULPTURE BY ARTIST THEO JANSEN

SURFBOARD SMARTFIN

IT'S DEFINITELY THE MOST RAD way of monitoring the ocean's health. Scientists created a smart surfboard fin that records information about the ocean and lent several of the devices to surfers. With it, surfers collect information about the health of the ocean while they ride waves. The first Smartfins included temperature sensors, a GPS device, and circuit boards to relay the information back to the scientists, but eventually the scientists want to include more sensors to collect a lot more data about the ocean, including its levels of salt, acids, and oxygen.

SUPERPOWERS IN ANIMALS

MOVE OVER, Superman. You think leaping skyscrapers is impressive? Fleas can jump 200 times their own body length and 150 times their body height. They aren't the only little creatures with superpowers. Relative to their size, mantis shrimp deliver the fastest and most powerful punches in nature—easily cracking through the shell of a clam. The shocking pink dragon millipede shoots out poisonous hydrogen cyanide to protect itself, and the hairy frog—also called the horror frog—grows claws at will by breaking its own toe bones and pushing them out of its toe pads. Seriously creepy—but effective!

SURREALISM

CLOCKS DRAPED LIKE WET LAUNDRY over tree branches, colorful blobs that transform into animals, bizarre creatures that rise from the landscape. If these seem like strange dreams, then the surrealist artists who painted them—Salvador Dalí, Joan Miró, and Max Ernst—met their goals. An art movement from the 1920s to 1960s, surrealists wanted to delve into the unconscious mind, the source of imagination. The surrealists' thinking was influenced by the work of Sigmund Freud, the father of psychoanalysis. Freud believed that our unconscious mind—the part of our mind we're not consciously aware of—holds many of our feelings, desires, and thoughts, which sometimes fuel dreams.

ACCORDING TO OUR CALCULATIONS ...

This stick insect should be renamed. It's not stick size. It's more like the size of an entire tree branch. Bred by a museum in China, the record-breaking stick insect measures 25 inches (64 cm) long. Typical stick insects are only a half inch to 13 inches (1 to 33 cm) long.

THE WORLD WIDE WEB, designed by British computer scientist **TIM BERNERS-LEE,** was inspired by Arthur C. Clarke's *Dial F for Frankenstein.* The 1964 sci-fi story, which Berners-Lee read as a kid, described a system that let **computers communicate with each other.**

In *Back to the Future Part II,* Marty McFly sports a pair of **self-lacing sneakers.** Those cool kicks, designed by **NIKE,** were just a movie prop—but people petitioned for the real deal. Nike finally delivered with the self-lacing HYPERADAPT.

Mary Shelley's 1818 classic sci-fi novel *Frankenstein,* in which a mad scientist builds a man and **brings him to life with an electric current,** is believed to have sparked the development of **DEFIBRILLATORS,** the gadgets that SHOCK HEARTS BACK INTO ACTION after a heart attack.

The 1920 play *R.U.R.,* or Rossum's Universal Robots, by Czech author **KAREL ČAPEK,** introduced the word "ROBOT" to the world and inspired their creation. In *R.U.R.,* the robots are actually **live, artificial people**—not machines—but the word stuck.

Jules Verne's 1886 novel *The Clipper of the Clouds,* which envisioned **the future of flight,** captured the imagination of **IGOR SIKORSKY,** the inventor of the MODERN HELICOPTER.

As a kid, physicist **JAMES KAKALIOS** read Iron Man comics and was amazed by the superhero's ability to set off pulsar rays just by thinking. It inspired him to develop a BRAIN-COMPUTER INTERFACE that people can use to move things, including remote-controlled quadcopters and prosthetic limbs, **using only their thoughts.**

26 SUPER SCI-FI INSPIRED INVENTIONS

H. G. Wells's classic 1898 novel, *The War of the Worlds,* about a **Martian invasion,** made American scientist **ROBERT H. GODDARD** become fascinated with spaceflight. He went on to invent the FIRST LIQUID-FUELED ROCKET.

GOOGLE created a pin-on, BLUETOOTH COMMUNICATION DEVICE modeled on *Star Trek* communicators. In the sci-fi show, crew members wore communicators on their shirts and tapped them to talk to their ship's artificial intelligence. Google's worked the same way—**only connected with Google Assistant instead of a starship.**

In 1942, Robert Heinlein published a short story about **WALDO F. JONES,** a disabled inventor who created a remotely operated mechanical hand. In the 1940s, inventors created real MANIPULATOR ARMS and called them **waldos.**

Inspired by *Back to the Future Part II,* a couple of companies, **LEXUS** and **HENDO,** have invented real HOVERBOARDS that actually **float above the ground,** Marty McFly style.

DXTER, a medical scanner that measures lung and heart function and more, won a competition where participants created real medical tricorders, the HANDHELD DIAGNOSTIC TOOLS used by *Star Trek's* doctors.

American inventor **SIMON LAKE,** the "FATHER OF THE MODERN SUBMARINE," got some ideas—such as ballast tanks, periscope, and divers' compartments—from the **Nautilus,** the fictional submarine in Jules Verne's 1870 novel *Twenty Thousand Leagues Under the Sea.*

Tech company **NVIDIA** is working on PROJECT HOLODECK, **a virtual reality environment**—inspired by *Star Trek's* holodecks—that people can share. Engineers, for example, may be able to design something together, seeing a life-size model that they can change on the (virtual) spot.

Ernest Cline's 2011 science fiction novel *Ready Player One* follows a teen's quest in a **virtual utopia.** The book inspired PALMER LUCKEY to design the OCULUS RIFT virtual reality headset. In fact, the novel was given to all new employees at the Oculus company.

The **speeders** that zip LUKE SKYWALKER and REY around their planets in the *Star Wars* movies inspired several companies to create real, PERSONAL HOVERBIKES.

They're nowhere near the power of tractor beams in the *Star Wars* films and *Star Trek,* but RESEARCHERS have created real-life TRACTOR BEAMS that can **trap tiny particles in their beams** and move them around.

The novels in the Lensmen series, published in the 1930s and 1940s by E. E. "Doc" Smith, featured a command ship, the Directrix, that coordinated the Galactic Patrol fleet. It inspired a U.S. NAVAL OFFICER to introduce the concept of COMBAT INFORMATION CENTERS aboard **naval ships.**

Superhero Wolverine's rapidly healing skin inspired chemists and ENGINEERS AT STANFORD UNIVERSITY to create a **synthetic material** that can sense subtle pressure and HEAL ITSELF WHEN TORN OR CUT.

R2-D2 and C-3PO, the amazing droids from the *Star Wars* movies, inspired the founders of iROBOT, a company that CREATES A VARIETY OF ROBOTS.

ELON MUSK credits Douglas Adams's *The Hitchhiker's Guide to the Galaxy* for instilling in him a desire to **find out the big questions in life** that need to be answered. That led him to start SPACEX AND TESLA.

The **handheld communicators** in the *Star Trek* series inspired MARTIN COOPER, who led Motorola's research and development team, to create the FIRST MOBILE PHONES in the 1970s.

Sci-fi doesn't just inspire what gets made—it can inspire what things look like, too. According to designer JONY IVE, the white STORMTROOPER helmets in the *Star Wars* films **influenced the look of the Apple's signature earbuds.** (See page 45 for more sci-fi styles.)

The **universal translator** that allowed the Enterprise crew on *Star Trek* to instantly UNDERSTAND ALIENS influenced the development of GOOGLE TRANSLATE.

Tom Swift, the famous main character in a series of sci-fi and adventure books in the early 1900s, was a favorite of NASA physicist JACK COVER. Cover invented the TASER, a stun gun that **shoots out two electrodes.** In fact, "Taser" stands for "Thomas A. Swift Electric Rifle."

H. G. Wells's 1914 novel *The World Set Free,* which predicted highly destructive nuclear weapons and a world war, may have inspired physicist LEO SZILARD in two ways: to figure out how to CREATE A NUCLEAR CHAIN REACTION in 1933 and, after World War II, to campaign for arms control and the **peaceful use of nuclear power.**

In an episode of *Star Trek: The Next Generation,* the android Commander Data listens to multiple tracks of music on his computer. It gave STEVE PERLMAN, a scientist at Apple, the idea for QUICKTIME, a groundbreaking **multimedia player.**

·TALONS·

T

·TUT'S FOLDING BED·

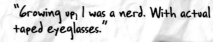

"Growing up, I was a nerd. With actual taped eyeglasses."

TAYE DIGGS, actor and singer

TALONS

HERE ARE SOME FACTS you can sink your teeth ... er, claws ... into: Birds' talons—the sharp, hooked claws at the end of their toes—vary a lot in size and shape depending on the birds' needs. All birds have them. They use them to grip branches and other things they perch on, to carry food or materials to build nests, and even to scratch itchy spots. But birds of prey have especially long, sharp, strong talons so they can pierce the skin of a potential meal and hold on tight. Like your fingernails, talons are made of a tough, protective protein called keratin, and keep growing through a bird's life.

TARDIGRADE

THE TOUGHEST CRITTER on the face of the Earth is probably the tardigrade. Also known as the "water bear," it's a tiny creature with eight legs, a scrunchy face, and a long, plump body. These awesome animals, which usually don't grow longer than 4/100 of an inch (1 mm), are almost indestructible. They can survive in outer space and in about any environment you can throw at them: extreme temperatures, radiation, you name it. How do they do it? They hibernate! They curl up into a tiny pellet, and their metabolism—all the body processes that work together to give them energy—slows to less than .01 percent of its normal rate.

TARDIS

THE TARDIS—short for Time and Relative Dimension In Space—is a fictional spacecraft that carries quirky sci-fi hero Dr. Who through time and space. And it is seriously awesome. Unlike the super streamlined spacecraft in other science fiction series, the TARDIS is shaped like an old-timey police box, a type of telephone booth for contacting the police. But that's just its outside. Inside, it's *waaay* bigger, consisting of many rooms and a couple of floors. The TARDIS is not merely machine; it's more living being. The first time the Doctor touched the TARDIS controls, he said it was the most beautiful ship he'd ever seen. Then he stole it. Ever since, he's traveled in the TARDIS to save people and planets.

TELEKINESIS

IN THE WORLD OF THE X-MEN, Jean Grey's powers include telekinesis, the ability to levitate and manipulate objects—and other beings—with her mind. But that's fiction. Are there people in real life with the power of telekinesis? We want to believe! For years, individuals have claimed to have the power, often giving astonishing demonstrations of bending spoons, starting dead watches, rolling pencils, or moving the pages of a book. And scientists have designed laboratory experiments to look for evidence that telekinesis exists. But the experiments found nothing, and the supposed psychics turned out to be fakers. We'll have to stick to fiction. At least for now.

ACCORDING TO OUR CALCULATIONS ...

You don't want to get into a hand-to-talon combat with these birds: The harpy eagle, which lives in Central and South America, grows talons as long as four inches (10 cm). If that's not extreme enough, check out the nails on the cassowary, a native of Australia. Its talons reach nearly five inches (13 cm) long.

TIME MACHINE

SCIENCE FICTION AND TIME MACHINES go together like peanut butter and jelly. But in 1895, when H. G. Wells published *The Time Machine,* it was a mind-blowing idea. Ever since, writers have devised various time machines that have let them travel into the past or future. Many of the stories focus on the effects of time travel itself—whether it changes the course of history, or what happens if you bump into a future or past version of yourself. Wells was actually more interested in what happens when people depend too much on technology and the effects of a society of "haves" and "have-nots."

TINY TOWNS

TINY HOUSES ARE A THING. But how about tiny towns? Turns out, there are several towns in the United States with total populations of fewer than 15 people—and they all have a story to tell. Some were thriving towns in the past, but residents left after a key employer closed down or an accident or natural disaster occurred. Centralia, Pennsylvania, was a coal-mining town of 3,000 until the mine caught fire in 1962, forcing most residents to leave. Ten residents kept living there, despite the underground mine fire. The town of Tortilla Flat, Arizona—population, six residents—once tried to sell itself in an online auction. The one-and-only resident of Monowi, Nebraska, serves as mayor, watches over the local library, and runs the local tavern.

TITANIC

THE LUXURY STEAMSHIP R.M.S. *TITANIC* was thought to be "unsinkable." So confident were her builders that they didn't include enough lifeboats for all the passengers. It was a tragic decision. On her first voyage, in April 1912, *Titanic* sideswiped an iceberg, which ripped six thin slits in the ship's hull, flooding compartments inside. Within hours, the luxury liner sank. It was one of the most infamous disasters at sea—one that has been retold in numerous books and movies. The ship carried about 2,200 passengers and 900 crew members but had only enough lifeboats for 1,178 people—if they were filled to capacity, which they weren't. Only 705 survived.

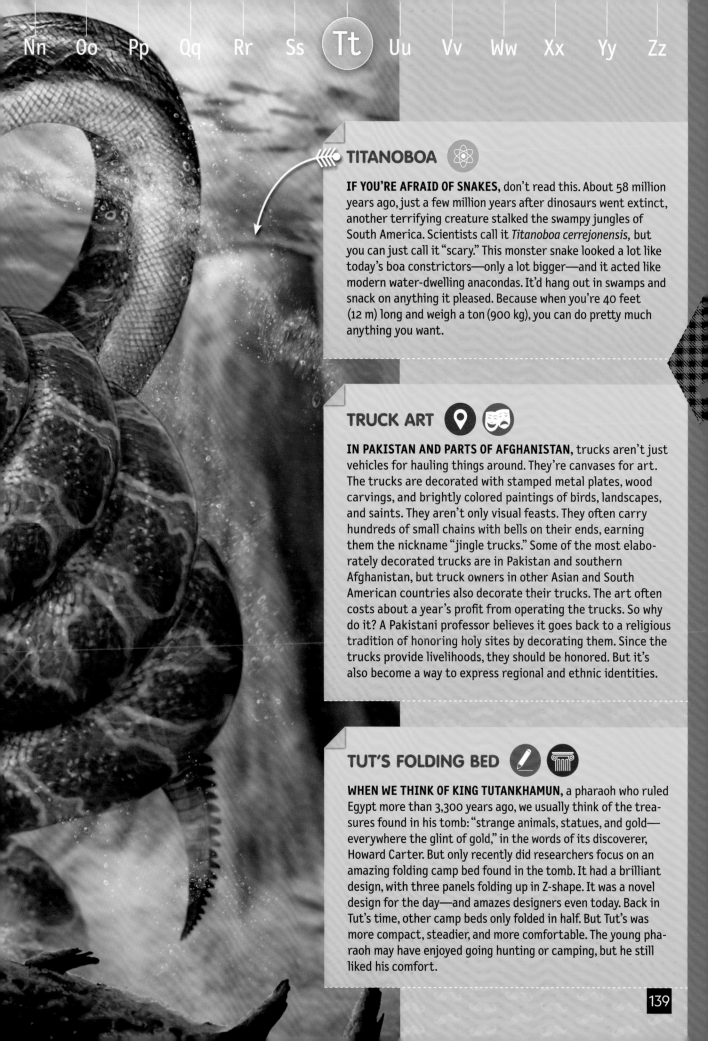

TITANOBOA

IF YOU'RE AFRAID OF SNAKES, don't read this. About 58 million years ago, just a few million years after dinosaurs went extinct, another terrifying creature stalked the swampy jungles of South America. Scientists call it *Titanoboa cerrejonensis*, but you can just call it "scary." This monster snake looked a lot like today's boa constrictors—only a lot bigger—and it acted like modern water-dwelling anacondas. It'd hang out in swamps and snack on anything it pleased. Because when you're 40 feet (12 m) long and weigh a ton (900 kg), you can do pretty much anything you want.

TRUCK ART

IN PAKISTAN AND PARTS OF AFGHANISTAN, trucks aren't just vehicles for hauling things around. They're canvases for art. The trucks are decorated with stamped metal plates, wood carvings, and brightly colored paintings of birds, landscapes, and saints. They aren't only visual feasts. They often carry hundreds of small chains with bells on their ends, earning them the nickname "jingle trucks." Some of the most elaborately decorated trucks are in Pakistan and southern Afghanistan, but truck owners in other Asian and South American countries also decorate their trucks. The art often costs about a year's profit from operating the trucks. So why do it? A Pakistani professor believes it goes back to a religious tradition of honoring holy sites by decorating them. Since the trucks provide livelihoods, they should be honored. But it's also become a way to express regional and ethnic identities.

TUT'S FOLDING BED

WHEN WE THINK OF KING TUTANKHAMUN, a pharaoh who ruled Egypt more than 3,300 years ago, we usually think of the treasures found in his tomb: "strange animals, statues, and gold—everywhere the glint of gold," in the words of its discoverer, Howard Carter. But only recently did researchers focus on an amazing folding camp bed found in the tomb. It had a brilliant design, with three panels folding up in Z-shape. It was a novel design for the day—and amazes designers even today. Back in Tut's time, other camp beds only folded in half. But Tut's was more compact, steadier, and more comfortable. The young pharaoh may have enjoyed going hunting or camping, but he still liked his comfort.

TREE HOUSES

Why hang out on the ground when you can be perched in a tree? Tree houses can be anything your imagination makes them: a secret hideout, a clubhouse where you hang with your friends, a getaway where you read comics or do art.

Kids have always known how awesome tree houses are. But, guess what? So have grown-ups.

Tree houses built for adults and families can be retreats, art studios, or even homes! Some are like cabins perched among the leaves, but others are luxury, multistory mini-homes, hotels, and restaurants built by designers who specialize in building super-awesome tree houses. So what's the appeal of tree houses? Partly, it's a way people can get closer to nature—and has been for ages.

As far back as the first century, Roman Emperor Caligula held banquets in a tree-house dining room large enough to hold 15 guests, their servants, and acrobats and jugglers for entertainment. Many centuries later, during the Renaissance, tree houses were a "must-have" feature of fancy European gardens. Even Britain's Queen Elizabeth I enjoyed dining in a tree house.

FUN FACT

In southeastern Papua, in Indonesia, the Korowai people live in tree homes built as high as 114 feet (35 m) around large banyan or wanbom trees. The height protects them from swarming mosquitoes, rival groups and, as the Korowai believe, evil spirits.

Not all tree houses were as fancy as the royal variety. Franciscan monks climbed into basic tree houses to meditate—and some Hindu monks still do. By the 19th century, poets escaped to tree houses to soak in nature and free their imaginations.

Tree houses built centuries ago still exist. They're great examples of designs that stood the test of time.

FOR OTHER TREE-MENDOUS DWELLINGS, CHECK OUT BAMBOO HOUSES ON PAGE 14.

FAQ

HOW BIG CAN TREE HOUSES GET?

It depends on your tree—and your imagination! To hold a simple tree house, one that's roughly eight feet (2.4 m) long and eight feet wide, you need a tree with a trunk diameter of 12 inches (30 cm) or more. But why stop there? People build tree houses that are supported by multiple trees (often with help from additional human-made supports), sometimes the size of a castle.

DO TREE HOUSES HURT TREES?

Unfortunately, yes. So good tree-house builders do everything possible to keep damage to a minimum. Bark is a tree's defense against harmful bacteria and viruses, so tree-friendly builders don't put many holes or cuts in the bark. They use a few large bolts for support instead of lots of little nails and screws, and they avoid rope that can rub against the tree as it grows.

A lot of builders also design tree houses to wrap around the tree's trunk to avoid adding too much weight to one side, and they leave enough room for the tree to keep growing. Good engineering makes sure that the trees stay healthy.

NERD OF NOTE:
ANDY AND SIMON PAYNE

GROWN-UPS don't have to be boring. If you need proof, consider this: Some design tree houses for a living.

Founded by brothers Andy and Simon Payne, the British design company Blue Forest builds tree-house getaways of all shapes and sizes. The wilder, the better.

It was a natural career choice for Andy and Simon. Growing up in Kenya, the brothers spent a lot of time outdoors, building basic tree houses, jungle swings, and ziplines. Those fun experiences inspired the designs they do for Blue Forest.

They've built spiral-shaped hideaways inspired by nature and huge tree houses shaped like castles, complete with ziplines to make speedy getaways. They try to turn their clients' dreams into reality, capturing both the fun of adventure and love of nature.

The interiors are as wild as the outside. In one tree house, they hid a slide behind an armoire that looked like it was straight from Narnia. They also made a bookcase spin to reveal a hidden spiral staircase.

The designers think about what they loved as kids and make it part of their designs— just taking it up another level.

It's pretty much a dream job.

IMAGINING TREE-HOUSE ADVENTURES

WHEN YOU HAVE A MAGICAL SETTING LIKE A TREE HOUSE— OR A TREE VILLAGE!—IT'S CERTAIN TO BE THE START OF AN ADVENTURE. JUST LOOK AT THESE AWESOME TREE HOUSES FROM BOOKS AND MOVIES.

- **IN THE MAGIC TREE HOUSE BOOKS,** siblings Annie and Jack discover a mysterious tree house full of books and are soon whisked away on a series of adventures in different places and times.

- **THE EWOKS,** the fluffy teddy bear-looking inhabitants of Endor in the *Star Wars* movies, live in Bright Tree Village in the canopy of a forest. Wooden bridges connect huts that are built around individual trees. As C-3PO says, "A village in the treetops! Isn't this splendid?"

UNCONSCIOUS MIND · U · UPSIDE-DOWN LIGHTNING

"I doubt that the imagination can be suppressed. If you truly eradicated it in a child, he would grow up to be an eggplant."

URSULA K. LE GUIN, author

UNCONSCIOUS MIND

IF YOU'VE EVER HAD A "gut feeling" about something, thank your unconscious mind. It's your source of intuition and dreams and other things you're not even aware of. In fact, that's what it's all about: things you're not aware of. Your unconscious mind holds memories, beliefs, and thoughts, but not ones that you can mull over or wonder about. It's like they're hidden from you—at least until they show up in dreams or as gut feelings. Your unconscious mind is hard at work processing information all the time. It may even register something new long before you're aware of it—if ever.

UNDERGROUND RAILROAD

THE UNDERGROUND RAILROAD wasn't trains running through buried tunnels. It was a network of people, mainly African American but also white, who worked in secret to help escaped slaves from the South to safety farther north. From the late 1700s to the Civil War (1861 to 1865), the Underground Railroad provided shelter and assistance, including "conductors" who guided people to safe hiding places in private homes, schoolhouses, and churches. The railroad theme was picked up in the names used in the network. The hiding places were called stations, safe houses, and depots, and the people operating them were called the station masters.

HARRIET TUBMAN, A CONDUCTOR OF THE UNDERGROUND RAILROAD, LEADS A GROUP TO FREEDOM.

UNDERWATER ART MUSEUM

OFF THE COAST OF SPAIN'S CANARY ISLANDS, dozens of sculptures are exhibited in an unusual setting: an underwater art museum. The brain-child of artist Jason deCaires Taylor, the Museo Atlántico includes thought-provoking sculptures: kids rowing boats on the floor of the ocean, people walking toward a long wall, businessmen in fancy suits playing on children's swing sets, human-animal hybrids, and many others. The artwork is intended to make people think about the state of our oceans. But more than that, it is creating an artificial reef to provide shelter for fish and other sea life.

UNMELTABLE ICE CREAM

FINALLY! Ice cream that doesn't melt. Lucky for us, Japanese researchers developed a type of ice cream that, unlike the regular treat, won't drip in the heat while you eat it (a good five minutes or more). It uses special micronutrients, called polyphenols, found in strawberries and other natural plant foods. Polyphenol liquid makes it harder for the water and fat molecules inside ice cream to separate, which normally happens during melting.

UPSIDE-DOWN LIGHTNING

HERE'S HOW LIGHTNING USUALLY WORKS: A big electrical charge—drawn from an incoming storm—builds up near the bottom of a storm cloud. If enough energy builds up, zap! A lightning bolt shoots toward Earth. But on rare occasions, it breaks out of the top of the cloud, sending a big bolt of lightning up to the edge of space. Upside-down lightning! (It's really called a gigantic jet, but that's not as fun.) The crazy lightning show is more likely in the tropics, where storms are taller and have more violent winds.

UFOs

No, we're not talking about little green people from outer space ... or are we?

Truth is, it's a big leap from unidentified flying objects to spaceships piloted by aliens. UFO just means someone spotted something flying and couldn't figure out what it was.

When most people talk about UFOs, they wonder if extraterrestrials have buzzed over Earth—maybe even stopped by. According to a recent poll, more than half of Americans believe UFOs exist, though less than half think space aliens have actually visited. But the thing is, if they had, would our governments even tell us? Or would they keep it a secret so we don't freak out? Those questions keep some people up at night. Let's sort it out so you don't lose any sleep.

If you were hoping for a visit from ET, we've got some bad news. Most UFO sightings have been "debunked"—proved to be some normal earthly thing. Those mysterious lights and weird-looking aircraft that move in bizarre ways? Just flares, rockets, weather balloons, and strange weather phenomena. Sometimes they're even hoaxes.

But, notice: We said most UFO sightings have been debunked—not all.

There have been enough mysterious sightings that the government has studied UFOs.

It found several reports of aircraft that zoom through the sky at high speeds but don't have any sign of propulsion, like jet engines. An Air Force pilot who in 2004 saw a bizarre flying craft that flew incredibly fast, rotating while it moved, was convinced it wasn't from Earth.

So does that mean UFOs definitely exist and are probably aliens? Not necessarily. Even with all our scientific know-how, sometimes we just don't have explanations for unusual phenomena—yet.

IMAGINING EXTRATERRESTRIAL VISITS
IN SCIENCE FICTION, YOU DON'T EVEN ASK IF UFOS ARE REAL. OF COURSE THEY ARE! THE REAL QUESTIONS ARE: WHAT KIND OF COOL SPACESHIPS ARE THE ETS FLYING, AND DID THEY COME BY FOR A FRIENDLY VISIT OR ... GULP.

- **IN THE 1956 CULT CLASSIC MOVIE *EARTH VS. THE FLYING SAUCERS*,** aliens in high-tech flying saucers contact a scientist working on a satellite program. Their message? We're coming to take over, so surrender peacefully. Yeah, not going to happen.

- **AFTER ENCOUNTERS WITH UFOS,** people are mysteriously drawn to the strangely shaped landform called Devils Tower in Wyoming, U.S.A., where alien visitors make their first scheduled contact with Earthlings. Luckily, the aliens in the 1977 blockbuster movie *Close Encounters of the Third Kind* are friendly.

EXTRATERRESTRIALS DON'T HAVE TO VISIT EARTH FOR US TO COMMUNICATE WITH THEM.
READ ABOUT THE GREETINGS WE SENT INTO SPACE ON THE VOYAGER PLATES ON PAGE 151.

FAQ HAVE ALIENS REALLY TAKEN PEOPLE FROM EARTH INTO THEIR SPACESHIPS?

OK, here's what we know: Several people have reported contact with intelligent nonhuman beings. They call themselves "experiencers," people who have experienced alien abductions. They have time periods they can't recall, strange dreams, flashbacks about things they can't understand. Some even describe alien beings and UFOs. Many recalled their experiences after being hypnotized.

The thing is, alien abduction isn't the only thing that can create such experiences. Some medical conditions also create disturbing sensory feelings and can even make people lose consciousness for a period of time. Plus, hypnosis turns out to be an unreliable way to recall memories. It's just too hard to tell the difference between memories of actual events and imagined events.

Put it all together, and most of the reported alien abductions can be explained by other phenomena. But not all of them. The experiencers clearly went through something very powerful and unusual—but not necessarily alien abduction.

DOES THE U.S. GOVERNMENT REALLY HAVE AN ALIEN'S SPACESHIP AND BODY AT AREA 51?

Area 51, a top-secret U.S. Air Force base, is way out in the middle of a desert in Nevada. Perfect place to be hiding alien spacecraft, right? People say the U.S. government got its hands on not just an alien spacecraft, but its alien pilots, too—possibly those from a crash landing in Roswell, New Mexico. They took them to Area 51, where they've been studying them ever since. Don't believe it? Well, ever since the 1950s, airline pilots have seen UFOs in the area. Convinced now?

Don't be. It's true that there's lots of supersecret stuff at Area 51. But that stuff isn't aliens and alien spacecraft. In the mid-1950s, the Air Force pilots at Area 51 tested U-2 spy planes, which flew much higher than some believed possible—accounting for the UFO sightings. Since then, the Air Force has developed and tested other top-secret military planes, including stealth aircraft and probably even secretly obtained Soviet fighter jets, as well as advanced weapons at Area 51. Of course, the last thing Air Force officials want to do is blab all about those. So, secrets. Lots of them. But alien spacecraft? Probably not.

FUN FACT

Aliens attract a lot of interest—and the people of Nevada know it. The state renamed a highway "Extraterrestrial Highway," and along that route, you'll find the Alien Research Center with a giant alien statue.

NERD OF NOTE:
LUIS ELIZONDO

LUIS ELIZONDO IS, by nature, skeptical. But he believes we need to take UFOs seriously.

For years, Luis led the U.S. Defense Department's secret program that investigated UFOs.

"We have identified some very, very interesting, anomalous type of aircraft," Luis says. The aircraft weren't like any aircraft that we know. They didn't have any obvious forms of propulsion, were difficult to see, and moved at high speeds and in weird ways.

Luis and his team tried to figure out what the aircraft were, how they worked, and whether they were a threat to us. They didn't try to answer the question on everyone's minds: Were they alien?

"I don't know where it's from. But we're pretty sure it's not here," Luis says. "Now does that mean it's 'out there'? Whether or not it's Russian or Chinese inside or little green men from Mars or frankly your neighbor's dog, I wanted to purposely steer away from [that question]."

He's not the kind of guy to jump to conclusions, and he doesn't think others should either. But after all he's seen, he's not going to dismiss reports of UFOs. "My personal belief is that there is very compelling evidence that we may not be alone," he says. "Whatever that means."

VALLEY OF THE WHALES

WHALES IN A DESERT. It's not the most common sight—unless you're in the Wadi Al-Hitan region of Egypt's Western Desert, about 100 miles (160 km) southwest of Cairo. There, a graveyard of hundreds of whale skeletons lies among the rocks and sand. If the setting isn't weird enough, the whales definitely are. They had hind legs. The long-extinct ancient whales, known as archaeoceti, lived 40 million years ago, when the area was underwater. They give us a look at a time in evolution when whales were making the move from land to sea.

VAMPIRES

VAMPIRES, FANGED CREATURES, rise from their graves to suck the blood from innocent victims. Lucky for us, they don't exist. Unfortunately, for centuries people didn't know that. When their family and friends got sick, they suspected vampires. Part of the reason is that dead bodies go through changes that make them look like vampires. Their skin shrinks, making teeth and fingernails look like they've grown (fangs and claws!). And when insides decompose, a dark fluid can leak out of the mouth and nose (blood!). To prevent "vampires" from rising from their graves people sometimes stuffed dead bodies with soil, stones, bricks, or a coin (for good luck).

VENOMOUS PLANTS

POISONOUS PLANTS—like poison ivy—are bad enough. Their oils get on your skin and make you break out. But at least they don't prick you! Like some snakes that inject venom through their fangs, venomous plants, like nettles, have hollow "hairs" that can get into your skin. That's how they deliver toxins. Most just create itchy red welts. But the tree nettle, found in New Zealand, has toxins that can sting for days. Worse yet, the gympie gympie, found in Australia, creates a burning pain that can last months.

VIDEO GAMES

WITH STUNNING GRAPHICS, complex worlds , and virtual reality technology, today's video games are seriously awesome. But they had humble beginnings. When the 1961 video game *Spacewar!* was invented it was impossible to copyright computer programs, so anyone could use programming that went into it. And they soon did. The game was expanded into *Galaxy Game,* one of the first coin-operated video games. *Spacewar!* also inspired Nolan Bushnell, the founder of Atari. In 1972, Atari released *Pong,* a simple table-tennis game for arcades. It became a huge hit, and many other arcade and home games followed. In 1977, Atari stepped up gaming with a home game console that let people play a variety of games. By the early 1980s, video games were part of popular culture, with hits like *Pac-Man* and *Donkey Kong.*

VILLAINS

VILLAINS, those story characters who torment our heroes with their sinister plans, creep us out and send chills down our spines. But we wouldn't want it any other way. Thing is, we love to hate villains. The Joker, the Wicked Witch of the West, Darth Vader, Lord Voldemort, and Simba's uncle Scar are some of the most memorable characters in stories. But they're more than that. They help propel the story forward.

ACCORDING TO OUR CALCULATIONS ...

In 1993, Russian cosmonaut Aleksandr A. Serebrov brought along a Nintendo Game Boy with a *Tetris* game cartridge for his 197-day stay on the Mir space station. It was the first video game played in space (at least by humans). Later, back on Earth, Serebrov's Game Boy sold for $1,220.

VIKINGS

FUN FACT

Viking raids were so feared that coastal cities in other lands began building stone walls facing the sea and walling in their harbors.

Please, note: This is not the way to make friends. The first time Vikings headed out from Scandinavia, in 793, they went to Lindisfarne, a pretty little island off the northeast coast of England. It was a center of learning, with an awesome library and book-loving monks who took care of the abbey. The Vikings promptly stole the church's treasures, destroyed the library, and either tossed the monks into the sea, killed them, or enslaved them.

That single raid pretty much cemented the Vikings' reputations as savage warriors with little respect for learning and even less for the Christian religion. But it's a bit of a one-sided picture. Vikings definitely were fearless warriors, but they also were traders, explorers—and peaceful farmers back in Norway, Denmark, and Sweden.

But it was their seafaring and raids that made Vikings famous—or infamous. From their earliest raids in the eighth century and through the early 11th century, Vikings set sail from their homelands to raid monasteries, villages, and cities in other lands. Ireland, England, and Scotland were early and frequent targets, but not the only ones.

By the end of the Viking age, the Vikings not only ruled the seas of northern Europe, but they had spread their influence as far as North America and Russia. They also didn't limit their attacks to coastal villages. After establishing bases along the coasts, they'd travel inland, attacking great cities of Europe, such as Paris and Seville.

Why'd they do it? They went on raids to get riches and goods to survive the harsh northern winters back home. Many Vikings were farmers back in Scandinavia, but good farming land was scarce. Other Vikings took to the seas to trade, especially in lands east of Scandinavia. As they pushed farther overseas, many Vikings established settlements in new lands. The culture of these mighty sea-going people shaped much of the world for centuries.

VIKINGS MAY HAVE TAKEN RAIDING TO A NEW LEVEL, BUT THEY WEREN'T THE ONLY SEAFARING MARAUDERS. CHECK OUT THE PIRATES ON PAGE 112.

FAQ

DID VIKINGS REALLY WEAR HELMETS WITH HORNS STICKING OUT THE SIDES?

You can't be a Viking warrior without horns sticking out of your helmet, right? At least, that's what stories lead us to believe. It's true that some Vikings wore cool helmets as they traveled around raiding and pillaging in Europe, North America, and West Asia. But helmets with horns? Nope. And, for that matter, the helmets didn't have antlers or wings either. Vikings either wore iron or leather helmets or went bareheaded.

So why do we associate Vikings with horned helmets? In the 1800s, both a Swedish artist and a costume designer for an opera decided to put Viking characters in horned helmets. Because, you know, even if the helmets weren't historically accurate, they were still seriously awesome. So awesome that the idea stuck.

DID WOMEN WARRIORS FIGHT WITH THE VIKINGS?

It's one of the great mysteries of history: Were fierce Viking women warriors real, or did they exist only in mythology and folklore? Historical accounts of the Viking age tell of communities of women warriors, called shield maidens, who battled beside Viking men.

But many of those accounts were written after the Viking age, and some of them were exaggerated to make the stories livelier. Researchers needed to find evidence directly from the Viking age. And they did: figurines and images of armed women warriors in artwork from the early Viking years. But researchers still weren't satisfied. What if those were depictions of Valkyries, mythical female warriors that the war god Odin sent into battle?

VALKYRIES

The researchers needed to find an actual flesh-and-blood woman warrior ... or, at least, her skeleton. They searched burial sites and found Viking women buried with weapons, but not buried in the typical way Vikings treated their warriors. Then, archaeologists unearthed the most amazing, classic warrior grave. It was absolutely packed with weapons—sword, ax, spear, arrows, knife, two shields, even a pair of warhorses—and clearly a high-ranking warrior. The skeleton hinted that it might be a woman, and recent DNA tests confirmed it. It was a woman warrior—maybe a real shield maiden!

NERD OF NOTE:
RAGNAR LOTHBROK

A HERO FROM THE EARLY DAYS of the Viking age, Ragnar Lothbrok's exploits were so amazing that he became almost mythical, celebrated in epics and poetry. Ragnar was the son of the king of Sweden and Denmark, but he liked to claim he was a direct descendant of the Norse god Odin.

With his fearless reputation and godly connections, you'd expect him to have a noble Viking nickname. But Ragnar's was "Shaggy Breeches," referring to the animal-skin pants he wore. Not like anyone dared tease him about it.

Ragnar led so many successful raids that he was viewed as a "Sea King"—rich, powerful, and famous. His most infamous raid was on Paris in 845. He led a fleet of 120 long-ships and thousands of Viking warriors up the Seine River to attack the city, but news of his approach arrived before he did. You'd think that would give the Parisians time to prepare a defense. But, no. Ragnar was so feared that the residents of Paris fled, making the city super easy to plunder.

There are different accounts of how Ragnar died. As far as historians can tell, he met his death in a dramatic way: The Anglo-Saxon king of Northumbria finally caught the raider and threw him into a snake pit.

VIRTUAL REALITY

VIRTUAL REALITY—OR VR—is a computer-generated, 3D environment that you can interact with in a way that feels totally real—as long as you strap on one of the weird-looking, bulky headsets. A lot of people think VR takes gaming to the next level. But it can be used for a lot of things. Medical and dental students use VR to practice surgeries and procedures. Home designers may use VR to try out different options before actually building them. Someday, you may strap on a VR headset to visit a live volcano, go back in time to look around a medieval village, or follow sharks in the ocean.

VIRUSES

VIRUSES are tiny invaders. They get inside your body and create havoc. The viruses that give us colds, the flu, or other illnesses are living organisms. When they're inside us they can grow and spread to other people. Outside of hosts, they live only a little while. Computer viruses are not living organisms, like cold viruses, but they act a lot alike. They're tiny programs that can get inside a computer and copy themselves, often creating problems, such as destroying data stored on the computer or making it work badly. If only computers could wash their hands ...

VOLCANOES

YOU MAY PICTURE A CONE-SHAPED mountain with steam spewing out its top. But volcanoes actually come in different shapes and sizes, and they don't all erupt the same way. What all volcanoes have in common is that they're created when magma—the flowing, hot, molten rock under Earth's crust—pushes up through vents and fissures in Earth's surface. Some volcanoes have thin, runny magma that spills out and runs down their sides as lava flows. Others have thick, sticky magma that holds gases inside until the pressure builds up too much. Then they violently explode, sending rocks, ash, gas, and steam high into the air.

VOMIT COMET

SPOILER ALERT: That's not its real name. We're actually talking about the reduced-gravity program that gives future astronauts a chance to train for life in space. They ride a plane on a two- to three-hour wild flight, climbing and diving 30 to 40 times, to experience weightlessness over and over for about half a minute each time. Astronauts aren't the only ones who take the rollicking ride. Aerospace engineers try out new gear in the plane, and even students and celebrities have flown in it. The downside to all the sudden dips? You can probably figure that out from the plane's nickname.

VOODOO

YES, RITUALS WITH VOODOO DOLLS are part of the voodoo (or vodou) religion's practices. But Voodoo followers don't stick pins in them to hurt their enemies. They use them to ask spirits to help heal or guide them. Voodoo, a religion first practiced by Africans forced into slavery in the Caribbean and Americas, blends beliefs and traditions from Roman Catholicism and native African religions. It's found mainly in Haiti, some other Caribbean countries, and New Orleans, Louisiana, in the U.S.A., but the rituals and practices vary a lot from temple to temple.

VOYAGER PLATES

IN 1977, when NASA launched the Voyager 1 and 2 spacecrafts to explore the far reaches of our solar system and beyond, they included a message to introduce Earth to any extraterrestrials who might happen to come upon them. The message was included in gold-plated discs and included greetings recorded in 55 languages and music that spanned many eras, genres, and cultures. The recordings also included nature sounds, such as tweeting birds, crashing waves, and crackling thunder. They also included a key to decoding the message: a diagram of hydrogen, the most common element in the universe.

151

WATER HARVESTING
W
WOUND-HEALING NANOCHIP

"Even when [comedy] was hard ... it didn't make me quit ... It felt like what I was supposed to be doing."

WANDA SYKES, actor, comedian, and writer

WATER HARVESTING

IN THE FIRST EVER *Star Wars* movie, Luke Skywalker's family lived on a dry, dusty planet, Tatooine, where they farmed moisture from the atmosphere using gadgets called vaporators. Researchers are trying to make that possible on Earth. To get an idea of how that'd work, think about when you're holding a cold drink outside where it's hot. You know how water droplets form on the outside of your glass or can? When warm air cools down, the water vapor in the air condenses, forming the liquid droplets. Engineers are creating different devices to cool the air and extract the water from it. They can already pull the moisture from fog. Now they're working on devices that could do it in hotter, drier areas. Luke would be proud.

WAX FIGURES

IN 18TH-CENTURY EUROPE, many wax figures started out as death masks of people who had recently died. That might creep out a lot of people, but not Marie Tussaud. She learned the trade at the time of the French Revolution when much of the French ruling class was executed by guillotine. Sometimes she'd have to make a death mask from a head that had just been chopped off. But Marie realized that people were intrigued by gruesome murders—and by the lives of the rich and famous. She put together a traveling show of her wax figures and eventually opened a gallery in London. The public loved it, and Madame Tussaud became as famous as the people she carved in wax.

A WAX FIGURE OF MADAME TUSSAUD

WAX WORMS

WAX WORMS CAN INFEST BEEHIVES, eating bees' food and harming young bees. No surprise, then, that a Spanish beekeeper, Federica Bertocchini, plucked the unwanted invaders out of her beehives and threw them in an old plastic bag. But an hour later, the wax worms had eaten holes in the bag. Good thing Bertocchini is also a biologist. She teamed up with other scientists and studied how the worms can eat plastic—and whether they can help us tackle our huge plastic pollution problem. Every year, we produce 300 million tons of plastic. And it's really hard to break down. The wax worms wouldn't be a total solution, but maybe they can help.

WEIRD WORDS

ONLY A TUNKLEHEAD WOULD THINK OF taking a sno-go out in bluebird weather. It's just dingy, inso? You got that, right? It's English, after all—words and phrases spoken in the United States. But here's the thing: You wouldn't hear anyone say those two sentences. They're strung together from regional dialects all over the United States. Even when a language is spoken throughout an entire country, different regions put their own spin on it. They have their own vocabulary, grammar, and pronunciation that people in other regions might not understand. So here's how to decipher those first two sentences: in Maine, a "tunklehead" is a fool; a "sno-go" is what some Alaskans call a snowmobile; "bluebird weather" means a brief period of warm weather in autumn to a Marylander; "dingy" may be how a Californian refers to something foolish or crazy; and "inso" is a quick way of saying "isn't that so?" in Wisconsin.

WOUND-HEALING NANOCHIP

THIS NEW MEDICAL DEVICE seems straight out of *Star Trek*. It's a tiny chip, smaller than a dime, that can repair injuries. You place it on your skin and zap it with a small electrical current (not enough to hurt). In just a second or so, the chip reprograms skin cells to become any type of cell your body needs. Researchers tried it on a mouse that had a badly injured leg. Within a week, the device helped regrow blood vessels in the mouse's leg. Two weeks later, the leg was healed. The researchers hope someday the device will help people recover from injuries and other medical conditions.

153

Dozens of **waterfalls** tumble through a series of 16 interconnected, cascading lakes in central Croatia. THE PLITVICE LAKES are distinct colors—GREENS, GRAYS, OR BLUES—and were carved by water flowing through limestone and chalk.

A BAY IN PUERTO RICO TWINKLES WITH BLUE-WHITE LIGHTS as you paddle or swim through it at night. The light show is courtesy of **hundreds of thousands of phosphorescent single-celled organisms** that light up when disturbed.

A bridge in Seoul, South Korea, **squirts water out both sides.** The MOONLIGHT RAINBOW FOUNTAIN even GLOWS DIFFERENT COLORS, thanks to LEDs.

26 WATERY WONDERS

Nicknamed the "LIQUID RAINBOW," the Caño Cristales River in Colombia bursts with VIBRANT REDS, BLUES, YELLOWS, ORANGES, and GREENS late in the year. The colorful display is thanks to **algae, mosses,** and a **plant** that grows only in that river's environment.

GLISTENING POOLS OF TURQUOISE water step down a hillside at the Pamukkale travertine terraces in Turkey. Also called the "COTTON CASTLE," the white terraces were **created by hot springs** that deposited minerals as they flowed by.

An EIGHT-STORY-TALL WATER FEATURE resembling a large waterfall plunges straight down all levels of the DUBAI MALL in the United Arab Emirates. **Dozens of divers plunge with it**—but they're just statues.

The "CROWN FOUNTAIN," created by artist Jaume Plensa for Millennium Park in Chicago, Illinois, U.S.A., is PART FOUNTAIN, PART VIDEO SCULPTURE. Water cascades from the mouths of people portrayed on **two glass-brick towers** and falls into a black granite reflecting pool.

In Greek mythology, sirens were magical women who lured unwary sailors off course. According to legend, Zeus struck the siren with a thunderbolt, turning her into a whirlpool. **Inspired by the tale,** water sculptor William Pye created "CHARYBDIS" as a WHIRLING WATER SCULPTURE in northern England.

WHITE MOUNDS SEEM TO FLOAT in a watery sky at the world's largest salt flat, SALAR DE UYUNI in Bolivia. The unusual water feature happens during the wet season, when the salt flat gets flooded by nearby lakes and, **like a mirror, reflects the sky.**

The largest hot spring in Yellowstone National Park, U.S.A., the **GRAND PRISMATIC SPRING** is ringed with BANDS OF COLORS ranging from red to green, caused by **pigmented bacteria.**

Huge rings, called **PHUMDIS,** dot LOKTAK LAKE in India. The phumdis are made of intertwined plants, soil, and other organic matter. **The largest ring covers as much as 15 square miles** (39 sq km)—almost two-thirds the size of Manhattan, in New York City.

THE CENOTE IK KIL, an ANCIENT SINKHOLE in Mexico, was **used by the ancient Maya** for religious rituals. From an opening on top, vines reach all the way down to the dark waters below.

LAKE RETBA (or Lac Rose) in Senegal ranges from a PALE ROSE color during the rainy season (July through October) to a BRIGHT BUBBLE GUM color during the dry season (November to June)— thanks to a **high salt content, salt-loving microbes, and algae.**

FLOWERS AND PATTERNS flow down a wall of water in Osaka Station City in Japan. A computer-controlled **"PRINTER"** ejects water droplets and streams in different sizes and patterns.

THE "GIANT" is a large MOSS-COVERED FACE WITH SPARKLING EYES at **Swarovski Crystal Worlds.** A waterfall pours from the Giant's mouth into a pool below, and visitors must step through the Giant's head to enter a "magical world" made of crystal.

Sitting in shallow water at the **Playa de la Malvarrosa** in Valencia, Spain, a small **SAILBOAT** shimmers in the sun. It's actually a fountain: THE SAIL AND BOAT ARE MADE OF WATER! Good luck trying to set sail in it.

The most famous fountain in Brussels, Belgium, is the **MANNEKEN-PIS.** It's a **statue of a little boy,** who's … uh … GOING NUMBER 1. Put up in 1619, it replaced a fountain that dated back to 1388. That one was of a little boy who also had to go too bad to hold it.

You've seen the CARTOONS where a car knocks over a fire hydrant and gets lifted up on a burst of water? In Italy, the **"CAR FOUNTAIN,"** created by **artist Juan Galdeano,** looks just like that. A support hidden by the water actually holds the car up.

CHAMPAGNE POOL, in New Zealand, CONSTANTLY BUBBLES, thanks to **carbon dioxide gas** rising from the hot spring. A vibrant orange color, caused by minerals, rings the pool, adding to its celebratory style.

A HUMONGOUS WATER FAUCET seems to **float in the air** at Aqualand in Cadiz, Spain. The **"MAGIC TAP"** continually pours into a pool below it.

WILD MUSTANGS seem to gallop through a fountain, kicking up water at their heels, in **LAS COLINAS** in Irving, Texas, U.S.A. The bronze statues, among the largest equestrian sculptures in the world, **commemorate the wild legacy of Texas.**

When its **water evaporates** during the summer, **SPOTTED LAKE,** in British Columbia, Canada, becomes a MOSAIC OF NEARLY 400 YELLOW, GREEN, WHITE, AND PALE BLUE POOLS. The colors come from salts and other minerals.

VICTORIA FALLS, in Zimbabwe, is the LARGEST SINGULAR WATERFALL IN THE WORLD. Stretching more than a mile across (1.6 km) and plunging 354 feet (108 m), spray from the falls rises up 1,600 feet (500 m).

ABRAHAM LAKE in Alberta, Canada, looks like A PIECE OF MODERN ART with big drops of white paint on a blue surface. The natural art display happens only during winter, when **bubbles freeze just under the water's surface.**

Most fountains shoot water upward, but in Osaka, Japan, the **"NINE FLOATING FOUNTAINS"**—LARGE CUBES THAT SEEM TO HOVER IN THE AIR—**spray downward.**

A HUMONGOUS MIRRORED HUMAN HEAD towers above a fountain in Charlotte, North Carolina, U.S.A. Created by Czech sculptor David Černý and called **"METALMORPHOSIS,"** it's made of 35 layers that rotate to rearrange its face. **And, yes, it spits water out.**

WEAPONS
From Ages Past

So, this definitely isn't anything to brag about, but humans can get pretty creative when it comes to vanquishing their enemies. Among their inventions: huge catapults that hurled stones at castle walls, contraptions that squirted flaming liquid at enemy ships, sharp stones lashed to wooden handles. The unfortunate truth is, weapons helped shape history. Superior weapons helped win wars—even when armies or navies were outnumbered—and they helped those forces defend or expand empires.

The earliest were weapons designed for close combat. Picture the movies with vast fighting forces rushing toward each other and battling one-on-one. Even unskilled foot soldiers could swing axes or clubs. By 14,000 B.C., trained warriors used swords. And, of course, fists came in handy, too—especially after 600 B.C., if soldiers wore battle gloves, called cestuses. Some even had metal or spikes embedded in them. Ouch.

Of course, even the winners of hand-to-hand battles could end up in really bad shape. How to deal with that problem? Ranged weapons—those that could be used from a distance! The earliest ranged weapons were spears. Developed 300,000 to 400,000 years ago, they were cheap, easy to make, and effective. They were a favorite of armies throughout the ages, especially when paired with shields for protection. Bows became common much later, around 40,000 B.C., but in skilled hands they were much more accurate. Thousands of years later, arrows were put to a more frightening use. The Chinese developed "fire arrows"— basically, the first rockets—that they launched at their enemies. Even if the fire arrows didn't hit their mark, they probably scared the enemy to death.

As weapons developed, so did protection from them.

FUN FACT
A massive 14th-century trebuchet nicknamed "War Wolf," possibly the largest and most powerful ever built, hurled missiles as heavy as 300 pounds (136 kg)— almost as much as an upright piano. The English used it to smash through the outer defenses of Stirling Castle in Scotland.

In the era of castles and other fortresses— with archers shooting through skinny windows way up high—armies needed some serious power to go up against those odds. They got that power in the form of siege weapons or siege engines. First developed as far back as the third and fourth centuries B.C., siege engines reached the height of engineering genius in the Middle Ages. Some were battering rams—heavy logs either carried by several warriors or suspended from wheeled frames—that pounded castle gates, doors, and walls. But others were massive trebuchets, huge catapults that flung stones or other objects at the castle walls. Many siege engines were so huge that they had to be transported in pieces and built on the spot. But they ended up being a smashing success.

TO LEARN ABOUT ANOTHER WEAPON THAT CHANGED HISTORY, READ UP ON ARCHERY ON PAGE 10.

FAQ DID ANCIENT WARRIORS REALLY USE FLAMETHROWERS?

Unfortunately, yes. In 678, the Byzantine Empire, whose capital was Constantinople (present-day Istanbul, Turkey), unleashed a weapon so destructive that nothing could withstand it. Known as "Greek fire" (also "sea fire" or "Roman fire"), Byzantines used it to defend their empire for more than seven centuries.

Greek fire was a flammable liquid—its exact recipe was a secret—that was shot under pressure through long bronze tubes with swiveling nozzles at their ends. Its first use was against an invading navy that besieged Constantinople for four years and seemed intent on capturing the capital. But armed with Greek fire, a small Byzantine fleet sailed out to meet the enemy ships. The Byzantine ships shot out the Greek fire, and everything it hit was instantly set ablaze. Water couldn't put it out. In fact, Byzantines even pumped it onto the water surrounding enemy ships so their sailors couldn't swim to safety. Harsh. No surprise, then, that a historian wrote that Greek fire "caused enemies to shiver in terror."

WHAT WAS THE MOST IMPORTANT WEAPON INNOVATION EVER?

It's impossible to name the one most important innovation ever. But if we had to choose, we'd say horses. Yes, horses. And, no, they don't shoot laser beams from their nostrils or anything like that. But those swift, four-legged animals were used all over the world to speed warriors into battle. Their impact was huge. In fact, they helped change the very nature of European society in the 12th century. How? They allowed the rise of the mounted knight! Protected by their suits of armor and armed with lances, mounted knights would gallop their warhorses at full speed straight into the enemy's ranks. For centuries, mounted knights ruled the European battlefield.

The knights provided military muscle for royal empires that otherwise couldn't support large cavalries. In exchange for their military service to their monarchs, warrior nobility were granted land that they then controlled. That was a change that shook up society back then. With property under the control of these noble warriors, they soon had more influence in other aspects of society. European empires were never the same afterward.

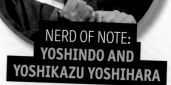

NERD OF NOTE:
YOSHINDO AND YOSHIKAZU YOSHIHARA

IF ANYONE CAPTURES the spirit of a samurai warrior, it's the Yoshiharas. The father and son are master swordsmiths, keeping alive the ancient tradition of Japanese sword making.

When Yoshindo, the father, was only 10 years old, he started to learn sword making from his grandfather. Yoshindo operated the bellows, pumping air into a furnace so steel could be heated. It gave him an up-close view of all the steps in making a sword: heating the steel until it glowed red, then hammering it into a blade, red sparks jumping from the hot metal. And when it was perfectly shaped, plunging the blade into cool liquid to harden its edges.

Over time, he developed a fine eye for the details of a sword's shape. Now the master of his own workshop, Yoshindo expects his apprentices to learn the same way he did—by observing. It takes 10 or more years to become an expert swordsmith. One of Yoshindo's star pupils was his own son, Yoshikazu, who mastered sword making quickly. When the Yoshiharas go to swordsmith competitions, their swords are too good to be judged. They're displayed for others to admire.

XIBALBA
X
X-RAY

"Football's still a hobby. That's the secret. If I didn't have training every day, I'd [still] go and play five-a-side with my mates."

XAVI HERNANDEZ, soccer star

XIBALBA

XIBALBA (pronounced shee-bal-ba) is the name the ancient K'iche Maya gave to their underworld, the place they believed dead souls ended up. Xibalba means "place of fright," and that pretty much sums up how the Maya viewed it: Death gods ruled the underworld, subjecting souls to horrible trials and dangers, like having to cross rivers of blood, undergo attacks by spinning knives, and sacrifice their own hearts. To survive such an unpleasant afterlife, the dead were buried or cremated with weapons, tools, food, and even dogs (sometimes only clay sculptures) to guide them. If the Maya used all their skills and intelligence, they might outwit the death gods.

X-MANSION

THE X-MANSION, also known as the Xavier Institute for Higher Learning (and formerly known as Charles Xavier's School for Gifted Youngsters), is the training site of the X-Men and a school for mutant teenagers in the Marvel Comics' universe. It's also a real place. You can be forgiven if you didn't know that. After all, if the X-Men are fictional superheroes, it should be safe to assume the place is made up, too. But you can actually find the X-Mansion at times on Google maps—and GPS will guide you there. (It's in New York State.) Good to know in case you ever develop strange superpowers that you need to learn how to control.

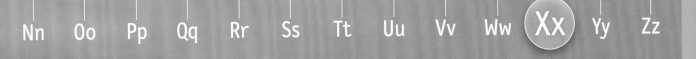

X-PLANE

THE X-PLANE IS A SUPER-STREAMLINED experimental jet that NASA and Lockheed Martin are developing to carry passengers over land faster than the speed of sound, about 767 miles an hour (1,234 km/h). Supersonic passenger travel over land has faced a serious challenge: sonic booms. Those are the huge, thunder-like cracks created by shock waves, rapid changes in pressure at supersonic speeds. They're not just annoying. They can even damage property on the ground. So NASA is trying a new technology in the X-plane that limits the effect to a soft "thump" instead of a big boom. In fact, the X-plane's formal name is Quiet Supersonic Transport, or QueSST.

XOLOITZCUINTLI

THIS RARE BREED OF HAIRLESS DOG (pronounced show-loh-etts-KWEENT-lee), believed to be the first dog in the Americas, was named after the Aztec god Xolotl (with the Aztec word for dog, *itzcuintli*, added on). Long ago, in Mexico, dogs were considered sacred, guarding homes from evil spirits. In some remote Mexican and Central American villages, the pups still have a reputation as healers. People hold their warm bodies close to ease joint pain and even toothaches.

X-RAY

YOU MAY HAVE SEEN an x-ray at your doctor's or dentist's office. These black-and-white pictures show your insides. Ever wonder how they do it? X-rays, like the light we see around us, are a type of electromagnetic wave. X-ray machines use them to see inside your body, to check for broken bones, cavities in teeth, or cancer. Calcium in your bones absorb x-rays the most, so they show up white in the images. Soft tissues and fat absorb less and look gray, while lungs look black because air absorbs the least. X-rays contain a little radiation, and doctors want to keep that to a minimum. They'll make x-rays only when really needed, and they'll cover up other parts of your body with lead aprons to block x-rays from getting into those parts.

WHAT KIND OF
DESIGN DEVOTEE
ARE YOU?

START HERE.

IF YOU GOT A BONUS DAY OFF SCHOOL, WHAT WOULD YOU DO?

Hang out at home, maybe with friends.

Go out somewhere and do something different.

WHAT DO YOU LIKE TO DO?

Just chill. Maybe play some games.

ON A COMPUTER?

Make stuff.

WHICH WOULD YOU CHOOSE: LEGOS OR MARKERS?

Art—it's the best way to express my creative side.

Hand me the bricks! I'm a master builder.

WHAT'S YOUR FAVORITE THING TO MAKE?

WHERE WOULD YOU RATHER EXPLORE: A MUSEUM OR A BOTANICAL GARDEN?

I can totally nerd out in a museum.

WHAT'S COOLER: THE PLACES THEMSELVES OR THE ARTIFACTS ON DISPLAY?

I love them both!

I have a serious green thumb!

LANDSCAPE DESIGNERS combine garden and design expertise to create awesome outdoor spaces.

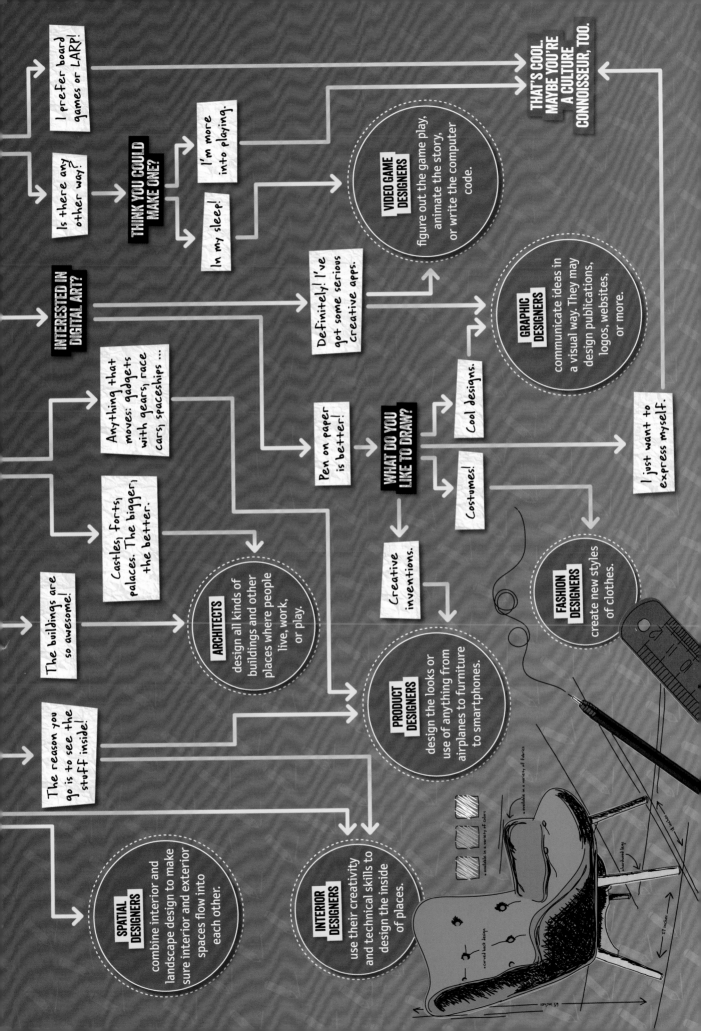

I prefer board games or LARP!

Is there any other way?

THINK YOU COULD MAKE ONE?

I'm more into playing.

In my sleep!

THAT'S COOL. MAYBE YOU'RE A CULTURE CONNOISSEUR, TOO.

VIDEO GAME DESIGNERS
figure out the game play, animate the story, or write the computer code.

INTERESTED IN DIGITAL ART?

Definitely! I've got some serious creative apps.

GRAPHIC DESIGNERS
communicate ideas in a visual way. They may design publications, logos, websites, or more.

Anything that moves: gadgets with gears, race cars, spaceships ...

Cool designs.

Pen on paper is better!

WHAT DO YOU LIKE TO DRAW?

Costumes!

I just want to express myself.

Castles, forts, palaces. The bigger, the better.

FASHION DESIGNERS
create new styles of clothes.

The buildings are so awesome!

ARCHITECTS
design all kinds of buildings and other places where people live, work, or play.

Creative inventions.

PRODUCT DESIGNERS
design the looks or use of anything from airplanes to furniture to smartphones.

The reason you go is to see the stuff inside.

SPATIAL DESIGNERS
combine interior and landscape design to make sure interior and exterior spaces flow into each other.

INTERIOR DESIGNERS
use their creativity and technical skills to design the inside of places.

•YAKS•
Y
•YURTS•

"I'm usually not on my phone that much. I prefer listening to old radio shows and watching foreign films than tweeting."

YARA SHAHIDI, actor

YAKS

IN CHINA, they're known as "hairy cattle," and it's easy to see why. Yaks, short-legged oxlike animals, are covered with thick, shaggy hair. They need the warmth. They live on high plateaus in Central Asia, Tibet, Mongolia, and Nepal. But they're well adapted to their environment. Besides their warm insulation, yaks' lungs can hold about three times more air than most cattle. They also have more red blood cells, so they're better at moving oxygen through their bodies—a definite advantage at elevations where the air is thin.

YODELING

YODELING IS A KIND OF wordless singing style where you rapidly switch back and forth between your normal "chest voice" and a high-pitched note range known as "head register" or "falsetto." People probably started yodeling thousands of years ago, when they wanted to round up cattle or send a message to someone on a faraway hillside. A lot of people picture yodelers in the Alpine countries—Switzerland, Austria, southern Germany—and it's still part of folk music there. But it has deep roots in Africa, especially among Bantu and Pygmy tribes, and later became a popular style in American country music from the 1920s through 1940s.

YOGI-ISMS

YOGI BERRA, A HALL OF FAME BASEBALL PLAYER and one of the greatest catchers in the history of the sport, was probably even better known for the funny things he said. Sometimes he created a catchy new expression that actually didn't make sense—but may have hidden a pearl of wisdom. People love these "Yogi-isms," and they became part of American culture. Here are a few favorites: "It ain't over till it's over," "The future ain't what it used to be," "A nickel ain't worth a dime anymore," and "When you come to a fork in the road, take it."

YO-YOS

YO-YOS, THOSE SWIRLING DISCS ON A STRING, haven't always been playthings. Ancient Greek kids offered them up to the gods as a rite of passage into adulthood. In the 16th century, hunters in the Philippines used weapons similar to yo-yos, which they'd fling at enemies or prey and then yank back. But in most places, yo-yos were just plain fun. The secret behind how yo-yos work—other than the skills of their handlers—is momentum, the force that makes a moving thing continue moving. Yo-yos have two kinds of momentum: linear, moving in a straight line, up and down the string; and angular, moving in a spinning motion. They keep the disc steady as you put it through its tricks.

YURTS

FOR THOUSANDS OF YEARS in Central Asia, especially Mongolia, people have lived in yurts. These sturdy, slightly domed, circular dwellings are lightweight and easily moved from one place to another using a few pack animals—ideal homes for herding communities that move often. Made from flexible crisscrossing poles and roof beams, and covered with layers of felt and an outer waterproof layer, a yurt can be set up in 30 minutes to three hours. Fancy "crowns," ring-shaped windows on top of the dome, can be handed down for generations. Inside, the yurt is divided into separate spaces for different purposes, such as food preparation, sleeping, and prayer.

ZEBRA
ZYDECO

"Nerd: One whose unbridled passion for something, or things, defines who they are as a person, without fear of other people's judgment."

ZACHARY LEVI, actor and singer

ZEBRA

ZEBRAS' FLASHY DESIGN IS ONE OF A KIND. Like our fingerprints, no two zebras have the same pattern of stripes. But just why do zebras have stripes in the first place? Scientists have several theories. It turns out that zebras living in the warmest regions of Africa have more stripes. Some researchers think those extra stripes may help keep them cool. How? It has to do with black absorbing more heat than white. When air hits a zebra, it moves faster over the black parts and slower over the white. That creates little swirls of air, like mini-fans, that help cool zebras. On the other hand, the stripes might help protect zebras in different ways. Disease-carrying biting flies don't like landing on striped surfaces. The stripes also may confuse predators, such as lions or leopards. Someday, zebra researchers hope to solve the mystery.

ZEBRAFISH

THESE FISH HAVE AN AMAZING POWER: When their spinal cords are injured, zebrafish can heal themselves. Good as new—no more paralysis. It's a marvel of nature, and scientists have worked hard to figure out how they do it. Turns out, zebrafish build a bridge between the cells on either side of the injury, and nerve cells grow across it over about eight weeks. By the time the gap is filled in, the injury is healed. Scientists are studying the zebrafish's remarkable powers in hopes of finding new ways to help people recover from injuries that create paralysis.

ZEBRA ORCHID

HAVEN'T HAD ENOUGH OF STRIPES YET? Check out these awesome flowers. Zebra orchids are definitely not black and white, but they are seriously striped. The small orchids are greenish yellow but have red stripes on their labellum, the large part that serves as a landing pad for insects that come and pollinate the flowers. Zebra orchids are common in parts of Western Australia, where they often grow in clumps of more than 10 plants (kind of like little plant herds!) or in other scattered groups.

ZODIAC

MAYBE YOU'VE HEARD PEOPLE SAY they're Scorpios, Virgos, or Leos. They're referring to their zodiac signs, ties between their birthdays and the night sky. How'd the two get connected? Back as far as the eighth to seventh centuries B.C., Babylonian astronomers mapped the sky so they could determine the best times to plant and harvest crops based on the rising and setting of stars and constellations. Around the fifth century B.C., they sliced their view of the night sky into 12 divisions, based on how the sun appeared to travel over the course of the year (its "ecliptic"). During a particular time of the year, the ecliptic would intersect with a certain constellation: Aries, Pisces, Gemini, and so on. Whoever was born during that time period would get that zodiac sign. (It doesn't line up perfectly anymore. The sky has changed a bit since the zodiac signs were assigned.) These days, the zodiac is more important to astrologers— people who believe the planets and stars influence earthly affairs and try to make predictions based on the connections—than to astronomers, scientists who study space, the universe, and celestial objects.

ZYDECO

ZYDECO IS A MUSICAL GENRE that captures the spirit of the Creole community of southern Louisiana, U.S.A. It blends Cajun dance music from the same region with soul and rhythm and blues. Accordions star in both zydeco and Cajun music, but zydeco often adds electric bass, horns, and sometimes keyboards to the mix, while Cajun bands may add fiddles. The music was popular in Louisiana for all of the 1900s, but it became popular throughout the country in the 1980s—about the same time that Americans developed a taste for Cajun and Creole food.

ZOMBIES

The living dead. Rotting corpses that shuffle and stumble toward you, never giving up, never satisfied. They want only one thing: braaaiiiinnnnns.

Zombies aren't sophisticated like vampires, mysterious like phantoms, cool like werewolves, or awe-inspiring like hulking monsters. Zombies are just plain disgusting. Their blank eyes stare at you without a hint of recognition. Blood and brain bits drip down their grotesque faces. (Hello? Ever hear of napkins?)

So, where do zombies come from? Originally, they appeared in Haitian folklore as corpses that voodoo sorcerers, called bokors, could bring back to life as servants. By the 1950s and '60s, though, the zombies portrayed in books and movies had little in common with their Haitian origins. And that's largely the same today. Here's how the modern stories go: Zombies are dead people who come back to life (kinda). Some rise straight from the dead. But others start out like regular, nice people who get turned into zombies.

How does that happen? The scariest way is by a zombie bite. Zombie-bitten people get violently ill and die. How fast depends on where the zombie bites them, how often, and so on. But it doesn't take a zombie bite to turn someone into a zombie. Anyone who dies during a zombie invasion becomes a zombie (unless they die from a massive brain trauma). The whole point is that zombies become an epidemic, quickly spreading their affliction.

How the zombie epidemic starts in the first place varies, depending on the story and the era when it was made. The early zombie movies, made in the 1960s during the space race between the United States and Soviet Union, hinted that some mysterious space radiation was at fault. These days, when people are worried about catching nasty diseases, the zombie epidemic usually starts when some awful virus escapes a laboratory.

Sometimes we don't know how a zombie epidemic starts, only how it ends: a zombie apocalypse, the destruction of human civilization. It's our worst nightmare—and that's exactly why zombie shows are so popular. We love to be scared and see humans battling their worst fears—as long as we're safe in our homes and cozy movie theaters. And eating popcorn (not brains).

NEED MORE MONSTERS IN YOUR LIFE?
CHECK OUT VAMPIRES ON PAGE 146.

FAQ

IF MOST ZOMBIES EAT BRAINS, WHAT DO VEGETARIAN ZOMBIES EAT?

Graaaiiiinnnnns! (Sorry, couldn't resist.) No, actually, here's the thing: In movies, zombies don't retain any traits of their hosts. Nice people don't become nice zombies. They're just zombies. Same thing with vegetarians. They don't stick to the values they had as actual, totally living people. As zombies, they eat brains, too. Or, at least, flesh. Books and movies vary a lot on zombie eating habits.

Eating brains is the favorite zombie trait (among zombie fans, not among zombie victims). Moviemakers don't usually say why zombies eat brains. It's probably just because it's the creepiest thing they could think of. But fans of the genre fill in the blanks and offer an explanation: Our brains contain feel-good hormones. The zombies must be going for those. Either that or the ooey-gooey texture.

SO, YOU'RE SURE THAT ZOMBIES DON'T EXIST IN REAL LIFE, RIGHT?

Well, it's complicated. The zombies of human nightmares won't be bothering us any time soon, but other species aren't so lucky.

Cockroach zombies are totally real, thanks to a parasite called the jewel wasp. This wasp uses roaches as nurseries for its eggs, and to do that, it first turns the roaches into— you guessed it— zombies. How? It injects venom into a part of the roach's brain that controls movement. Then, by tugging on the roach's antenna, the wasp can control the roach and lead it towards its burrow. There, the wasp lays its eggs in the zombie roach.

Another monster parasite, single-celled *Toxoplasma gondii* is scary in a big way— if you happen to be a mouse. *T. gondii* reproduces inside cats' intestines, and it has a very special way of getting there. The parasite is commonly found out in the everyday world. When a mouse eats or drinks something infected with *T. gondii,* the organism changes the mouse's brain, making it less fearful. An infected mouse might walk right up to its natural predator, a cat. When the cat takes the bait (the zombified mouse), *T. gondii* infects the cat and reproduces in its body.

These are just a couple of examples, but nature is full of creepy creatures. These organisms aren't actually monsters, though. They've simply adapted really interesting, and sometimes spooky, ways to survive.

A NEW JEWEL WASP EMERGES FROM ITS COCKROACH INCUBATOR.

NERD OF NOTE: ZOMBIE RESEARCH SOCIETY

YES, the Zombie Research Society is a thing.

You might think they're a bunch of horror movie-crazed people who nerd out about the details of brain eating and rotting flesh. Well, they probably are. But they're also professors, doctors, and serious researchers. Yes, really.

Members of the Zombie Research Society think through all aspects of zombies and a possible zombie apocalypse. In the words of their mission statement, they're "dedicated to the historic, cultural, and scientific study of the living dead."

ZRS researchers study how zombie epidemics would spread in real life and how a zombie apocalypse would affect the world. They delve into the biology of the undead and the anatomy of the zombie brain. They figure out the best way to prepare for and survive a zombie apocalypse. Many have written books and articles about their subjects or consulted for documentaries. Has the world gone mad? No— and neither have the members of the Zombie Research Society. They don't actually think there are real brain-eating zombies. It just turns out that studying zombies and a possible zombie apocalypse is a fun way to think through actual problems.

FIND OUT MORE!

FUN FACT

Britain's MI6 trained two mice, Micky and Tricky, to help bug the home of a suspected Russian spy in Portugal. In the early 1990s, the mice carried a wire through a drainpipe, so the spy agency could get better reception when listening into the Russian's conversations.

Books

Billions of Years, Amazing Changes: The Story of Evolution
By Laurence Pringle, illustrated by Steve Jenkins (Boyds Mills Press, 2011)
One of the best books on the subject, packed with fascinating info and art. Best for grades 3 and higher.

Chasing Cheetahs: The Race to Save Africa's Fastest Cat
By Sy Montgomery (Houghton Mifflin Harcourt, 2014)
How the Cheetah Conservation Fund works with locals to save the big cats. Best for about grades 5 to 8.

Cleared for Takeoff: The Ultimate Book of Flight
By Rowland White (Chronicle Books, 2016)
Aviation's most exciting and important moments, aircraft, and pioneers. Best for about grades 3 to 7.

Comics Confidential: Thirteen Graphic Novelists Talk Story, Craft, and Life Outside the Box
Compiled by Leonard S. Marcus (Candlewick Press, 2016)
Interviews and original comics by graphic novel artists, who talk about their backgrounds and creative processes. Best for about grades 6 and higher.

Courage and Defiance: Stories of Spies, Saboteurs, and Survivors in World War II Denmark
By Deborah Hopkinson (Scholastic, 2015)
Stories of the heroic young men and women who secretly fought Nazi occupation. Best for about grades 3 to 7.

Hopping Ahead of Climate Change: Snowshoe Hares, Science, and Survival
By Sneed B. Collard (Bucking Horse Books, 2016)
How climate change affects snowshoe hares. Best for about grades 2 to 5.

FUN FACT

Watson, the computer that beat former champions on the television quiz show *Jeopardy*, now uses its "smarts"—or its ability to analyze lots of information—to help medical pros fight lung cancer.

Scaly Spotted Feathered Frilled: How Do We Know What Dinosaurs Really Looked Like?
By Catherine Thimmesh
(Houghton Mifflin, 2013)
How paleoartists put together clues to bring dinosaurs to life on paper. Best for about grades 4 to 7.

Super Cool Tech
(DK, 2016)
Gadgets, gizmos, cutting-edge technology, and how it's shaping the future. Best for about grades 4 and higher.

The Whydah: A Pirate Ship Feared, Wrecked, and Found
By Martin W. Sandler (Candlewick Press, 2017)
The true story of the only pirate ship ever found and what its riches have revealed about pirates' lives. Best for about grades 4 to 7.

Websites/Online

AMERICA'S STORY FROM AMERICA'S LIBRARY
americaslibrary.gov
The Library of Congress presents biographies, history, sports, entertainment, games, and more.

KIDS THINK DESIGN
kidsthinkdesign.org
All areas of design, including cool info, profiles of designers, and projects to try.

NASA
nasa.gov/audience/forstudents/index.html
Space, science, interviews, and much more.

NATIONAL GEOGRAPHIC KIDS
natgeokids.com
Animals, nature, science, and more cool stuff.

WOW IN THE WORLD PODCAST, National Public Radio
npr.org/podcasts/510321/wow-in-the-world
The wonders of science, technology, discovery, and inventions.

FUN FACT

In 1947, a pilot in Washington State saw speedy, crescent-shaped objects that moved "like a saucer if you skip it across the water." A newspaper mistakenly reported them as "saucer-shaped." It was the first reported UFO sighting, and ever since, UFOs have been called flying saucers.

SELECT BIBLIOGRAPHY

Adams, Tim. "Norman Doidge: The Man Teaching Us To Change Our Minds." *Guardian*, Feb. 8, 2015. Available online at www.theguardian.com/science/2015/feb/08/norman-doidge-brain-healing-neuroplasticity-interview.

Buller, Laura, et al. *Top Secret: Shady Tales of Spies and Spying.* DK, 2011.

Crew, Bec. "In Conversation With Lisa-Anne Gershwin, Jellyfish Savant." Scientific American Running Ponies blog, Feb. 25, 2014. Available online at blogs.scientificamerican.com/running-ponies/in-conversation-with-lisa-anne-gershwin-jellyfish-savant/.

Davis, Janet M. "America's Big Circus Spectacular Has a Long and Cherished History." Smithsonian.com, March 22, 2017. Available online at www.smithsonianmag.com/history/americas-big-circus-spectacular-has-long-and-cherished-history-180962621/.

Doudna, Jennifer. "How CRISPR Lets Us Edit Our DNA." TED Global, London, Sept. 2015. Available online at www.ted.com/talks/jennifer_doudna_we_can_now_edit_our_dna_but_let_s_do_it_wisely/transcript.

Elizondo, Luis. Interview. CNN, Dec. 18, 2017. Available online at www.youtube.com/watch?v=wqwsaypXh6w.

"Elon Musk: How I Became the Real 'Iron Man.'" Bloomberg Risk Takers, Aug 3, 2011. Available online at www.youtube.com/watch?v=mh45igK4Esw.

Flatow, Ira, and David Scheel. "Eight Arms That Send a Message." Science Friday, Jan. 29, 2016. Available online at www.sciencefriday.com/segments/eight-arms-that-send-a-message/.

Gershwin, Lisa-Ann. "Perilous Bloom—Rise of the Jellyfish." TEDx Dublin, Nov. 20, 2014. Available online at www.youtube.com/watch?v=r-yGbHYyLS0.

Golden Age of Piracy. Available online at www.goldenageofpiracy.org/.

Goodrich, Ryan. "Viking History: Facts & Myths." Live Science, April 20, 2016. Available online at www.livescience.com/32087-viking-history-facts-myths.html.

Hall, Stephanie. "Kites Rise on the Wind: The Origin of Kites." Library of Congress Folklife Today blog, March 16, 2017. Available online at blogs.loc.gov/folklife/2017/03/kites-rise-on-the-wind/.

Herzog, Katie. "Mushroom Burial Suit Turns Dead Bodies Into Clean Compost." Grist, Jan. 28, 2016. Available online at grist.org/living/mushroom-burial-suit-turns-dead-bodies-into-clean-compost/.

FUN FACT

Samurai walked on the left side of a path to make sure the long tips of their swords' scabbards, which hung off their left hips, didn't touch. Because if they did, it could lead to a sword fight! Japanese still walk—and drive—on the left, a legacy of the samurai.

FUN FACT

The lion's mane jellyfish, found in the Arctic and other frigid waters, can grow tentacles as long as 120 feet (37 m), about one-third the length of a football field (including the end zones).

FUN FACT

Octopuses have hand preferences—just like we do! Researchers noticed that octopuses only reach out to each other using their front arms—not the other six—during a certain type of communication. The researchers are still figuring out what it means.

SELECT BIBLIOGRAPHY
CONTINUED

"History of UFOs." History. Available online at www.history.com/topics/history-of-ufos.

Kean, Leslie. "Fmr. Manager of DOD Aerospace Threat Program: 'UFOs are Real.'" Huffington Post, Oct. 23, 2017. Available online at www.huffingtonpost.com/entry /fmr-manager-of-dod-aerospace-threat-program-ufos _us_59de2f4be4b0b992a8214874.

Kohen, Yael. "3 Cool Jobs You Didn't Even Know Existed." *Marie Claire,* Dec. 21, 2016. Available online at www.marieclaire.com/culture/news/a24263 /in-your-dreams/?src=socialflowFB.

Leahy, Stephen. "Electric Cars May Rule the World's Roads by 2040." *National Geographic,* Sept. 13, 2017. Available online at news.nationalgeographic .com/2017/09 /electric-cars-replace -gasoline-engines-2040/.

Lee, Jae Rhim. "My Mushroom Burial Suit." TED Global, 2011. Available online at www.ted.com/talks/jae_rhim _lee/transcript.

Leveen, Lois. "Mary Richards Bowser (fl. 1846–1867)." Encyclopedia Virginia, Jan. 2014. Available online at www.encyclopediavirginia.org/ Bowser_Mary_Richards_fl_1846-1867.

Metz, Cade. "Building A.I. That Can Build A.I." *New York Times,* Nov. 5, 2017. Available online at www.nytimes .com/2017/11/05/technology/machine-learning -artificial-intelligence-ai.html.

Minster, Christopher. "The Golden Age of Piracy." ThoughtCo., Aug. 27, 2017. Available online at www .thoughtco.com/the-golden-age-of-piracy-2136277.

Nield, David. "Biologists Have Discovered an Underwater Octopus City and They're Calling It Octlantis." *Science Alert,* June 10, 2018. Available online at www.sciencealert.com/marine-biologists -discover-an-underwater-octopus-city-octlantis -jervis-bay-australia.

FUN FACT

If Vikings wanted to get to a river that was connected to where they were sailing, they'd carry their ships and cargo over the land to reach it.

"Portrait of a Pirate: Myths and Unexpected Truths."
Georgetown University, Feb. 24, 2017. Available online
at scs.georgetown.edu/news-and-events/article/5958
portrait-pirate-myths-and-unexpected-truths.

Scott, Sophie. "Why We Laugh." TED 2015, March 2015.
Available online at www.ted.com/talks/sophie_scott
_why_we_laugh/transcript.

"Shifting Colors of an Octopus May Hint at a Rich,
Nasty Social Life." NPR the Two-Way, Jan. 28, 2016.
Available online at www.npr.org/templates
/transcript/transcript.php?storyId=464447457.

Thakrar, Raju. "Deadly Weapons Forged as Art."
Japan Times, April 27, 2008. Available online at
www.japantimes.co.jp/life/2008/04/27/general
/deadly-weapons-forged-as-art/.

"Timeline: History of the Electric Car." PBS Now, Oct. 10,
2009. Available online at www.pbs.org/now/shows/223
/electric-car-timeline.html .

"Under the Sea With Invasive Species Expert Erin Spencer."
GenHERation, March 1, 2016. Available online at
genheration.com/under-the-sea-with-invasive
-species-expert-erin-spencer/.

Varghese, Sanjana. "Zombie Studies: The Scientists
Taking the Living Dead Seriously." NewStatesman,
Aug. 3, 2017. Available online at
www.newstatesman.com/politics/health/2017/08
/zombie-studies-scientists-taking-living-dead-seriously.

FUN FACT

You probably "speak circus"
and don't even know it! If someone's
ever told you to get your "show on the
road" or "jump on the bandwagon,"
they're using circus lingo. Let's just
hope they don't "ditch" you. Way back,
circuses wouldn't formally fire you;
they just left you standing in the
ditch beside the railroad tracks
when the circus train
pulled away.

FUN FACT

Humans weren't the first
farmers. That honor probably goes to
a species of small black ants that live in
and eat a lumpy, brown plant in Fiji. They
gather the plant's seeds, plop them into the
cracks of trees, and fertilize them with their
own poop. When the plants produce fruit,
the ants harvest the seeds and do it all
over. They've lived—and worked—
that way for three million years.

Viviano, Frank. "This Tiny Country Feeds the World."
National Geographic, Sept. 2017. Available online at
www.nationalgeographic.com/magazine/2017/09
/holland-agriculture-sustainable-farming/.

Whitley, Tori. "'I Don't Know Where It's From': Former UFO
Program Head On Navy Jet Footage." NPR Morning
Edition, Dec. 19, 2017. Available online at
www.npr.org/2017/12/19/571868263/secret-program-at
-the-pentagon-spent-million-to-study-ufos.

CREDITS

CREDITS

For Alex McCauley, whose science smarts shine among nerds everywhere —TJR

Copyright © 2019 National Geographic Partners, LLC

Published by National Geographic Partners, LLC. All rights reserved. Reproduction of the whole or any part of the contents without written permission from the publisher is prohibited.

Since 1888, the National Geographic Society has funded more than 12,000 research, exploration, and preservation projects around the world. The Society receives funds from National Geographic Partners, LLC, funded in part by your purchase. A portion of the proceeds from this book supports this vital work. To learn more, visit natgeo.com/info.

NATIONAL GEOGRAPHIC and Yellow Border Design are trademarks of the National Geographic Society, used under license.

For more information, visit nationalgeographic.com, call 1-800-647-5463, or write to the following address:

National Geographic Partners
1145 17th Street N.W.
Washington, D.C. 20036-4688 U.S.A.

Visit us online at nationalgeographic.com/books

For librarians and teachers: ngchildrensbooks.org

More for kids from National Geographic: natgeokids.com

National Geographic Kids magazine inspires children to explore their world with fun yet educational articles on animals, science, nature, and more. Using fresh storytelling and amazing photography, *Nat Geo Kids* shows kids ages 6 to 14 the fascinating truth about the world—and why they should care.
kids.nationalgeographic.com/subscribe

For information about special discounts for bulk purchases, please contact National Geographic Books Special Sales: specialsales@natgeo.com

For rights or permissions inquiries, please contact National Geographic Books Subsidiary Rights: bookrights@natgeo.com

Designed by Brett Challos

Names: Resler, Tamara J., author. | National Geographic Kids (Firm), publisher. | National Geographic Society (U.S.)
Title: Nerd A to Z / by TJ Resler.
Description: Washington, DC : National Geographic Kids, [2019] | Audience: Ages 7-10. | Audience: K to grade 3.
Identifiers: LCCN 2018035824| ISBN 9781426334740 (hardcover) | ISBN 9781426334757 (hardcover)
Subjects: LCSH: Science--Juvenile literature. | Science--Encyclopedias, Juvenile.
Classification: LCC Q163 .R3925 2019 | DDC 503--dc23
LC record available at https://lccn.loc.gov/2018035824

Many thanks to the multitalented National Geographic Kids Books team—Kathryn Williams, Brett Challos, Sarah Mock, Danny Meldung, Shelby Lees, Molly Reid, Anne LeongSon, and Gus Tello—who made this a truly nerdworthy book; to Michelle Harris for her fact-checking; to Susie McCauley for her inspiration and friendship; and to Jim Monke for putting up with this nerd.

Printed in China
19/RRDS/1